COUNTING THE DAYS WHILE MY MIND
SLIPS AWAY

A Love Letter to My Family

BEN UTECHT
with Mark Tabb

HOWARD BOOKS
AN IMPRINT OF SIMON & SCHUSTER, INC.

New York   Nashville   London   Toronto   Sydney   New Delhi

Howard Books
An Imprint of Simon & Schuster, Inc.
1230 Avenue of the Americas
New York, NY 10020

First Howard Books hardcover edition August 2016

HOWARD and colophon are trademarks of Simon & Schuster, Inc.

For information about special discounts for bulk purchases, please contact Simon &
Schuster Special Sales at 1-866-506-1949 or business@simonandschuster.com.

The Simon & Schuster Speakers Bureau can bring authors to your live event.
For more information or to book an event, contact the Simon & Schuster Speakers
Bureau at 1-866-248-3049 or visit our website at www.simonspeakers.com.

Manufactured in the United States of America

10 9 8 7 6 5 4 3 2 1

Library of Congress Cataloging-in-Publication Data is available.

ISBN 978-1-5011-3660-3
ISBN 978-1-5011-3669-6 (ebook)

This story was written for my daughters:
Elleora—God is my light
Katriel—God is my crown
Amy Joan—Beloved gift from God
Haven—Place of safety and refuge

And dedicated first to:
My beautiful wife, Karyn; you are my rock and my hope.
And second, to:
All the family and friends who have filled
my life full of memories.

CONTENTS

Contents

PROLOGUE

I WAS A LITTLE NERVOUS LEAVING my wife, Karyn, at home while I joined my church's worship band for a Friday afternoon practice. Karyn's OB-GYN told us that the baby could come at any moment. However, our first daughter came a week late, and we had no reason to expect our last daughter would be in any more of a hurry.

I walked into the church at 3:00 p.m. wondering if I had made the right decision by coming to practice. It wasn't comforting that my good friend and lead worship pastor, Terry, greeted me sarcastically with "Your wife had better not go into labor tonight!"

"If I thought she was going to, I wouldn't be here," I replied with a laugh.

We got right down to business and started playing. I wanted to get home as quickly as I could. In spite of my bold statement to Terry, I couldn't stop thinking Karyn might actually go into labor while I was playing a guitar. We worked through the first song several times until it felt right and then moved on to the next, a song called "I Surrender." Terry asked me to sing the lead on the second song because the song has played a huge role in my life. I scrolled ahead to the beginning of the lyrics on my iPad as our keyboardist played the intro. The song is powerful, and the opening melody is almost haunting. I counted off the time in my head, breathed, and began singing, "Here I am, down on my knees again, Surrendering all, Surrendering all. . . ."

Before I could sing the next line a text message popped up on my iPad screen. "My water broke. Please come home immediately." My heart rate jumped through the roof. All I could think was, *You have got to be kidding me!* My voice cracked. "Terry, you're not going to believe this. . . . I gotta go, guys. Karyn's water broke. We're going to have a baby!"

Even though this was our third pregnancy and fourth child (thanks to a surprise set of identical twin girls), Karyn and I had never experienced the frantic race to the hospital. Doctors induced labor with our oldest, Elleora, and the twins were born via emergency C-section. When we found out Karyn was pregnant a third time, she was determined to experience a natural birth from beginning to end. A VBAC birth, that is, vaginal birth after cesarean, is risky, but since Karyn was a strong candidate to be successful, we decided to go for it.

I ran out of the church and jumped in my truck. The ten-minute drive to our house took me maybe eight minutes. I pulled into the driveway, ran through the front door, and immediately panicked as I found Karyn sitting in the bathroom in the middle of a contraction with amniotic fluid everywhere. I ran over to her and asked, "Are you okay? What can I do? How long do you think we have?" I don't think I waited for any answers before running upstairs to our room and throwing clothes into a suitcase. Karyn had already packed her bag, but I had not. I knew she could go into labor at any time but I had it in my mind that we still had at least a week. After throwing a bunch of random things into my bag, I ran back downstairs and asked Karyn, "Are you ready?"

She was calm. "Yes, Ben. Slow down. We have time."

I tried slowing down, but I couldn't. I got her to the truck and took off for the hospital, which was about twenty-five minutes away. The drive never seemed long before, but now it felt like we had to drive across the country. I flew down our driveway and out onto the narrow road that leads to our house. I barely stopped at the stop sign, then turned onto the main road that leads to Interstate 35. All I could think about was getting to the hospital and keeping Karyn comfortable on the drive. "Do you want me to turn on some music?" I asked. "Is there anything I can do for you? What can I do to help?"

"Just get us there safely. I'm okay," Karyn said. I kept asking the last question every couple of minutes.

Another contraction came right after we merged onto the interstate. This was no small contraction. Karyn reached over and grabbed my right hand and squeezed hard. She did the whole Lamaze breathing thing. The faster she breathed, the harder I pressed on the gas pedal. I didn't want to say it out loud, but I was certain we were going to have the baby right there in the front seat of my truck.

Thankfully, we reached the hospital before the baby arrived. I pulled up to the emergency entrance, where an orderly came out with a wheelchair for Karyn. When I returned from parking the truck I expected to find her in a room about to give birth. Instead, I found her in a triage room where nurses were calmly and casually asking her all sorts of questions. "What are you doing?" I wanted to yell. "The baby is about to pop out!" But I held back, trying to be as patient as I could.

Within ten minutes, they determined Karyn was in active labor and wheeled her to a labor/delivery room. I anxiously followed her into the room and began trying to act like I knew what I was doing. The doctor came in and did the first examination. I was surprised she even had to. I thought the baby was about to jump right out. "It's going to be a while," she said. "You are only dilated to a four." That is four on a scale of ten.

My first reaction was "What? Is that it?" But then I settled down and realized we were in for the long haul. Our doula, Nyki, arrived about fifteen minutes after we did. She continuously massaged Karyn's back and helped her find new positions as Karyn tried desperately to find comfort. The continuous onslaught of contractions transformed me into Hall of Fame Lamaze coach mode. "Breathe, honey, just breathe," I said as calmly as I could. I did the breathing with her on a lot of the contractions. After several hours of labor, Karyn looked at me and said, "I don't know if I can do this."

"You don't have to do this all natural. Do you want something for the pain?" I asked. I hated to see my wife suffer.

"No, I want to do this. I can do this," she said, her mind resolved. That was the tough, strong athlete I fell in love with.

Five hours after we arrived at the hospital the doctor finally told Karyn it was time to push. When she pushed she let out a scream like nothing I had ever heard in my life. It sounded like something out of a horror movie. Then she let out another one. I was sure the whole hospital heard it. People had to wonder what was going on in our room. One more push and scream did it. My baby girl's head appeared, all covered in dark hair like mine. What a beautiful sight.

However, the moment of joy turned into panic. The doctor immediately noticed something was wrong. I moved back out of the way as the doctor desperately tried to unwrap the umbilical cord from around my baby's neck, but without success. Finally, she pulled my baby girl out by her head and unwrapped the cord as she slid on out. The doctor held my baby and I held my breath, waiting for my little girl to make a sound, but nothing came out. Then, all at once, my baby girl let out the most beautiful little cry. "Dad, would you like to cut the cord?" the doctor asked, as if nothing out of the ordinary had happened.

"Of course," I replied.

Once the cord was cut, a nurse quickly wiped off my daughter, then handed her to Karyn for some skin-to-skin time. "You worked hard for that baby," the nurse said. "You hold her as long as you want."

I leaned down to Karyn. We both had tears in our eyes. "You did it," I said. "I am so proud of you." I stroked Karyn's hair, then softly stroked my baby's back. "Welcome, Haven," I said to my fourth daughter. "Do you know how much I love you?" After going back and forth between two or three names we had finally decided on Haven because this was our prayer for her, that she would be someone who provides peace and rest.

After thirty minutes, the nurse came over and took Haven. I went out into the hallway and found my parents while the nurse weighed Haven and measured her and did all the things nurses have to do for babies when they first enter the world. Karyn's parents had also just arrived. I ushered them all into the room for their first look at their newest grandbaby. The four of them crowded around her, joy overflowing. I stood back and breathed it all in.

Finally, the nurse wrapped my baby tight in a blanket and placed her in my arms. She looked so tiny, her little seven-and-a-half-pound, twenty-two-inch-long body in my huge hands and arms. I cradled her close to my body and looked down at her face, in awe of how perfect she was. Staring into my little girl's eyes, the finality of the moment hit me. Karyn and I had already decided that Haven was to be the last of our children, at least via birth. We might adopt someday, but this was the last time I was ever going to get to rush my wife to the hospital and the last time I was going to get to coach her through childbirth and the last time I would hold my daughter in my arms for the very first time.

The last time. This is it. There is not going to be a son. Ever, I thought. *This may very well be the end of the Utecht name in my immediate family.* I was my mother and father's only son, and now, with my fourth daughter, no one was going to carry the name along. And then another thought hit me, one that I hated, but it came anyway. *Is the same thing going to happen to my mind as to my name? Is my mind also going to slip away and be gone forever?* I held on to Haven just a little tighter. I stared into her eyes almost in desperation. I wanted to hold on to this moment and never let it go.

"Oh God," I pleaded, "please don't let this memory be taken away from me. Please don't let me forget this moment like I have so many others. Please, God. Please."

CHAPTER 1

WHERE IT ALL BEGAN

MY HEART POUNDED IN MY EARS. Adrenaline pumped, mixing with excitement and nerves. I jumped up and down in place trying to shake the butterflies out of my stomach. It didn't work. I could hear my teammate Adam Vinatieri's advice from the week before ringing in my ears. "Keep calm. Focus. And don't you dare blink at kickoff." The guy already had three championship rings and kicked the Super Bowl–winning field goal as time expired not once but twice, so I knew I needed to listen to him. But no matter how hard I tried, I couldn't help but get caught up in the moment as I stood in the tunnel leading out onto the field, waiting to run out for Super Bowl XLI, the ultimate game I'd dreamed about my entire life.

The week leading up to the game felt surreal. The team flew down to Miami for the game the previous Sunday. On Monday we spent a couple of hours out on the Sun Life Stadium field for media day, which is more like a media circus. I remember standing out there, talking to my buddy Bryan Fletcher, when all of the sudden a horn sounded and people came pouring out of the stadium gates like ants and descended on us. Besides reporters from the usual media outlets like ESPN and *Sports Illustrated*, there were people there from every publication and website on earth, most of which had nothing to do with football or sports. Some of the "reporters" came dressed in outrageous costumes. It was nuts.

And then the real craziness began.

During Super Bowl week we practiced at the Miami Dolphins' training facility. Whenever we traveled from the team hotel to the practice facility, Florida state troopers shut down the highway for our team buses. Cars had to pull over on the shoulder while police cars also blocked entrance ramps. Our buses drove down the middle of the five-lane highway like we owned the road. We weren't a football team. We were royalty. The royal treatment carried over to the practice field. Celebrities crowded around the field to watch us. Sometimes it was hard to concentrate on what we were there for, especially when Hall of Fame tight end Shannon Sharpe watched whether or not I caught the pass just thrown to me. He was the gold standard for tight ends, which is what I played on offense.

After another royal ride down the freeway we returned to our hotel rooms, where we all found gift bags with the Super Bowl logo on the outside, bags loaded down with new iPods and clothes and hats and all sorts of cool memorabilia. The week felt more like a really nice vacation instead of the buildup to a championship game.

In spite of the distractions, we had a great week of practice. The team felt really confident going into the game against the Chicago Bears. Just to get to the Super Bowl we had to beat the team that had won three of the previous five championships, and to do that we put together the biggest comeback in AFC Championship history. Every Colts player knew that if we played in the Super Bowl like we did in the second half of the AFC Championship, we had a good chance of becoming world champions.

I, too, felt confident when Super Bowl Sunday finally rolled around. I'd had a couple of nagging injuries I had to deal with toward the end of the season, but having two weeks between the AFC Championship Game and the Super Bowl gave me time to heal.

On the day of the game I woke up early, since I couldn't really sleep anyway, and looked out the window to see a dark, overcast sky. It rained off and on most of the day. Never before had weather affected the Super Bowl, but the forecast said this was going to be the first. I didn't really care. We'd played in worse conditions and won. I went downstairs for breakfast and sat through one meeting with the tight ends and another with the offensive linemen. After that I had nothing to do but sit around and watch movies and stare at the clock. Finally, around 2:00 p.m. I climbed on the team bus for the ride to the stadium. Of course, we had another police escort down a blocked-off freeway.

I thought I was keyed up as I got dressed in the locker room, but nothing compared to what I felt standing in the tunnel waiting to go out onto the field for the first time. The game wasn't due to start for at least an hour, but the stadium was already starting to fill. Music blared in the stadium and blasted through the tunnel where I stood with our punter, Hunter Smith; kicker Adam Vinatieri; and our starting long snapper, Justin Snow. I backed up Justin. The four of us were going to go out on the field to warm up. Justin and I just looked at each other with smiles filled with joy and anxiousness. "Can you believe we're here?" I asked.

"I know, it's crazy," Justin replied.

Finally a stadium attendant looked up from a clipboard and said, "Okay, you're set. Go." Hunter, Adam, Justin, and I all huddled close, gave the traditional embrace, then turned to go.

I trotted down the tunnel toward the field. The sound of cleats on the concrete ramp echoed all around me. I had just cleared the tunnel and put one foot on the turf when I heard one voice ring out over all the rest of the stadium noise. "Ben! Ben!"

I looked back over my shoulder and spotted my dad in his

Colts rain jacket and ball cap leaning onto the railing just above the tunnel. He had a big smile on his face. "Benjamin!" he yelled again, waving his hand down toward me. I didn't know how he was able to work his way through the crowd over to this spot. He and my mom and the rest of our family had seats on the other side of the field. "Ben, up here!" he said again.

I raised my hand to acknowledge I'd heard him, and to get him to stop calling my name. Then I sort of flicked my hand with a dismissive wave like I was trying to shoo off a pesky fly. All I could think was, *Not now, Dad. Don't you see I'm working? Don't you understand I am about to go out on the field for the biggest game of my life on the biggest stage in the world?!* After waving my dad off, I turned back toward the field and started to run out onto the turf.

But a voice in my head stopped me in my tracks. From deep inside I heard my father calling to me, not in the stadium, but in my backyard.

My mind took me back to a day when I felt the same mix of adrenaline, nerves, and excitement as I walked out on the freshly cut grass, my brand-new cleats laced up tight. "Ready, Ben?" my dad asked then. I nodded my head, bent over, and planted my hand in the turf as I got in a three-point stance. Tiny beads of sweat gathered on my brow; my legs shook in anticipation. I was like a spring, wound up tight, just waiting to go off. Suddenly the football moved. "Now," my dad said. I took off like a bullet. Legs churning, head down, I lowered my shoulders, closed my eyes, and lunged with all my might into the man with the football. I landed right in the middle of my dad's chest. He fell backward from his knees and wrapped his arms around my four-year-old body. "Good job, Ben," he said as he lifted me up, a huge grin on his face. "Want to try it again?"

I didn't even answer. I just raced back over to where I started and got back down in a three-point stance, ready to go.

From the back porch I heard my mom clapping like I'd just made the game-winning tackle in the Super Bowl. "Way to go, Beno-Button," she called out. "And be careful," she had to add because she's my mom. Then she called over to my dad, "Jeff, you take it easy on him."

My dad just smiled and nodded. "Okay, Lori," he said while giving me a little wink. "All right, Ben, let's do it again," he said.

I also heard my dad's voice call my name a few years later when my hands were big enough to catch a football. "Go long, Ben," he said, motioning with his left arm and winding up the football with his right. The backyard of the parsonage where we lived wasn't big enough for me to run real pass routes. Instead my dad went across the street from our corner lot and had me stand on the curb right in front of our house. "That's it, go long." I took off running down the side of our lot, right up next to the six-foot-tall cedar fence that surrounded the property. For a preacher, my dad had a really good arm. He lofted a spiral in my direction. I scrambled to get under it, moving right up next to the fence. Most of the time I caught the ball. Sometimes I smashed into the fence. There were times I did both. But catching the ball up against a tall fence was really good practice for me. I got used to grabbing the ball out of the air in tight places, even when that meant the catch was followed by a collision.

After I made the catch I took off running toward the make-believe end zone at the end of the fence line. Then I quickly sprinted back toward my dad. If there weren't any cars coming, I stopped at the curb and threw the ball across the street to him. "Nice catch, Ben. Good hands. Ready to do it again?" I always was. And my dad's arm never seemed to get tired. He'd stay outside throwing passes to me as long as I wanted. I loved the game. He loved spending time with me. It took me a while to figure out that that's what I loved about the game as well. Football meant time with my dad.

I still heard my father's voice calling my name when I signed up for my first real full-contact football team, right after my family moved to a new town. My father is a Methodist pastor. The Methodist church moves their ministers every five to ten years. Right before the start of my sixth-grade year it was our turn to go. We left the little town of Lindstrom, Minnesota, a place where everyone knows everyone else, to go to the historic Mississippi River town of Hastings, Minnesota. Hastings was ten times bigger than Lindstrom, but it was still basically a small town. I worried about fitting in and being accepted there. My mom and dad told me not to worry, that everything was going to be okay, but I wasn't so sure.

I joined my first football team and had gone through a few weeks of practice, but I still didn't really know anyone. Most everyone already seemed to have their circle of friends. Breaking into social circles can be tough in small towns. On top of that, I had a late birthday, which meant I was a year younger than most of my classmates all the way through college.

I may have been younger than most of the other sixth graders, but I was one of the biggest guys on my team. The coach had me play end on defense and wide receiver on offense. On the first play of the first game of my life, I lined up on defense directly across from the offensive tackle, just as the coach had shown me. I leaned over, planted my fingers in the grass in a three-point stance, and dug in my cleats. My dad stood on the sideline next to one of the coaches. Like me, my dad didn't yet know anyone in town.

The quarterback barked off the signals. I looked up and down the offensive line and saw a huge gap between the tackle and the guard. *Why am I lined up directly across from this guy where he can easily block me when I could jump the gap and avoid him?* I wondered. Before the ball could snap, I jumped over into the gap. The moment the center moved the ball I fired off the line as fast as I could and headed straight toward the quarterback. I got to the quarterback as he was about to hand the ball off to the running back. I grabbed the ball out of his hand and took off running down the field. As I ran toward the end zone my dad yelled from the sidelines, "Run, Ben! Run, son!" No one came close to me as I trotted across the goal line, untouched, to score my first touchdown.

The coach standing next to my dad turned to him as I crossed the goal line. "That kid, now that's an athlete," he said. Then he introduced himself to my father. I didn't have to worry about fitting in any longer.

After I started playing organized football my dad and I still tossed the football around the backyard, but more and more he watched as I played. After Little Raiders football came junior high, then high school. My dad and my mom were always on the sidelines or up in the stands. When I went off to college they came to as many games as they could, but they had to watch all the road games on television or listen on the radio. After the Indianapolis Colts signed me to a free agent contract out of college, my dad went down to the local Irish sports bar and grill and made an arrangement with the owner. "My son plays for the Colts, but the local stations don't show many of their games," my dad explained to him. "Do you think you could have one of your televisions show the Colts game so we can watch?" The owner could not turn him down.

Through my first year playing for the Colts my dad and mom went straight from my dad's church to the Irish bar and grill every Sunday. When we played early games that started at noon Minnesota time they sometimes missed part of the first quarter. In my second year my dad bought the NFL cable package so he could watch, and DVR, the Colts' games at home. They came to games in Indy when they could. They were in the stands in the

RCA Dome when we beat the New England Patriots in a miracle comeback to advance to the Super Bowl. Of course they were here, in Miami, for the biggest game of my life.

And I had just blown my dad off when he tried to share a moment with me before the Super Bowl. I felt sick to my stomach. I could not take another step. Me playing in this game wasn't just my dream. It was his as well. *Go back to where it all started*, came to me in a gentle whisper. *Go back to where it all started*. I knew right then that in this moment the biggest game of my life was not the most important thing. I turned around and scanned the stands for my father. He'd left the railing and started walking back to his seat. I caught sight of him just up the ramp a little ways. "Dad! Dad!" I called out to him.

He stopped and turned.

I waved for him to come back down to where he had been a few moments earlier. He came back to the rail. I reached up my hand as high as I could as he reached down to me. I grabbed his hand tight. Tears filled my eyes. "It all started in the backyard with you, Dad. I love you. Thank you so much," I said.

My dad smiled. "I love you, too." We were in the backyard again, playing football, my mom cheering me on from the porch. It was as if no one else were there, just the two of us.

The sound of the crowd returned. I had to go. I let go of my dad's hand and ran out onto the field with my teammates. The game started with a huge play by the Bears and ended with our team holding the Lombardi Trophy as world champions. The Super Bowl was all I imagined it to be. Yet I came away from the game reflecting on how I almost lost something irreplaceable before the game even started. Standing in the tunnel, caught up in the hype and excitement of the Super Bowl, I nearly let the game consume me. I almost lost myself, my real identity, all because of a game.

I now look back on that moment with a sense of irony. Even though I made a conscious choice to go back to where it all began for me and there recover my true self, I now face a battle in which I may not have a choice in how this ends. The game has already changed me in ways from which I may never recover. Future changes could well lie in front of me. The odds are troubling. In all fairness, it is not the game of football in and of itself that extracted such a heavy toll on me, but rather the lasting results of what medical books call mild traumatic brain injury. Most people simply call them concussions. I suffered five documented concussions over the course of my playing career, which stretched across four years of college ball and six seasons in the National Football League. I never thought about the long-term effects of this injury until it was too late.

However, this is not a book about concussions, or even football. Both play a major role in my story, but they do not define me. Mine is a story about a preacher's son who grew up in a loving family, a boy who grew up praying for a family of his own someday. When I found the woman with whom I now share my life, I knew I had found everything I had ever dreamed of. Now all of us, my mom and dad, my wife, my sister, and myself, are locked in a battle as I hope to hold on to those I love. They are not going anywhere. Unfortunately, my memories are. I have already lost some I once treasured.

I now understand that our essence as human beings lies in our ability to remember. Everything that matters about our identities—our very sense of self—comes from our memories. We may live in the present, but the present doesn't last. Every moment quickly slips into the stream of short-term memory and journeys toward the ocean that is the long-term memory center of the brain. There our memories take root, shaping us, refining us, defining who we are. We are the culmination of all we have experienced, all we have thought and read and believed, all we have loved. We are living memories. Without memories we cease to be ourselves. In a very real way we cease to be.

And that is the very real possibility I now face. My memories appear to have an expiration date even as I fight to hold on to them. I don't know who will win this battle. That is why I am compelled to write this book. Yes, this is my story, but it is also a love letter to my wife and four daughters. Someday all that you are about to read may be nothing but a blur to me. But with this book in their hands, my family will always remember who I was and why I loved them so much.

CHAPTER 2

FOUNDATIONS

My dad is a pastor, which makes me a preacher's kid. When people hear that, most automatically assume I was either a hellion or one of those perfect kids who never did anything wrong. Those are the two main stereotypes of preachers' kids. I didn't fit either picture. I didn't even know there was supposed to be anything different about my family until I was around eight or nine. My mom and dad were just my mom and dad. We went to church a lot, but that was where my dad worked. I didn't think it any stranger that we spent a lot of time at church than a football coach's kids think it odd that they spend a lot of time at football stadiums.

I was never intimidated by my dad's job. Honestly, I thought it was kind of cool to watch him up in front of the church on Sundays preaching a sermon. He has a gift for holding people's attention, and I don't just say that because he's my dad. I once overheard someone call him "the Velvet Hammer" because of his preaching style. I really like that. It's him. As I got a little older I looked around at people during church and I could tell that they were into what he was saying. Sure, I could always find someone who hadn't slept enough the night before, but you can find that anytime anyone gives a speech. When I played for the Colts I had one of the most dynamic, inspiring head coaches ever in Tony Dungy. I too had days where my eyelids got a little heavy listening to him, but that was on me, not him.

But it wasn't just the way my dad did his job that caught my attention. He and my mother lived out the things he taught as a pastor. They didn't make a big deal about it, nor did they act different when church members were around. The two of them simply set an example for my sister, Ashley, and me about what is really important in life and what a life worth living looks like. I saw it first and foremost in their relationship with one another. My mom and dad love one another, but more than that, they are *in love* with each other. Their example showed me the kind of relationship I wanted to have with my future wife someday.

Don't get me wrong. We were a normal family and there were times my parents lost it with my sister and me. Growing up I was always such a high-energy, ultracompetitive kid that my mom, who grew up in a family of girls, thought something must be wrong with me. I didn't always know when to stop and I pushed every boundary she ever set for me. But those moments became teaching times for us. My parents held weekly family meetings where we actually talked, all of us, together. Neither my mom nor dad turned these meetings into a lecture or a time to point out everything I had done wrong in the past week. I'll never forget, or I hope I don't, all the times my mom and dad truly listened and even apologized at times for things they had done that might have hurt my sister or me. Now that I am a dad I understand how hard it is to admit to your child that you were wrong. That only makes me respect my parents that much more.

This was the environment in which I grew up. Faith was a big part of who we were as a family, but it was a faith that was more than talk. It was a way of life. This faith shaped the way we interacted with one another and with other people. It also shaped the way in which my parents approached the big questions and problems of life. And one of the biggest challenges they faced was one they shared with a lot of families: how to send their children to college without leaving them drowning in student loan debt. Football, believe it or not, became an answer to prayer.

By the time I started high school my mom and dad started to think sports might be more than a way for me to build friendships and work off excess energy. From the time I was a little boy, coaches told them I was a bit of a natural, especially in football. I didn't play football in eighth grade, I played soccer instead, but some of my friends talked me into coming back on the team in my freshman year of high school. That year I played wide receiver, defensive end, and punter. My greatest growth and improvement came as a sophomore. I remember my sophomore coach, Pete Zach, telling me he was sending great reports up to the varsity head coach, Bob Majeski. When I played in high school Coach Majeski rarely, if ever, allowed sophomores to play varsity football. When I was a junior my body started to fill out and catch up with my height. I had my best season yet as our football team, the Hastings Raiders, made it to the Minnesota State Football Tournament, held in Minneapolis at the Hubert H. Humphrey Metrodome, where the Vikings played.

In addition to football I also played hockey through the winter. Believe it or not, I was a goalie. At six feet six inches without skates, I was probably the tallest in the state. I probably should have played basketball but in Minnesota hockey is a way of life and there was no exception for me, especially since my grandfather Bob Utecht was the legendary rinkside voice of the Minnesota North Stars. He even coined the phrase "Let's Play Hockey," which is now proclaimed before hockey games at every level all over the country.

I loved hockey, and I was good at it, but football was my sport.

One of the men in my dad's church, a guy named Terry, had played college football at the University of Minnesota. After my stand-out junior season, he and my dad were talking after church one Sunday. Terry told my dad he thought I had what it took to play Division I college football. "So what can we do to get him noticed by colleges?" my dad asked. Terry suggested making a VHS high-light tape of my best plays and sending it off to whatever colleges I might want to attend. My dad then contacted another man in the church, David, who ran the local cable news station. He also called his brother, my uncle Greg, who was the technology director in another school district. David went through all the footage avail-able from my games, both football and hockey (at this point, I still hadn't decided which to concentrate on), and picked out the best plays. My uncle Greg then turned those into a VHS highlight tape.

My mom and dad made several copies of the tape, then prayed over them. They said, "Lord, we want what's best for our son, and you know we have little money to send Ben to college. If it is your will, please bless him with a scholarship." With that, they sent the tapes off to the head football coach at every Big 10 school (there were only ten back then), along with Stanford, Syracuse, and Notre Dame.

It didn't take long for their prayers to be answered. Through-out the winter and spring of my junior year in high school I re-ceived recruiting letters from every school to which we sent tapes. The letters all said basically the same thing. "We're interested in what Ben can do. We would like to see more of him. Is there any chance he can come to our summer football camp so that we can evaluate him firsthand?"

Getting these letters was a huge honor. However, the football camps, along with the travel there and back, were very expensive. My mom and dad asked me which schools I was most interested in since there was no way I could go to camps at all of them. I thought and prayed about it for a while, and narrowed my list down to two: Penn State, which was coached by the legendary Joe Paterno, and Minnesota, which was only thirty miles from our home in Hastings. Minnesota was coached by Glen Mason. When Coach Mason took over, more than twenty years had passed since the Golden Gophers had won a Big 10 championship. The team hadn't been good in a while, but Coach Mason now had it on the rise. I liked the prospect of playing for a rapidly improving team. I also liked the idea of playing close enough to home that my family could come to my games.

The U of M camp just happened to come first that summer. I planned on attending it in June. Then I was going to go to the Penn State camp, a trip my family would work into a summer vacation.

On the first day of the U of M camp the coaches lined up all the players by position and had us run the forty-yard dash. The forty is the standard by which coaches and scouts evaluate all football players' speed. I don't know how or why they settled on the forty, but your forty time is crucial. I ran it in 4.4 seconds, which is a really, really good time. Vic Adamle, the Gophers' wide receivers coach who was recruiting me, immediately noticed.

A couple of days into the camp I participated in seven-on-seven passing drills. In a seven-on-seven drill, the offensive and defensive lines sit out. Instead, the receivers go up against the defensive backs. I ran a fade route down the sideline. On a fade route I try to move the defender in, then I fade out toward the sideline. The quarterback threw a high, arcing pass toward me. However, he threw the ball short. I had already beaten my man, but I had to come back to the ball. The defender, the ball, and I all converged on the same place at the same time. I jumped up high, and reached back over the defender, who already had his hands on the ball. While I was still in the air I grabbed the ball and ripped it out of the defender's hands. When my feet touched the ground I took off running and didn't stop until I hit the end zone.

After the whistle blew I heard a loud, high-pitched scream. I looked over and saw Vic Adamle sprinting down the field, yelling at the top of his lungs, "Yeah! That's what I'm looking for! Yeah! Now that's what I'm looking for." Vic ran all the way up to me and actually jumped in my arms. After his excitement played out, he slapped me on the back and had me run back to the line for another play.

At the end of the camp I was asked by Coach Mason and Coach Adamle to come back the next day with my dad for a personal meeting with Coach Mason.

"Sure, Coach," I said. I didn't know what Coach wanted to meet with me about, but I hoped it was something good. I called my dad and he agreed to come out the next day. Right after he hung up with me, my father called Terry, the man in our church who helped him put together my highlight video. My dad thought he knew why they wanted to see me, but he wanted Terry's opinion. Terry agreed with my dad and gave him several questions to ask in the meeting.

The next day I went back for the specialists camp, which is for the kickers, punters, and snappers. At the end of camp my dad and I went to see Coach Mason. He led us into his office, which was impressive. Dark woods, leather chairs and sofas; he made an immediate impression on me. My father and I took our seats across from Coach Mason as he sat behind his desk. Coach got right to the point. "We thought Ben had a fantastic camp; in fact with his talent we believe he could play for us this season!" My eyes grew wide when I heard this. At the time I was still only sixteen. Coach Mason continued, "We want Ben to be a Gopher. We want to offer him a full scholarship to come to the University of Minnesota."

I wanted to jump up and down, but I didn't. I looked over at my dad, who remained perfectly calm, which only a minister would. "That sounds really great," my dad said. "Would it be all right if I asked a few questions?"

"Sure," Coach said. "Fire away."

"What if Ben gets injured and the injury is career threatening and he cannot play? What happens to his scholarship then?"

Coach Mason shook his head. "Don't worry. His scholarship will remain intact even if he gets hurt."

"That's reassuring. Thank you," my dad said. Then he added, "Now, Ben is only sixteen years old and still growing." I was already six-six, but still pretty thin. "What do you think will happen if Ben gains forty pounds?"

Coach Mason broke out in a huge grin. "If that happens, he'll be the best tight end in the Big 10. I can promise you that."

My dad looked over at me. I didn't have any questions except where do I sign. We sat there without saying anything for a moment or two when Coach Mason broke the silence. "Well, what do you think?" he asked the two of us.

"Glen, Ben has another camp he's scheduled to go out to at Penn State next month," my dad said.

"I know," Coach Mason said. "That's why we wanted you to come in today." Then he looked right at me. "Ben, here's what you have to decide. Do you want to wake up standing on third base thinking you hit a triple, or do you want to start at home plate, standing in the batter's box, and knock the ball out of the park yourself?" It was the coach's way of telling me I could go to a powerhouse school like Penn State and start out on top in terms of the team's standing, or I could be a part of the rebuilding process at Minnesota, with a chance to do something really special.

I looked over at my dad. "Well, son, what do you think?" my dad asked.

"You know I want to play where you and mom can come watch me every week," I said.

"Your mother and I will support you whatever you choose to do," my dad replied.

I sat there for just a moment. "I want to be a Gopher," I said.

Coach Mason stood up and extended his hand toward me. "Ben, I think you've made the right choice. Congratulations. Welcome to the University of Minnesota family." He then shook hands with my dad as well.

My dad and I walked out into the hall, where my dad gave me a huge hug. "I'm so proud of you, son," he said to me. We both had tears in our eyes. It was such a special moment with my father.

After the meeting my dad and I went to the Golden Gopher Locker Room store, where I bought my mom a University of Minnesota sweatshirt. On the drive home I called her on my dad's cell phone. When she answered I said, "Hi, Mom. How are you doing?" in a very low-key tone of voice.

My mom took the bait. "I'm fine, Ben. How did the meeting go?" she said with that concerned-mom tone of voice.

"Unfortunately, it didn't go as well as we had hoped."

"Why? What did they say?" I could tell she was deflated.

"I'll tell you about it when we get home. Are you going to be there?" I asked.

"Yes. Oh, Ben, I'm sorry," she said.

"It's all right, Mom. They said they're going to watch me this season and told me to keep up the good work." I knew I had to get off the phone fast before I blew it. "I don't want to talk about it right now, Mom. We'll be home soon." I hung up the phone, and my dad and I had a good chuckle.

When I walked in the front door of our house I kept up the downtrodden-athlete act. My mom was waiting for me. She started toward me to give me a big mom hug. As we got close I pulled the Gopher sweatshirt out from behind my back and said, "Hey, Mom, how do you feel about wearing this for the next four years?"

My mom let out a scream. "Are you kidding me!?" she yelled. "Are *you* kidding me!?" She then fell back to the stairs and began to weep tears of joy. "Oh, thank you, Lord," she prayed. "Thank you, Lord." We all cried, laughed, hugged, and thanked God together in the entrance to our home.

I went into my senior year of high school with some lofty goals along with a pretty lofty view of myself. I'd be lying if I told you receiving a full-ride scholarship to play football at a Division I school didn't go to my head. Football had always been a game that started in the backyard with my dad, a game where friendships were formed, where I loved hanging out with the other guys on the team. All of that was still true, but going into my senior season football was now also the way I was going to make a name for myself. I planned on dominating games and being named all-state. Every game people would see why the Golden Gophers wanted me to come be a vital part of their team.

My plans lasted until the first half of the second game of the season. I took off down the field on a corner route. I was supposed to run straight up the field for about ten yards, then make a sharp 45-degree cut toward the sideline. Since the defender is on my inside shoulder, the cut sets up an open lane for the quarterback to get me the ball. I'd run this route so many times I could do it in my sleep. The ball snapped. I took off down the field. The defender was right where I wanted him to be. I reached my mark, planted my foot, and made a sharp cut toward the sideline. As I did I heard and felt a heavy pop in my hip like someone had just punched me hard. Pain shot through my body. My leg gave out and I collapsed to the ground. I had no idea what had just happened to me. It was almost like I had just been shot. The crowd gasped, then fell completely silent.

The next thing I knew my mom ran the fastest forty-yard dash in the history of Hastings High. She reached me on the field before the coaches or trainers got there. I looked up at her. She tells me my eyes were as big as saucers. "Mom, I don't know what happened," I said, confused and about to panic. I had never been injured in a football game before.

My mother didn't miss a beat. "Ben, look at me. Do you trust Jesus?" she asked.

"Yeah," I said.

"Then trust Him now. He's in control. You'll be okay," she said.

"But my scholarship—"

She cut me off. "He's in control. You will be okay," she repeated. In that moment a peace I can't even describe came over the two of us.

The following Monday my parents took me to see an orthopedic specialist. X-rays confirmed a pelvic avulsion fracture at the growth plate. "Ben shouldn't play football the rest of the season," he told us. When my mom asked how this injury could occur, the doctor explained: "He's growing so fast that it puts pressure on the bones. The good news is that this should heal completely and not give him any more problems."

I still had one problem, however. When Coach Mason offered me a scholarship, we could not sign anything. All we had was a verbal commitment and a handshake. The national letter of intent, the official document that committed me to the university, could not be signed for a few more months. I didn't know what the Gophers would do now that I was hurt. The pain in my hip was replaced by the fear that my Division I football career was over even before it started. Helpless to fix anything, I had nothing else to fall back on except faith. "Do you trust Jesus?" my mother had asked as I lay on the field in pain. I had nothing else to go on. "God, I put this in your hands," I prayed repeatedly. My cockiness was gone. The injury brought "Mr. Division I scholarship BMOC (Big Man on Campus)" back down to earth. The injury stripped everything away except the only thing that lasts, the only thing I can always count on. "Do you trust Jesus? He's in control. You will be okay," echoed through my head.

My mother was right. Everything was okay. Coach Mason honored his commitment to me. I still had my scholarship even though I wasn't supposed to play again that season. The game that I fell in love with in the backyard with my dad was going to pay for my college education. It was a dream come true.

CHAPTER 3

UP AND DOWN

THE FRACTURED HIP I SUFFERED IN the second game of my senior year of high school did not cost me my scholarship. Nor did it cost me the entire football season, as the doctor had predicted. After the doctor told me my season was over, my high school coach, Bob Majeski, called my father. Coach Majeski is the most successful coach in Hastings history and was inducted into the Minnesota State High School Coaches Association Hall of Fame. More important, he is a great man who played a major role in my life as an athlete and a person. Coach had talked to the high school principal, who had wrestled in college at a Division I school. The principal had suffered the same injury when he was in high school. However, he was able to continue competing even with the injury through toughness and by taking ibuprofen. "The question we need answered is will Ben make his injury worse by playing," Coach Majeski asked my father. "Playing at all this season could depend on his pain management. Is that something you'd like to check with your doctor about, because we'd love to have Ben back on the field?"

"Why is it so important to have Ben back?" my dad asked.

"Because he's one of our team leaders. We all know Ben is an outstanding player, but he brings much more to the team. I don't expect him to play at his normal level, and I will not do anything that might risk further injury. More than anything, I want Ben back for what he brings to the locker room. Even if he can't do anything but stand on the sideline, he makes us a better team," Coach Majeski said.

"Thank you," my dad said. "I can see that, but this really comes down to Ben and what he wants to do. How do you feel about that possibility?" my dad asked me.

I couldn't believe my dad even had to ask. I wanted to get back on the football field with my team more than anything. But I played it cool. "Sounds good to me," I responded as low-key as possible.

"We will get back with you and let you know," my father said to Coach Majeski.

My father seemed unsure about the whole prospect of me playing with a fractured hip, but he left the decision up to me. Well, me and our family doctor. To me, the choice was easy. The broken pelvis dashed my dreams of having a breakout year, but I had more than my own personal statistics in mind. We had a really good football team my senior year at Hastings High School. From the start of our first two-a-day practice we all knew we had a chance to do something special. When I went down with the hip injury, I felt I had let my team down. They counted on me, which made me willing to do whatever it took to get back on the field to help the team any way I could. One of the great lessons you learn in football is to put the team first. That is why when my dad asked how I felt about using over-the-counter anti-inflammatories and playing through the pain I didn't have to give it a thought. The answer was an absolute yes. If it would get me back on the field with the team, I was ready to give it a try.

My dad then called the doctor and asked him if my playing would make my injury any worse. "No, it's still going to heal, but there will be a lot of pain with it. It really comes down to how much pain he can stand and if he is willing to try." When my dad told me what the doctor said, there really was no question about what I was going to do. Every day before football practice I took the full dose of ibuprofen, then repeated that process afterward. The hip hurt like nothing I had ever experienced, but in football you play through pain.

Even though this was the first real injury I had suffered on a football field, this was far from my first time to play through pain. You can't play football without getting something hurt. You leave every game bruised and bloodied and your body just hurts. Those don't count as injuries. That's just the game. By the time I retired from professional football in 2009, the hurts touched every part of my body, from the top of my head down to my feet. However, when I was in high school, my only real injury was this pelvic avulsion fracture.

I took the maximum amount of ibuprofen allowed and tried to work my way back into playing shape. I found that even with the medicine, my range of motion was severely limited. No matter how much I wanted to contribute to the team, and no matter how badly the coach wanted me to play, the reality is you don't come back from a hip fracture in a matter of a couple of weeks. It took me five full weeks after my injury before I felt well enough to run in straight lines. I still couldn't make cuts or run pass patterns. By then the season was almost over. I was finally ready to play in the last game of the season, the conference championship game.

The conference championship game of my senior year was the biggest game of my high school career. We played Woodbury High School, which went on to win the state championship that season. The hype leading up to the game was electric. When Friday night finally rolled around, the stadium was full, standing room only. Our team went out with a lot of emotion, but by the end of the first half we were down by three touchdowns, 21–0.

The game was basically over. However, we played inspired football the second half and came back to tie the game while shutting
them out. Woodbury scored a go-ahead touchdown late, but they
missed the extra point. We got the ball back late in the fourth
quarter, down 27–21. Our offense moved the ball to their thirty-
five-yard line. We missed on a couple of passes and the drive sort
of stalled out. We faced fourth down and long with only fifteen
seconds to play. We had one last shot. The entire game came
down to the final play.

Our coach called a time-out and told the quarterback to throw
a Hail Mary, that is, a desperation pass to the end zone. The offense started running back out on the field when wide receiver
coach Jake Moore looked around. "Where's Utecht?" he yelled.
I had not played on offense since breaking my hip. "Utecht?" he
called again.

I tapped him on the shoulder. "I'm right here, Coach."

"I need to know," he said, his eyes wide, "can you do this? I just
need you to run straight down the field and make a play. Can you
do it?"

"I'll make the catch," I replied.

"Get in there," Coach Moore said, a huge smile on his face.

I ran back out on the field and took my place at wide receiver
for the first time since my pelvic growth plate had snapped. The
center hiked the ball and I took off toward the end zone. Three
defensive backs converged on me. I kept running. The quarterback threw the ball as hard as he could. I went up high over the
three defensive backs. The ball hit me in the hands and rolled
into my chest. The defensive backs bounced off me and fell to
the ground as I ran into the end zone to tie the game. Our kicker
kicked the extra point and we were conference champs.

This was the kind of play I had imagined myself making while
running pass routes against the cedar fence in my yard with my
dad when I was a little boy. As far as high school went, this was

the biggest play of my life. After the game my hip was so sore that I could hardly walk, but in the euphoria of the victory, the pain didn't seem so bad. That's another part of the game of football. When you win, nothing hurts as bad as it does when you lose.

Once the football season ended my injury healed pretty quickly. Then it was on to my final season playing hockey, where our team had a really good year. Not only did the pain in my hip area subside, but so did the humility and brokenness I felt right after the injury happened. When I did not know whether I was going to be able to keep my scholarship I spent a lot of time asking God for help. Now not only did I have my scholarship, but I was also the big hero of the biggest game of the season. I didn't really need anyone's help. I had it all going on. I was still very involved in church with my family, and I sang there often. (I started singing in church when I was a little boy. Music has always been a love in my life.) I was also a fixture at our youth group meetings. Outwardly, I was still the same guy I had always been, but deep inside I was straddling the fence between arrogance and humility. I now fit the stereotype, not of a preacher's kid, but of the Big Man on Campus, full-of-himself jock. I knew I was going places, and the next stop was the University of Minnesota.

A month before I was to report for my first U of M training camp, I was selected to play in the Minnesota Football Coaches Association all-star high school football game. Playing in this game was a huge honor, a recognition as one of the best high school players in the state. Eighty-eight players from all over Minnesota came together for a week of practice before the game at Macalester College in St. Paul. Most of the guys were going to play college ball somewhere, but not many had full rides at Division I schools, much less a Big 10 school. That made me stand out on a team full of standouts. I enjoyed the attention. There's a verse in the Bible that says pride comes before the fall. Knowing that, I should have been ready for what came next. I wasn't.

On the last play of the all-star week of practice I took off across the practice field, running a pass route. I jumped up, grabbed the ball out of the air, then landed right on top of the only sprinkler head that was out in the middle of the field. What it was doing there is anyone's guess. Since I never expected to land directly on a sprinkler head, I wasn't watching out for it. When I hit it, I hit it hard. I came down awkwardly and heard another loud pop. My pelvic injury was fine, but I had broken my left ankle. Not only was my all-star game over before it started; in all likelihood so was my dream of starting for the Golden Gophers as a true freshman.

Just like with my broken pelvis, my ankle injury left me scared and worried. Any amount of ego was gone, replaced with humility. I had no idea what the university was going to do. They had honored my scholarship offer before, and I hoped they would again, but I wasn't sure. On top of that, I played a position predicated on speed. Exactly one year earlier I ran a 4.4 forty-yard dash. Now I had a broken ankle and was coming off a broken pelvis, both on my left side. I had no idea what that combination might do to my speed. If I couldn't run pass routes fast enough to gain separation from defensive backs, my career was pretty much over before it started. Again.

Once again, I started praying. I pleaded with God to make all the bones go back together the right way, and honestly, to keep my speed where it had once been. Yes, it was a selfish prayer, but it didn't feel like it then. I was depending on God to come through as I wondered what else could be done.

My prayers were answered. Coach Mason again proved good to his word. The university sent me to an orthopedic surgeon, who removed a bone chip that had broken off my ankle. Within four weeks my ankle was as good as new and I was cleared to practice. The season was just starting, so technically I could have still played.

However, when the injury happened Coach Mason decided to red-shirt me. Redshirting meant I still worked out with the team and went to class, but I could not suit up with the team for games for the entire season. Since a redshirt misses the season, the NCAA grants them another year of eligibility. Basically it meant I now had a five-year scholarship rather than four. With an extra year of school paid for courtesy of the football team, not only could I get my bachelor's degree, but I could also pursue a master's if I wanted.

Once the doctors cleared me to practice, I threw everything into proving myself once again. Thankfully my speed had not diminished, and I dominated the rookie squad. I played so well that the coaches actually considered bringing me off the list of players unable to perform (PUP) and putting me on the active roster. However, because I had already missed a few games, they decided they would rather have me play on the team for four full seasons rather than the three and a half. I agreed with the decision as being the right one. By the end of the year I was named offensive demonstration player (a player who has not yet made the active roster but plays a significant role in practice) of the year. Coach Mason and the rest of the staff had high hopes for me the next year.

When I moved to Hastings at ten years of age, all of my closest friendships started on a sports team. The same thing happened when I went to the University of Minnesota. Most of my closest friendships came from the football field. That's where I got to know Dan Nystrom. The two of us came to the university as freshmen the same year, although Dan did not sit out a year as a redshirt. He was our kicker, but he was also a singer, like me. Both of us had been in as many choirs as teams through high school. Dan even made the all-state choir his senior year. We also shared a common faith. On top of all that, we just hit it off, and our voices complemented one another.

Any player on the roster of a major college football team has dreams of playing in the National Football League. Dan and I were no exceptions. But we also harbored dreams of doing something with music. We sang a little together, which made us start talking about singing publicly. The conversations might not have led to anything, except Dan had a friend whose dad worked the penalty box at the University of Minnesota hockey games. Hockey is huge at the U of M. Dan and I made a demo tape of us singing the national anthem and sent it to his friend's dad. If this seems like a roundabout way of getting a singing gig, well, it is. The friend's dad passed the tape along to the hockey rink manager or someone who made decisions about who performs at Golden Gopher games. I don't know if we really knocked it out of the park on our demo tape, or if it was the novelty of having two football players sing the national anthem, but however it happened, Dan and I were invited to come and sing at one of the Gophers' games.

On the night we were to sing, the PA announcer introduced us. Dan and I went out to center ice, microphones in hand, waiting for the music to start. I guess I should have been nervous, but I wasn't. If I had known what all this night was going to lead to, I really would have been scared to death.

I didn't know it, but up in the stands, sitting with her parents, was a freshman member of the Minnesota women's golf team. Her dad had played college hockey for Minnesota, and they're season ticket holders who don't miss a game. When the PA announcer said, "Please rise and remove your hats for the national anthem. Tonight, the anthem will be performed by Minnesota Golden Gopher football players Dan Nystrom and Ben Utecht," the girl leaned over to her parents and whispered, sarcastically, "Well, this ought to be good." She thought we were going to be the typical football jocks.

Then we started singing. Dan and I nailed it that night.

"Okay," the girl said, "these guys can sing." That made her pay a little closer attention to the two guys down on the ice. At six-seven, I literally stood out. She noticed me. After Dan and I finished singing, she sat down, looked over at her mom, and said, "Now why can't I meet a guy like that?"

A couple of weeks later she got her wish at a midwinter Fellowship of Christian Athletes event. To say she was disappointed by the meeting is an understatement. She knew who I was after hearing me at the hockey game. Afterward, she learned a little more about me, including the fact that I was very active in the university's FCA. That only made her want to meet me even more. She was more than a little excited when a mutual friend and one of my teammates, Justin Hall, offered to introduce us. And that's where the excitement ends.

I walked into the FCA event feeling pretty good about myself. That is to say, I had already started to develop the Big Man on Campus attitude I had in high school after I got my scholarship. Even though I had redshirted my first year due to injury, the fact that I had played so well on the rookie squad and the recognition I received from singing had already started going to my head. (After that first hockey game, Dan and I received numerous invitations to sing for all the U of M sports teams. By the time we graduated we sang for all the area professional teams as well as for Presidents George H. W. and George W. Bush.) On top of that, I had a girlfriend, so I wasn't out to make a good impression on any other girl I might meet.

Justin came over and found me right after I arrived. Since this was winter in Minnesota, everyone was pretty well bundled up, even inside. "Hey, Ben," Justin said, "I want you to meet Karyn Stordahl." Honestly, the girl sort of looked to me like a stocking cap and sweater with a face in between. I didn't pay too much attention to her.

I reached out my hand. "Hi, Karyn. Ben Utecht. Nice to meet

you." As I said this my eyes scanned the room, looking around to see who else was there.

"You, too," Karyn replied.

The conversation ended there, as did Karyn's slight infatuation with the singing football player. She figured she'd already met plenty of guys like me, guys who looked through her and past her, you know, the typical stuck-on-himself jock type. Even though that was far from the type of man I was inside, my actions at times showed otherwise. Unfortunately, it was going to get worse before it got better.

CHAPTER 4

MILD TRAUMATIC
BRAIN INJURY

I SUFFERED MY FIRST HEAD INJURY when I was four years old. To be honest, it sort of surprised me. After all, when it happened, I thought I was Superman.

I loved Superman and still do. My dad introduced him to me when he bought me a model set of Superman bursting through a wall. The two of us built it together. After that, I wanted all things Superman. My parents bought me some Superman pajamas complete with a cape that Velcroed to the shoulders. After I watched Christopher Reeve's 1978 *Superman* a few dozen times, I convinced them to buy the John Williams soundtrack for me. The more I listened to the music the more I wondered, *Why not me? Why can't I be Superman?* The idea made perfect sense to my four-year-old mind.

One afternoon I learned why not me. My friend Tim came over and the two of us decided to play superheroes. I don't remember who he pretended to be, but there was no doubt about who I was. I put on my Superman pajamas and cape, cranked up the John Williams soundtrack on the stereo, and took off running, trying to get airborne. Tim took off in the opposite direction. All the upstairs rooms in the parsonage in which we then lived connected to one another, which made it possible to run a complete circle through every room in the house. That's what Tim and I did. We flew off in opposite directions, only to meet back in the dining room, running full speed, each one of us oblivious to where the other might be. I didn't see Tim until it was too late. However, employing my superhero reflexes, I dove under Tim, who jumped up as high as he could. I then flew right between his legs, and I might have kept on flying if it hadn't been for the wooden dresser that lay directly in my path. I slammed into the corner of the dresser, face-first.

I don't know if my mother first heard the loud bang of my head hitting the corner of the dresser or my scream that followed, but she came rushing into the room to find me sort of attached to the dresser. She pulled me free, carried me to the car, and rushed me to the emergency room. The doctors stitched up the cut, which went all the way down to the bone. I still have the scar today. It reminds me I am not from Krypton. The injury slowed me down, but only for a couple of days. It wasn't long before I was running around the house again. I only had one speed, and that was full-on with no fear.

My next confirmed head injury came fifteen years later. I never saw it coming, either.

My body had caught up with my height by the time football training camp came around for what was now to be my redshirt freshman season (that is, my first year of eligibility for football, making me a freshman, although academically I was a sophomore). I reported for camp twenty pounds heavier than the year before, when I had my ankle surgery. I was now six-seven and weighed 240 pounds. Coach Mason and the receivers coach took one look at me and declared, "You're our new tight end." I did not like the sound of that at all. All through high school I had played wide receiver. The name tells you what the position does. I split out wide and I caught passes. Occasionally a play called on me to throw a block, but when I did, I went up against defensive backs. Those guys are small and quick. The tight end catches passes, but he is also an offensive lineman who spends most of the game blocking very large men on the defensive line or very large and very fast men who play linebacker. My height gave me a great advantage as a receiver, since most of my routes had me go up against those same linebackers, who were shorter and slower. However, this advantage changed once I got the ball. When I went over the middle to make a catch, I was vulnerable to being laid out.

Privately, I hated the idea of changing positions. I went into it kicking and screaming. However, outwardly I didn't argue. It felt good just to be wanted. Coach Mason had told my dad that if I gained forty pounds, he would make me the top tight end in the Big 10. I trusted him. When Coach asked what I wanted to do, I told him I would play wherever he needed me to play. Timing-wise, making the switch could not have come at a better time in terms of the evolution of the receiving tight end. In the earlier de-cades of football, most teams ran the ball first and foremost. Tight ends blocked and only occasionally caught a pass. About the time I became a tight end, offenses had opened up and threw the ball much more.

After spending my first year on the redshirt rookie squad, I finally got my chance to suit up for the Golden Gophers at home against Louisiana-Monroe in the Metrodome on Sep-tember 2, 2000. All of my family was in the stands cheering me on. On the first play of the game, I took off down the field on a seam route. I flew past the linebacker, looked up, and pulled the football out of the air, landing in the end zone for a forty-yard touchdown reception. Coach Adamle, the coach who got so excited about me making a catch on a similar route in the summer camp where I was recruited to come to the school, could hardly contain his excitement. This was my welcome-to-college-football moment and I loved it. I had waited for what felt like forever to make a play like this. The moment felt as good as I dreamed it would.

We went on to win the game 47–10. I only made one other catch, a short seven-yard reception. Altogether, eight different receivers or running backs had catches that day. I spent most of the game blocking. The blocking schemes were still pretty new to me, but I was starting to get the hang of it. After the game I found I had reached a new level of acceptance in the locker room. Guys three and four years older than I was started treating me like an equal and fully accepting I was as a member of the team. I didn't get that during my redshirt season. I have to tell you, it felt really good.

We lost our next game to Ohio University. I made one catch for thirty-nine yards, which is great statistically, but good stats don't mean anything when you lose. Then we went on the road to Waco, Texas, to play the Baylor Bears. We won the game, but that's not the story.

My mom went over to a friend's house to watch the Baylor game on television. Dad had a wedding to officiate so he was at the church getting ready for the wedding to start when the game kicked off. After the opening kickoff our offense came out on the field. In typical mom fashion, my mom cheered loudly for me when she saw me on the TV screen. I think it was almost as much fun for her to watch me on television as it was to sit in the stands. Everyone in the house cheered for me as well. The place had a party atmosphere to it. Everyone was having a good time.

As a tight end, most of the plays we ran called for me to block someone to open up a path for our running backs. As I said, the blocking schemes were all pretty new to me, since I never did much blocking when I played wide receiver. As a tight end, I learned a blocking technique where I led with my head and hands to land the initial blow on the defensive player, then launched up to gain leverage and move him out of my way. Playing the position is more complicated than that sounds. We had several different blocking schemes, depending on the play that was called. Most of the time I knew what to do, but on one running play early in the first half against Baylor I got spun around and I slammed into our starting left tackle. It was a helmet-to-helmet hit, which is never good. The force of the collision sent me sprawling to the ground, where I stayed.

A thousand miles away, in a living room in Hastings, Minnesota, my mother saw this play. The moment I hit the ground, she gasped. When the camera zoomed in on me lying very still, she stood up and stared at the screen. The camera stayed on me. Normally, even after a big hit, a player slowly gets up or, at the very least, rolls around in pain. Not me. I did not move a muscle. I have no memory of any of this because I was out cold. My mother told me the television announcer then said, "This doesn't look good. Utecht's legs aren't moving. He's very still. It is possible he could have broken his neck or injured his spine."

And then they cut to a commercial.

The wedding over which my dad was to officiate was ten minutes from starting when a member of the wedding party found my dad in his office. "You're Ben Utecht's dad, right?"

My dad gave him a funny look and cautiously said, "Yes."

"I just heard on the radio that Ben got knocked down on a play. He's laid out on the field and they don't know if he is going to be okay," the man said. "I thought you would want to know," he added, then left.

Now it was crisis time for my father. He wanted to grab the

phone and call my mother, but he didn't have time. He had to go out and do the wedding right then. And that is what he did. He said a prayer for me, then went out and took his place in the front of the church as the groomsmen came in and the bridesmaids all marched down the aisle. All he could think about was me lying on a football field in Waco, Texas, when the bride's father escorted her down the aisle while the crowd stood at attention. For everyone else in the room it was a joyous celebration. For my dad it was the longest wedding of his life. He had the bride and groom recite their vows and exchange rings, then pronounced them man and wife, all the while wondering what news was waiting for him once the wedding was over.

Across town my mother paced around her friend's living room, crying and praying during the longest commercial break in the history of television. Finally, the network came back to the game. She rushed over to the television, looking for me in the huddle of trainers and coaches crowded on the field. Finally, she caught a glimpse of me. I was still on the ground, but my legs were moving back and forth. The announcers said, "It looks like we're seeing some movement."

I remember waking up on the ground with a bloody nose. My coaches talked to me, then did a few tests to make sure I had not sustained a neck or back injury. Then the coaches had me sit up.

Back in Minnesota my mother heard the announcers say, "All right, he's talking to his coaches. It looks like he might be okay." My mom slumped down in a chair, emotionally exhausted. On the screen I stood up and was helped to the sideline. "Thank God," she prayed. "Oh, thank you, Jesus." She didn't finish watching the game.

My coaches helped me to my feet. I felt groggy and disoriented. My ears were ringing and my head was pounding. The trainers walked me back to the locker room, where they did a few basic tests. "You have a concussion," one said, "that's all. It sure looked like it could have been something bad." I wanted to go back into the game, but the trainers didn't let me. "We should have you sit out the rest of today, just in case," one said. I took off my pads and changed into some sweats, then returned to the sidelines.

The moment the wedding service ended, my dad rushed next door to our house. He flipped on the television and switched to the game. Play had resumed. The camera focused on the Minnesota sideline, where my dad saw me sitting on the bench in street clothes. A coach sat next to me, talking with me. My day was over, but at least my father could relax. It looked like I was going to be okay.

This was my first diagnosed concussion. Fifteen years ago, when this injury occurred, I didn't know much about concussions, including their symptoms, treatment, or long-term effects. Basically, a concussion occurs when the brain collides with the skull. Our brains float in a protective bath of cerebrospinal fluid. Our brains are soft; the skull is hard. When the head snaps violently, either from a blow to the head or from the head being whipped about suddenly, the laws of physics take over and the cerebrospinal fluid is not enough to keep the brain from slamming into the skull. If the impact is violent enough, the brain can be bruised, which shows up on a CT scan or an MRI. Doctors refer to that as a traumatic brain injury. In a concussion, the injury to the brain may not show up on any scans. Commonly no apparent bruising can be seen. That is one reason why a concussion is called a *mild* traumatic brain injury.

And that's exactly how concussions were regarded during my playing time, as something mild. Unless someone got knocked out cold, like I did, we never even thought of these injuries as concussions. We all just referred to them as getting our bell rung, or getting lit up. You get your bell rung when you get hit so hard you see stars or you feel disoriented for a moment. It wasn't until I started researching concussions in 2009 that I learned these are the symptoms of a Grade 1 concussion (and there are three grades, or three levels of severity). When I include bell rings, I now understand that I cannot count the number of concussions I suffered going as far back as junior high. Back then we had a blocking drill called Bull in a Ring. In this drill, one player got in the middle of a circle of players. On the coach's signal, everyone started running in place. The coach walked around the outside of the circle, then tapped one guy on the shoulder. This guy then took off after the guy in the center and tried to knock him off his feet. I came away from those drills with my bell rung more times than I can count. I usually had a headache as well, which is another concussion symptom, but I never thought anything of it. The headaches went away and I kept on playing. Getting your bell rung was no big deal.

It wasn't just me. That was the culture of football in regard to head injuries fifteen years ago. That doesn't mean no one knew anything about concussions when I was knocked out against Baylor on September 16, 2000. Research into concussions and football goes back to the mid-1980s. University of Virginia neuropsychologist Jeff Barth did the first study of concussions in college football in 1984 with the University of Virginia, then expanded the study the next year to include 2,350 players from the Ivy League schools and the University of Pittsburgh.* The book *League of Denial,* by Mark Fainaru-Wada and Steve Fainaru, gives a very detailed history of how concussion research in football, both good and bad, took off after Barth's initial study. Dur-

---

* Mark Fainaru-Wada and Steve Fainaru, *League of Denial*, Kindle ed. (New York: Crown Archetype, 2013), chapter 2.

ing the 1990s researchers discovered that concussions were far more widespread than anyone had believed before, and that they had more serious long-term effects than previously understood. Researchers started studying former players and found that many exhibited the kind of "punch drunk" symptoms associated with former boxers who had spent too much time in the ring. In 1994 the NFL even established a committee to study concussions and find ways to make the game safer. Already, many researchers, like Dr. Robert Cantu, were speaking out, saying concussions must be taken far more seriously. In an interview I conducted with Dr. Cantu for this book, he told me that there is nothing mild about mild traumatic brain injuries. Traumatic is traumatic and should be treated as such.

I knew none of this when I suffered my first documented concussion. When I heard the trainer tell me I had suffered a concussion I thought it was about as serious as a paper cut. On the Monday after the Baylor game I went through the rudimentary concussion protocols in place at the time, passed them, and returned to practice either that day or the day after. The next Saturday I was back in the lineup at tight end against eventual Big 10 champion Purdue and their quarterback Drew Brees, now quarterback of the New Orleans Saints. We lost the game. I only had one catch, which was not unusual for a tight end back then. The position was still transitioning from primarily a blocker to a receiver.

I started the rest of the season. We ended up with a winning record and played in the Micron PC Bowl in Miami, held in the same stadium where I would one day play in Super Bowl XLI. All in all, I had a really good season for a first-year player. Not many freshmen see a lot of playing time. I not only played; I started every game that season. When the season ended, I wasn't thinking about concussions or injuries or anything else. Honestly, I wasn't even thinking that much about my schoolwork. I was already focused on the next season and building on what I had started in my redshirt freshman year. As a team, we had gone to back-to-back bowl games for the first time since 1960 and 1961. This was why I had come to the University of Minnesota. I wanted to be a part of something special, and now I was. It was a great place to be for a nineteen-year-old boy like me.

CHAPTER 5

GASTON

I CALLED MY DAD ONE DAY in early November, a little over a month after the Baylor game. "Dad, I think I found the girl I'm going to marry," I said.

"What?" my dad said with a tone that told me I had his full attention. "Where? I mean, who is she?"

"Her name is Karyn," I said. "She's just . . . I've never met anyone like her before."

"Where did you meet her?"

"At the FCA Halloween karaoke party. From the moment she walked in the door I couldn't take my eyes off of her," I said. Even today, I can still picture her in her costume that night. She wore an orange seventies disco-style jumpsuit with big white polka dots on it. Just thinking about her that night makes my heart race. I immediately went over to introduce myself to her, which wasn't easy because she seemed to be trying to avoid me. It turns out that she was! When I finally got close enough to introduce myself she said, "We've met before, Ben, but you probably don't remember."

I wish I could blame the blow to the head in the Baylor game for my mistake. As soon as she said that, I remembered we *had* met, or at least she had met me. I had looked right past her that first meeting. In my defense, I had a girlfriend back then, but that was no excuse for my really bad first impression. "I am so sorry about last time," I said.

"It's okay," she said, and I hoped she meant it.

I knew I had to think fast to change her perception of me. *Ask about HER!* I thought. So I asked, "You are on the golf team, right?" As it turns out, Karyn wasn't just on the golf team. By the time her college career ended she was named team captain and academic all-American.

"Yes, that's right," she said.

"So how is your season going?" I asked.

"Our season is over," she replied.

"Uhhh . . ." was all I could get out. Karyn just gave me a wry grin. I think I salvaged the moment by asking if I could get her some punch. My trip to the punch bowl was the farthest I let her get away from me that night. By the end of the evening I asked for her phone number and if she would mind if I called her sometime.

"If you want," she said with a little smile; if I wasn't hooked already, I now was. However, her tone of voice didn't really give away how she felt. I couldn't tell if she wanted me to call or not.

I didn't waste any time finding out. I called her the next day around five thirty. "Hi, Karyn. It's Ben. Ben Utecht."

"Oh. Hi, Ben," she said with a note of surprise.

"If you haven't eaten yet, would you like to go to dinner with me and another couple of my friends?" I asked.

"Sure, I would love to," she said. Only later did I learn that she had already eaten dinner.

In spite of what I told my father, I didn't approach this dinner as any kind of romantic encounter. I may be a hopeless romantic, but I did not truly believe that I was going to marry Karyn after spending a little time with her at a college karaoke party. However, I knew I wanted to get to know her better, and I hoped she might get to see the real me.

My friend Jake and his date came along with Karyn and me to a place called J. D. Hoyt's. All through the evening we all talked and laughed a lot. When I learned Karyn loved Disney movies, Jake and I sang every Disney song we could remember. Because I wasn't trying to make a love connection, both Karyn and I were free to just be ourselves. I didn't approach this date as a romantic encounter, but I have to tell you, by the end of the night I knew there was something very special about her. After we left the restaurant I walked her to the door of her sorority house and told her good night. We didn't have a good-night kiss or anything like that. The moment just wasn't right. The whole evening had just been fun.

But afterward I couldn't get her out of my mind.

The more I thought about her, the more I realized she was exactly the kind of girl I had always hoped to find. She had a great sense of humor. She was smart and loved to have fun. And from what I had already learned about her, I could tell she had a rock solid faith. She didn't seem to approach God like some religious duty. I could tell she had a real, personal, intimate relationship with Him. On top of that, she was a topflight athlete who could probably clean my clock at golf. If I had made a checklist of the qualities I had hoped to find in a girl, she would have marked all the right boxes.

That's when I called my dad and told him I thought I had found the girl I was going to marry someday. I do not mean I had already fallen head over heels in love with her. However, I knew that if I spent more time with her, that was exactly what would happen.

That may be why I froze and didn't call her again for a few weeks. More than once I picked up the phone but I couldn't bring myself to dial her number. I ran into her at FCA functions, and I always talked and kidded around with her. Okay, I was flirting. I couldn't help myself. But then I never pursued her. I know I confused her to death with all the mixed signals I sent her way.

Part of my hesitation in letting her know about the growing feelings inside me came from the fact that I had just come out of a yearlong relationship when I met her and I was a little hesitant to jump into another relationship that could turn serious. Looking back, I realize that's more of an excuse than a reason. I think the real issue had nothing to do with fear but with me. When I was with Karyn I felt like I didn't measure up, like I didn't deserve someone like her. She didn't do anything to make me feel that way. In fact, she did the exact opposite. My insecurities all came from deep inside myself. Deep down I was convinced that if I pursued her romantically, I would do something to hurt her and blow any chance of a future together.

Like a lot of people when they first go off to college, I was trying to figure out who I really was and who I wanted to be. A war was going on inside me. I felt pulled between the person my parents brought me up to be and the guy who felt a huge charge when the older guys on the team asked me to go out for beers after games. Beers after games led to dipping my toe in the campus party scene. I'm not going to lie, I liked it. I liked the way people reacted to me as a football player, especially when I had a really good game.

Don't get me wrong. I didn't suddenly start living up to all the stereotypes of a preacher's kid. In a lot of ways I remained who I had always been. All my life I had stood up for the underdog. That didn't change. I also tried to conduct myself with integrity in everything I did. Again, I did not change. However, consistently living out my faith was always a challenge. In some ways I reduced my Christian walk down to generally being a nice guy and nothing more. I didn't pray as much as I should have, not unless something bad happened, like another injury in a ball game. If I read the

Bible, it was because I felt like I had to so that I could check it off my to-do list. I had strong faith but wavered on pursuing a real, dynamic relationship with God. I was just a good guy who liked to have a good time without hurting other people. That was enough.

Straddling the fence always felt uncomfortable and it made me hesitant to pursue a real relationship with Karyn. I knew she wanted someone who was the real deal when it came to faith and commitment. Honestly, right then, I wasn't that guy. However, my hesitance didn't stop me from accepting her invitation to accompany her to her sorority's formal dance.

About a month after we went out to dinner Karyn called me for the first time. I don't think I had called her since that first invite to go out with some friends. We definitely had not gone on another date. However, I gave enough of an "I'm interested" vibe when we talked at FCA events that she felt confident I would accept her invitation if she asked me to go. Of course I said yes.

When I picked Karyn up for the dance, she greeted me at the door in a long blue sequined gown. She wore her long blond hair in the updo girls often get for proms and formals. All I could say was, "Wow, you look beautiful."

"You look handsome yourself," she replied. I had on my best suit. We made a good-looking couple that night, if I do say so myself.

I don't really know what my intentions were that night. When we danced, I wanted to be with her. She made me laugh and I did the same for her. The two of us just seemed to fit in such a natural way. I tried not to convey the wrong message, I tried not to lead her on, but I got caught up in the night. Late in the dance Brian McKnight's "6, 8, 12" came on. I took Karyn in my arms and we danced across the dance floor. As the music played, I looked down at her and began to sing, "It's been six months, eight days, twelve hours since you went away. I miss you so much and I don't know what to say." The look in her eye told me I had made an impression.

After the dance we rode a bus back to her sorority. She squeezed close to me as we rode along. When I walked her up to her front door, she turned and looked up at me. Whew. This was the kind of magical moment where first kisses are born. I hugged her and said, "Thank you so much for inviting me. I had a wonderful time." Then I leaned in toward her. She looked up at me. She closed her eyes as I leaned down closer, only to have me kiss her on the forehead and say, "Well, good night." It was the perfect ending to a perfect ending, if by perfect you mean the perfect way to send the ultimate mixed message. That was me, Mr. Relationship Confusion.

I didn't call Karyn for months afterward, which confused her even more. In the meantime, my life got even more complicated. In my redshirt sophomore season I had a solid year statistically even though we didn't play that well as a team. We lost some close games and ended up 3-7 on the year going into the last game of the season, against our biggest rivals, the University of Wisconsin Badgers. Our rivalry with the Badgers goes back to 1890. Unfortunately, we had lost the last six games. With our poor record, we went into the game as heavy underdogs. But as the old saying goes, that's why you play the game. Early on I made a seventy-five-yard catch and run for a touchdown. Later I went up in the end zone and made a one-handed forty-five-yard catch for another touchdown. We ended up winning the game 42–31. The ESPN announcers broadcasting the game interviewed me on national television after it was over. Me! They reserve those interviews for the stars of the game, and on this day, that star was me.

The Wisconsin game, on top of the season I'd had, put me right in the middle of the discussion of up-and-coming college tight ends. College football talking heads on television buzzed about how I was now one of the favorites for the next year's John Mackey Award, which is given to the top tight end in the country.

One afternoon I was sitting in my dorm room when the phone rang. My roommate answered the phone, then handed it to me. "This is Ben," I said.

"Hi, Ben, I'm"—the guy gave me his name but I don't remember it—"and I'm a sports agent. Let me tell you, I followed the season you just had and I am excited about your prospects for next year. I believe you have the potential to be one of the first, if not the first, tight ends taken in next year's draft."

I nearly dropped the phone. I could not believe my ears. "Really?" is all I could say.

"Yes, really. Now I know that NCAA rules keep you from signing with anyone until you formally declare for the draft, but I hope when you do you will keep me in mind." He then went on to tell me all his firm had to offer me, including avenues into the world of entertainment. "We know you are a gifted singer and that that might be something you want to pursue after football," he said.

I had no idea how this stranger knew so much about me. Clearly he had done his homework before making the call. When I hung up the phone my roommate asked, "What was that?"

"A sports agent," I said, in shock.

"You're kidding me! Oh man, that's AWESOME!" my roommate said. He jumped up and gave me a high five. "Dude, this is going to happen for you!"

That was just the first of many calls I received throughout the off-season and into the beginning of my redshirt junior year. If you thought my receiving a scholarship at the age of sixteen went to my head, having agents call took me to a whole new level. My college major was supposed to be communications, but once the possibility of playing on the next level presented itself, my major became football. Football not only became my major, it was my identity. When I watched NFL games on television, I started picturing myself on the field. I craved the fame and fortune. When another agent called, I ate up the attention. I still went to FCA meetings, and I went to church when I went home, but I also started slipping into the lifestyle that I thought I deserved. The party scene became normal and I started making compromises with my convictions that I never expected myself to make. But, at the time, I didn't feel too bad about it. After all, I was on my way to the NFL. This was going to be my life. I might as well enjoy it.

And then I would run into Karyn.

One evening that summer I called her. "Hey, Karyn, it's Ben. Would you like to go see a show?"

"Tonight?" she asked.

"Sure, if you don't have anything else going on," I said.

"Okay," Karyn said.

I took her to see the theatrical comedy *Triple Espresso*. I had already seen the play with my family and loved it so I was confident it would make for a good date. A long time had passed since I had seen Karyn, and in a way, I missed her. Maybe my feelings came because it was summer and my days were filled with nothing but summer school classes and football conditioning on a nearly empty campus. Perhaps I was lonely, but I found myself thinking about Karyn a lot. *This is so right. Why don't I pursue a real relationship with Karyn?* I found myself thinking over and over. *And what better way to bring two people together than comedy?*

My plan worked. The two of us had a great time laughing together and enjoying dinner after the show. The whole night I thought how I could get used to this. Then, once again, after I dropped her off at her off-campus apartment with just a hug, she didn't hear from me. I'm sure she thought that just like the comedy we watched, the joke was on her. But in reality, the joke was on me.

Around that time Karyn went home for a visit. She and her mother went to a special IMAX showing of one of her favorite movies from when she was a girl, *Beauty and the Beast.* In the middle of the movie, when Gaston sings his praises and all the girls swoon, Karyn sat up in her seat and said to her mom, "That's it! That's Ben. He's Gaston!" I have to be honest. She was right. I had allowed my success to go to my head and had become Gaston. All I needed was the hunting lodge and a goofy sidekick.

The hype surrounding me as a player peaked right before the start of my redshirt junior year. I was named to a couple of preseason all-American teams. ESPN listed me as a potential second- or third-round draft choice. Other publications called me a favorite for the Mackey Award. Before I signed with Minnesota, Coach Mason said I had the potential to be the best tight end in the Big 10. This was my chance to prove him right. If I had the kind of year I hoped to have, I planned on declaring myself eligible for the next NFL draft. Even though I had not put as much energy into my schoolwork as I should have, I was on track to graduate in May. The timing, to me, was perfect. I could graduate on time, land my dream job as a professional football player, then use that position to set me up for a life after football.

In our first game of the 2002 season I picked up where I left off in the previous year's Wisconsin game. I had three catches for eighty-six yards and one touchdown in a 42–0 win. The next week, against Louisiana-Lafayette, I led the team with seven catches for seventy-eight yards and three touchdowns in another Golden Gopher win, 35–11. Against Toledo in week three I only had three catches, but that still led the team. I also scored one touchdown as we went on to win, 31–21. I had four more catches in a big win over Buffalo. After the first month of the 2002 college football season I led the nation in receiving, not just among tight ends but for all receivers.

More calls from agents rolled in. National sports commentators talked about me. I was right where I wanted to be as a football player. All of my dreams appeared to be on the brink of coming true.

And then came a game against Purdue.

CHAPTER 6

TURNING POINT

As a team, my Golden Gophers went into the 2002 Big 10 opener riding a four-game winning streak and feeling good about our chances to make some noise in the conference. Although the 2001 season had been a disappointment, we ended the year beating our biggest rivals in Wisconsin. That was my breakout game, which was supposed to lead to 2002 becoming my breakout season. However, putting up big numbers against smaller schools Louisiana-Lafayette, Toledo, and Buffalo is very different than doing the same against the power schools of the Big 10. I was anxious to prove myself against the best teams in the best college football conference in the country. First stop: Ross-Ade Stadium in West Lafayette, Indiana, for a game against Purdue.

In 2002, Purdue was two years removed from a Big 10 title and playing in the Rose Bowl. Drew Brees had gone on to the NFL, but Purdue still had a good quarterback in Kyle Orton, who also went on to play in the NFL. On top of that, we had to go on the road for only the second time all season. We knew this was going to be a tough game, but everyone on the team, from Coach Mason on down, felt we had a good shot at coming home with a win.

Purdue jumped out in front with a touchdown drive midway

through the first quarter. However, we clawed back in front as Dan Nystrom kicked three field goals in the second quarter, including one with only a minute and a half remaining in the first half. We went into halftime in front 9–7 and were set to receive the opening kickoff of the second half. That meant we had a good chance both to score late in the first half and again at the beginning of the second, without Purdue even touching the football. I had three catches for twenty-nine yards in the first half, which isn't a bad way to start a game.

Unfortunately, Purdue intercepted a pass from our quarterback, Asad Abdul-Khaliq, on the first play from scrimmage in the half and ran it back for a touchdown. No one on our sideline panicked. Coach Mason walked up and down the line telling us, "That's all right. Let's get the ball back and put some more points on the board."

During the next series of plays, Asad called a play on which I was to run a corner route. On a corner route, I run out about ten yards, plant my foot, and cut hard at a 45-degree angle. I can run the route in my sleep. The moment the ball snapped, I took off from the line. A linebacker tried to stay with me but I blew past him. Ten yards out I planted my left foot and made a hard cut. No one was near me. I was wide open. The moment I planted my foot I heard a pop and a sharp pain shot right through the middle of my foot and up my leg. I pulled up from the route and kind of hopped up in pain. I don't remember if Asad threw the ball to me or not. The shooting pain in my foot sort of crowded out every other memory of the moment.

I limped back into the huddle. Asad looked over at me. He could tell I was in pain. "You okay, 'techt?" he asked.

"Yeah, I'm fine," I lied. In football you are taught to play through the pain and that's what I tried to do. The initial shot of pain grew into a deep, constant throbbing that got worse with every step I took. I should have taken myself out of the game, but

I didn't. The game was too important and I didn't want to let my coaches and teammates down. Unfortunately, Purdue scored two more touchdowns in the third quarter to take a 28–9 lead. We managed to cut it to 28–15 in the fourth quarter with a touchdown (the extra point failed), but we never got close to scoring again. The loss only made my foot hurt that much worse on the trip back to Minneapolis.

I thought the pain would go away, but when it was even worse on Monday I went in to see the team trainers. They sent me in for an X-ray. My worst fears came true. I had a significant stress fracture right in the middle of my foot. The team sent me to see an orthopedic doctor, who told me that I had made the injury worse by continuing to play on it after the initial break. So much for playing through pain. "You have a couple of options, Ben," he told me. "We can put your foot in a hard cast and you stay off of it for the next six to eight weeks. Unfortunately, your season will be over. However, you will qualify for a medical redshirt." A medical redshirt means I would receive an extra year of eligibility, which I didn't need or want. I was on track to graduate in four years. I didn't need a sixth year of college.

"I need to keep playing," I replied. "Is there any way I can stay on the field?"

"There is," the doctor said. "We can cast your foot, just as we discussed, and you stay off of it through the week. Then, on game days, we can remove the cast, give you strong anti-inflammatories, and let you play. It will be painful, but what we give you for the pain should help."

"Let's do that," I said without hesitating. I didn't need to think through the two options or consult anyone. If there was a way for me to stay on the field and contribute to the team, I was going to do it.

The doctor put my foot in a cast. For the rest of the week I hobbled around campus on crutches. I could not practice with the team, but I sat in on all the team meetings and film sessions in preparation for the next game. Then on Saturday mornings the trainers cut off my cast, gave me a shot of painkillers, and sent me out to play. I did not miss a game, but I never came close to matching my level of play from the first four games. Through the rest of the regular season I never led the team in receiving and I did not score another touchdown. All the hype about me possibly being a high draft choice evaporated. Agents stopped calling. I went from being a leading contender for the Mackey Award, as one of the premier tight ends in college football, to just another guy. The fact that I was playing every week on a broken foot did not matter to the scouts and commentators. I disappeared from everyone's radar screens. My dreams of playing the next season in the National Football League were all but dead.

And that really, really ticked me off.

I wasn't mad at the doctors or trainers who put me in and out of the cast. I wasn't mad at the scouts and sportswriters who had basically written me off as a flash in the pan who could put up great stats against little MAC (Mid-American Conference) schools but melted when the competition got tough. I couldn't blame them for moving on from me to whatever tight end happened to be lighting it up now. If I had their job, I would do the exact same thing. And I wasn't mad at my foot for giving out. That would just be dumb.

No, I was mad at God for letting my foot break and taking away all the hopes and dreams I had of a brighter future. This was my third major injury in basically four years, going back to my pelvic avulsion in high school. Every single injury happened on fluke plays where no one was around me. My pelvic fracture occurred when I planted my foot and cut hard on a pass route, which sounded extremely familiar now. Then I tore up my ankle when some bonehead put a sprinkler head in the middle of a football field. How can something like that even happen? And now I had broken another bone, not because some all-American linebacker plowed into me, but because I turned at the wrong angle while running. *God,* I yelled in my mind, *why do you keep doing this to me?!* He had to be the one doing it. There was no other explanation. Even if He wasn't responsible for causing the injuries, He sure could have kept them from happening.

And that is exactly what I expected Him to do. I felt like God owed that to me. After all, I was a good guy. All through high school I had gone out of my way to do good to other people. I even played with a broken hip, not for my own personal gain but because the team needed me. My high school coach, Bob Majeski, called me the eternal optimist because I always put the team first and I always did what I could to help others. *Always!* Coach Majeski even resurrected an old award at Hastings High that hadn't been given out in years. The Marvin "Tubby" Biskupski Award went to an athlete that showed exceptional character, integrity, compassion, and competitiveness. When he gave the award to me it hadn't been given out in forever, and it hasn't been given out since. I carried that same dedication into college. Deep down, I felt the accolades coming my way and the NFL buzz were God's ways of rewarding me for my solid character. And now He just up and decided to take it all away.

Week in and week out I hobbled about on those cursed crutches, then suffered through constant, throbbing pain as I limped through Saturday's games. The more my foot hurt, the angrier with God I got. Finally I flat-out told Him, "That's it, God. I'm done. I did my part. I lived the kind of life I thought You wanted from me. I didn't complain when my hip fractured, even though it cost me my season. And I didn't get angry with You when my ankle broke even though it cost me starting as a true freshman. I sucked it up and I did what You expected me to do. Then You let this happen to me? How? How could You do this to me? If You aren't going to be here for me, then why do I worry about being there for You and doing what *You* want?"

I hit my breaking point, which made me stop straddling the fence. I jumped down with both feet on the other side. Through the rest of that season I allowed myself to get swept up in the party culture on campus. Commitments I made when I was in high school, commitments to purity and integrity, I threw out the window. I'd always been a hopeless romantic who dreamed of a very special wedding night with my bride, where the two of us have saved ourselves for one another and that moment. At twenty-one, I stopped saving anything for anyone. In the back of my mind I was thinking, *I'll show You, God*. Through all this I remained part of FCA and played on their worship team. I had even become part of the leadership team prior to becoming so angry with God. Honestly, I should have stepped down because I wasn't living the kind of life one should expect from a person in a Christian leadership position. But I didn't. I guess that was also part of my way of sticking it to God.

I was still mad at God one afternoon as I hobbled through the training room next to our football locker room. Just being in the training room made me seethe. You only go see the trainers when you are injured, and that was me. I was finished with my treatments for the day and was on my way toward the door when I felt a tap on my shoulder. Turning around I looked down at a little five-feet, two-inch, blond-haired, blue-eyed girl I recognized as part of the training staff.

"Are you Ben?" she asked.

"Yeah," I said.

"We haven't met yet. I'm Melissa. Could I talk to you for a minute in the back room there?"

"Sure," I said, even though I didn't really want to. I followed her back toward one of the rooms the trainers use, and honestly, the whole time I thought she wanted to ask me out on a date. That's how full of myself I was. The whole way back to this room I'm trying to figure out what I am going to say because I didn't want to go out with this girl.

The moment we got to a private place she turned to me and said, "Are you a Christian?"

"Uh . . . yeah. Yes, I am," I stammered. She caught me completely off guard. Her question felt like a sucker punch in the gut, it was so out of the blue.

"Well, I'm a Christian, too, and . . ." She hesitated for a moment. "This may sound strange to you, I don't know. But I need to ask you another question."

"Okay," I said, completely unsure of what might come out of her mouth next.

"Do you believe God speaks to people?" she said.

I grew up in the home of a Methodist pastor in the Midwest. My parents took their faith very seriously, but we never talked a lot about supernatural encounters. She had to sense how uncomfortable her question made me when I sort of spit out, "Yeah, well, you know, I guess."

"Okay. Good. I was hesitant to tell you this, but last night I was praying with some of my friends and all of the sudden God just put your name on my heart so much that I couldn't focus on anything else. So I left the room and got down on my knees and started praying for you by name." Then she stopped and looked at me in a way that made me feel like my soul was laid bare before her. "Things aren't right in your life, are they? There's a darkness there. I don't have the answer for you, and I'm honestly really nervous about saying this to you because I don't know you, but the Lord told me to tell you something."

She had my full and undivided attention. "What?" I asked.

"He told me to tell you that you aren't giving Him something, Ben; do you know what that is?" she asked.

I broke out in a cold sweat. All I wanted to do was get out of there as fast as my crutches could carry me. "Uh, you know, I . . . I . . . I . . . I don't know. I gotta go," I said, and turned to leave right then. Melissa didn't chase me or press her question. She watched as I left.

Once I got outside and started toward my dorm the panic I felt in that little room grew. I felt tormented inside. A battle waged inside me between who I had once been and who I was now becoming. I tried to push Melissa's question out of my head as nothing but crazy talk, but I couldn't. *She knows. How can she possibly know about the choices I'm making?* I wondered. *And why would she care how I'm living my life? Why would she ask me these questions?*

When I got back to my room I tried to study or do something, anything, normal. I grabbed a book off my desk and started studying. But I couldn't concentrate. My mind kept dwelling on Melissa's questions. *You aren't giving Him something, Ben,* I could hear her say. Her words grew louder and louder in my mind until I was completely overwhelmed. The only thing I could think to do was the same thing I always did when I needed answers: I called my dad. I told him everything Melissa had said and then I asked, "Dad, what do I do?"

"Ben, you need to pray and ask God if this message is really from Him," my dad said.

Now, you have to understand that I hadn't been doing a lot of praying the past few months, except to tell God how mad I was at Him. But this episode so rattled me that I took my dad's advice. I got down on my knees for the first time in forever and said, "God, if this is from you, you need to tell me what to do. You need to tell me what I'm not giving to you."

I prayed like that for a while, and I didn't hear any answers coming down from heaven, so I got up and went back to my desk. When I opened my computer I noticed I had some new emails. I clicked on one from my aunt. At the top of the email was a Bible verse from Proverbs 3:5–6. The verse said, "Trust in the Lord with all your heart and lean not on your own understanding; in all your ways submit to Him, and He will make your paths straight." The moment I read this passage it felt like a bolt of lightning struck my room. The hair on my body stood up and warmth radiated all through me. I had the answer to Melissa's questions. I knew the one thing I had not completely given to God.

Me.

When I was ten years old I went to my mom and dad and asked them about Jesus. I heard my dad talk about him every Sunday, and, as a preacher's kid, my whole life had been immersed in God stuff. That night long ago my mom explained to me what it means to have an actual relationship with God through faith in Jesus, His Son. I prayed a prayer with my mom and dad right there in my room. After that, whenever anyone asked me if I was a Christian, I always went back to that night with my parents and said, "Yes, I am."

However, after my encounter with Melissa I realized that I had never completely given my entire self to God. I wanted faith in my life, and I certainly wanted God to bless me. After all, I felt like that was the least I deserved, since I always tried to do the right thing. But in this moment I realized there is a huge difference between wanting God to be part of your life and totally surrendering yourself to Him. I remembered the old movie *Chariots of Fire* and the story of Eric Liddell. Liddell once said, "You will know as much of God, and only as much of God, as you are willing to put into practice." I hadn't been willing to put that much into practice, at least not the hard sayings of Jesus, where He said, "If anyone would come after Me, let him deny himself and take up his cross and follow Me. For whoever would save his life will lose it, but whoever loses his life for My sake will find it. For what will it profit a man if he gains the whole world and forfeits his soul? Or what shall a man give in return for his soul?" (Matthew 16:24–26). Denying self means total surrender of oneself to Christ, including one's hopes and dreams for the future. When my first injury occurred, my mother asked me, "Do you trust Jesus?" Now I had to decide if I really did.

The conversation with Melissa proved to be a turning point for me. I apologized to God for growing so angry with Him. "If my future is going to turn out different than my dreams, so be it," I prayed. "I don't want my plan anymore but yours."

Blessings from heaven did not suddenly pour down on my life. In terms of football, life got a lot worse. Our team ended exactly the opposite of how it began. We started off the year with four straight wins as I led the nation in receiving. We ended with four straight losses. I did what I could, which wasn't much. But rather than get mad, I surrendered my season to the Lord. I felt a great deal of peace.

Even with our four straight losses at the end of the year, our team was invited to play in the Music City Bowl in Nashville, against Arkansas. We had five weeks between our last game against Wisconsin and the bowl game, five weeks where I could stay off my foot completely and let it heal. The next time my cast came off, it came off for good. A week or so before the bowl game I found I could run once again without pain. When it came time for the game, I played like I did in the first month of the season. I led the team with seven receptions and scored one touchdown. We won, 29–14. More than that, I felt like for the first time in a very long time I was back where I needed to be, not as a player, but as a man.

CHAPTER 7

MOVING FORWARD

I GOT A LITTLE AHEAD OF myself at the end of the last chapter. I wanted to complete the circle and tell you how my season ended. But having a great game and coming away with a win in the Music City Bowl was far from the most important thing that happened in Nashville with that game. I had a good game, but a couple of days before the game I had a conversation that altered the course of my life forever.

I also need to make it clear that my encounter with Melissa, while it proved to be a turning point in my life, did not result in an instantaneous transformation. Old habits die hard, even if they aren't very old. I had a lot of days where I took three steps forward and two steps back. However, one action I took proved to be the strongest cure to keep me from slipping back into the destructive patterns I wanted to leave behind. Not long after my conversation with Melissa, I picked up the phone and called Karyn. Calling her was a huge gamble. I hadn't called her since our last date, which had been months earlier. And that date came nearly a year after the one before. I couldn't blame her if she never wanted to hear from me again.

I wasn't so sure she didn't. Since that last date I'd noticed some subtle changes in her demeanor toward me. In the past, when I looked over her way at an FCA event we usually shared a flirtatious glance. Not anymore. Both of us were on the FCA leadership team, which meant we interacted as part of the group, but she never gave the slightest indication that she was still interested in me romantically. If I had been really perceptive, I would have realized that she had moved on. She'd dated other people, as had I, but there was more to it than that. I now know that when we first went out she had hoped the two of us might develop a very special relationship. That's why she invited me to the sorority formal. My tepid response afterward didn't help matters. The fact that I called about once a year made it clear to her that any kind of relationship with me was never going to happen, and she was perfectly fine with that.

But I called her anyway, not to ask her out but just to talk. Even with all the mixed signals I'd sent and our totally random, annual dates, Karyn and I were friends. I knew I could trust her. More than that, I needed her. Every time I was around her I felt Karyn was a kind of antidote to the garbage I had allowed to fill my life when I became so angry at God. However, I didn't say that when I called her that first time. I don't really remember how I started the conversation. I probably said something like, "I was just thinking about you and wanted to talk." I know she was surprised I called out of the blue. She was more surprised when I called her the next day. I may have called the day after that as well. All I know is our phone conversations became very frequent, and each one was longer than the one before. After a while the two of us talked for hours at a time.

A couple of weeks into our regular phone conversations, I mustered whatever courage I had left and asked her out. Luckily for me she said, "Yes." However, there's a lot more to the story. Before Karyn developed her college crush on me, she had a serious high school crush on a different guy, who ironically was in the same business school as Karyn in college. He was sort of like me in that he never really reciprocated the feelings that Karyn had shared for him. Fate, it seems, decided to put Karyn to the test.

Out of the blue he called and asked Karyn out. She said yes. He took her out to dinner and they returned to her apartment and started talking, then all of a sudden her phone rang. For whatever reason she felt compelled to answer. Yep, this was the moment I picked to call and finally ask her out on a date that I hoped was going to be the first step toward a lasting, long-term relationship. I had no idea she was on a date. I just said something like, "Hey, Karyn, some of my teammates and their girlfriends are getting together tonight. I was hoping you might go with me."

A long, awkward pause followed, which I now know was due to the other guy being in the next room. Finally Karyn answered, "Yes!"

"Great," I said, "I'll pick you up around seven."

The story doesn't end there, however. Karyn hung up the phone then said to her friend, "That was Ben. He called to ask me out. I told him yes."

Her high school crush reacted to the news in a way that shocked Karyn, and it shocked me when she told me about it later. He said something like, "Karyn, I know this may be too little, too late, but the reason I called and asked you out was to tell you that I like you a lot and I think the two of us are great together. I wanted to see where this relationship might lead." And then he leaned over and kissed her.

I will admit that when she first told me this story I was pretty upset that he kissed her, and she let him, but my reaction was only due to my own insecurity and a little jealousy. The miracle is how she responded to her date. She looked over at him and all she felt was a strong urging within herself to run toward me. A peace came over her. It was as though she could see her future and all she saw was me. She had made her decision.

"I want to thank you for a wonderful evening and for sharing your feelings with me," she said to him. "But I have to see where things lead with Ben. I hope you can understand that." When I think about this story today I have zero doubt that God's providence was at work, and that the timing of our relationship was being written by a divine hand. I cannot imagine a life where Karyn did not answer her phone or what might have happened if I had waited longer to call her.

After that date, I immediately called Karyn and asked her out again. However, I learned the hard way that I had much more to learn about what made a great date night for Karyn. On our second date I picked her up and took her to see a horror movie. Guys like horror movies because girls will often grab tightly on to us as if we can protect them. Karyn didn't grab on to me. Instead she spent the entire movie with her head buried in her hands. I don't think she looked at the screen one time after the opening credits. That wasn't what I had in mind when I picked the movie. We probably went out for something to eat afterward. To be honest, the details of the date are a little sketchy for me now. However, I do recall feeling different about her than I had any other time we went out. I also felt horrible for making her sit through that terrible zombie movie.

Looking back, I get angry at myself for not walking her out of the movie and asking Karyn what she would like to do! Trust me, I learned my lesson. Let's just say we don't watch those kinds of movies together anymore, or ever. After the zombie movie and dinner I took Karyn back to her apartment at University Village and walked her to the door. I didn't try to kiss her good night and she didn't expect me to, but this time, I wanted to.

I called the next day. "I had a great time last night," I said. "A bunch of us are going out for wings tonight. Would you like to go with me?" I wish I could have seen her face, because this had to surprise Karyn. Normally I let at least twelve months pass before asking her out again; now I had called twice in one week!

"Sure. That sounds like fun," Karyn said.

That night marked another change in our relationship. A couple of my friends from the football team were there along with their dates. Overall, the wings place was really crowded. We didn't have enough chairs for everyone. I told Karyn, "Why don't you sit here on my lap?" That gesture was my first bold step toward indicating to her that I wanted to be more than friends. Finally I had the courage to start showing some more physical affirmation.

We went out again a short time later. I don't really remember the date, but I hope to never forget what happened next. At the end of the date I invited Karyn to come back to my dorm room with me. When we walked in the door I had candles arranged strategically throughout the room. She gave me a sort of look like, *What are you up to?* The candlelight set the mood. I then took my guitar and began playing and singing Edwin McCain's "I'll Be." I know it sounds cheesy, but it worked! I finished the song and before she could say a word, I launched into the Ben Folds song "The Luckiest." The song starts off about how the person singing doesn't get many things right the first time, which was definitely true of how I had handled my relationship with Karyn. I wanted to find a way to tell her how I had really messed up and how I regretted confusing her and how blessed I felt that she had given me another chance. I couldn't think of a good way to say that, so I let Ben Folds say it for me.

By the time I finished the second song, Karyn's eyes glistened. I then dropped down on one knee, which, with my height, put us face-to-face as she sat on the edge of my bed. Setting my guitar aside, I leaned in and gave her a hug. As I slowly pulled out of the embrace I kissed her on the cheek. I drew back, and looked her in the eye for a sign of affirmation, which I received along with her beautiful smile. I then kissed her for real for the very first time.

The moment was magical for both of us. I pray I never lose this memory.

All of these phone calls and dates took place late in my redshirt junior football season and in the five-week gap between our last Big 10 game and the Music City Bowl. It was a pretty relaxed month. Practices were light up until a week or so before the game. Like I said in the last chapter, the closer we got to the game against Arkansas, the better my foot felt. I was able to run and regain the speed I lost when I could only limp across the field.

The team flew down to Nashville a week before the game. Every bowl game has all sorts of activities planned around it. We toured historic music places in Nashville and stayed at the Gaylord Opryland Resort and Conference Center, which is one of the largest hotels in the world. The place literally felt like the Mall of America in my home state of Minnesota, with rooms attached. With seventeen restaurants, indoor rivers, and walking paths along tree-lined paths, I had never stayed in anything quite like it.

Looking back, though, none of that mattered to me. The best part of the week was the fact that Karyn came down to Nashville for the game as a student-athlete representative on an athletics and academic advisory council for the university. On trips like this, our team has a pretty tight schedule. Between all the bowl committee activities we have to do and our practice sessions, there's not a lot of time for yourself. That made this a hard week. All I really wanted to do was find Karyn and spend time with her. But time was hard to come by.

One night I called her and said, "Let's meet. I have to see you."

"Me, too," she said, "but what about your curfew?" She knew that if we went out at that late hour, I was going to be in violation of team rules.

"I'll take my chances," I said. "We won't leave the hotel, so technically I won't be in violation. I'll meet you downstairs and we'll go to whatever restaurant we can find that is still open."

That was harder than I thought. We walked all around looking for a quiet place to sit and talk and grab a bite to eat, but most everything was closed for the night. The massive indoor atriums were pretty much empty. Finally we found a quiet table next to one of the indoor ponds where we could be alone. I pulled my chair over close to Karyn. "I've given this a lot of thought," I said, "and I, I want to be in a serious relationship with you." This was more than me saying I wanted us to be exclusive and see no one else. In my mind I was already looking ahead at a long-term future together.

Karyn gave me a big smile. "I want the same thing," she said.

"Really?" I said. I guess I sounded surprised, or maybe I was just relieved. I felt confident in Karyn's feelings toward me, but being vulnerable is always a nerve-racking experience.

"Yes, Ben. Really."

We shared a kiss and just sat there, holding hands, for a very long time. We talked a little, but mainly we just sat there, together. We never did get anything to eat, but I didn't care.

That moment, alone with Karyn at a secluded table under the trees and next to a pond in the middle of the Opryland hotel, was the only part of the trip that mattered to me. If I had not been able to play a single down in the game a couple of days later, the week would not have been diminished. This conversation changed the course of my life.

As it was, I did get to play, and I played well. Maybe it was because my foot was completely healed. Or maybe it was because my serious girlfriend was sitting in the stands next to my mom, cheering me on. Either way, I had the game of my life. A few years later, when I was with the Colts, one of my new teammates connected my name to that game. He had been on the opposing team. "Man, you tore us up," he said. I just smiled. I love this memory.

I could have ended my college football career with the Music City Bowl. I was on track to graduate in May, and while my draft stock had taken a hit after my foot injury, after my performance in the bowl game I thought I might still have a good chance of making an NFL team. However, as I considered declaring myself eligible for the April draft, I couldn't help but feel I still had unfinished business at the U of M to take care of. For one thing, if I was serious about making it in the NFL, I needed to skip the spring semester to prepare for the NFL Scouting Combine in Indianapolis in February, along with the personal tryouts that teams put prospective players through. Trying to do all of that while also maintaining the course load I needed to get my degree didn't exactly go together. And I really wanted to get my degree. That's the whole point of going to college.

More than that, I did not want to end my college career on the down note that was the last seven games of my redshirt junior season. Yes, I played well in our bowl game, but to me that did not compensate for the missed opportunities caused by my broken foot. I believed that if I came back for my senior year and played healthy all season long, the dreams I had of going high in the draft would come true.

Once I made a public decision to return for my final year of eligibility, the hype machine started back up. I wasn't the only one talking about what I might do now that I was completely healthy. Publications again talked about me as a possible Mackey Award winner and a potential high draft choice. However, unlike the year before, I worked very hard to keep everything in perspective. I made a conscious decision to surrender the hype and the upcoming season to God. Sometimes people think only bad things can trip us up, and that we must surrender those to God so that He can make everything better. That's just not true. When He asks us to surrender all to Him, He means everything, good, bad, and in between. I've found that's the only way life really makes sense and works.

Unfortunately, I never got to find out how good I could be if I played completely healthy. From the start of my senior season we became much more of a rushing team than a passing team. We had a group of really good running backs, led by Marion Barber III and Laurence Maroney, both of whom went on to play in the NFL. Barber was a 2005 fourth-round draft pick by the Dallas Cowboys, while Maroney went in the first round to the New England Patriots a year later. Instead of running pass routes, I spent most of my time blocking and opening holes for these guys to run through. Most games our quarterbacks hardly ever threw the ball. In our Big 10 opener, against Penn State, we ran the ball fifty times and passed it only seven. I still had a great game receiving that day. Of the seven passes thrown, I caught three for thirty-four yards. I had a really good game the next week as well, against Northwestern. We only passed the ball twelve times, but I caught four for sixty-four yards and my first touchdown of the season.

However, those games were the high point of my senior season. A dull ache in my lower abdominal area hit me after the second game. The dull ache grew into real pain with every game and eventually affected my play in a negative way. The team doctor diagnosed it as something called osteitis pubis, that is, an inflammation of the joint of the two major pelvic bones at the front of the pelvis. The condition is pretty rare, but that's what they told me I had. If I had known what was really going on, I would have shut down my season and called it a college career. Instead I kept pushing through the pain and hoping I would get better. The doctors treated the pain by inserting a four-inch-long needle into my lower abdomen just above places where no guy wants a needle to go and injecting me multiple times with cortisone. The shot hurt nearly as much as the injury.

The pain in my abdomen only grew worse in spite of the shots. Then, in our eleventh game of the year, the injury became debilitating. We were playing Wisconsin at home in the old Metrodome on Senior Day. Before kickoff I was recognized and honored as a four-year starter. My mom and dad and sister were up in the stands, cheering for me. So was Karyn. This was the kind of moment I dreamed about when I signed to play for Glen Mason and Minnesota.

Then the game started. Just like every game that season, we ran the ball nearly three times as much as we passed it. On one of only twelve pass plays called in the game, I took off on a corner route. This is the same route I ran when I broke my hip in high school and the same route on which I broke my foot against Purdue in my redshirt junior season. Just like those two games, I released from the line, ran about ten yards down the field, planted my left foot, and cut hard toward the sideline. As I turned I felt a pop-pop-pop-pop across my abdomen, like someone unsnapping a jacket. My legs started wobbling and my feet gave out from under me. My body tumbled to the ground. However, before I fell, I grabbed the football out of the air for a twenty-four-yard gain.

The stadium went nuts when I made the catch, then it fell silent when I didn't get up. The training staff ran out onto the field. I'm sure my mother wanted to as well, but she didn't. Thankfully. The trainers picked me up and helped me off the field to the bench, then proceeded to cart me off to the locker room. With that my senior season and college career was over. I did not suit up for our Big 10 finale at Iowa, nor did I play in the Sun Bowl against Oregon. I finished the year with only eighteen catches for 289 yards and two touchdowns. By comparison, the year before I had seventeen catches for 229 yards and five touchdowns . . . after four games! You could say I was more than a little disappointed with how the year turned out.

After the Wisconsin game I underwent an MRI but nothing showed up on the scans. No one could tell me what was actually wrong with me. And since no one knew exactly what was wrong with me, no one knew what to do to help me get better. Not only could I not play football—I could barely walk. That's not good, especially for a guy who needs to showcase his abilities for NFL teams.

With all the uncertainty swirling around me, I easily could have panicked. If I got angry with God the year before over a broken foot, I could have really gone off on Him over this unknown, debilitating injury. But I didn't. Instead I went back to the lesson the Lord taught me after my encounter with Melissa. I prayed, "God, I don't know what this is or how it is going to turn out, but I surrender it to You. I give it to You." I didn't know why God might let these things happen, but I kept going back to the fact that He always has a plan. Like my mother told me the first time I found myself lying on a football field unable to get up, I had to trust Jesus and the fact that He knew what He was doing even if I could not yet tell what it might be. Thankfully, His plan started coming into focus in a way that was better than anything I could have imagined, even if I couldn't quite make it out for a while.

CHAPTER 8

OUT OF THE ASHES

ALMOST FOUR MONTHS AFTER I FELT the pop-pop-pop-pop in my abdomen during the Wisconsin game, I flew down to Indianapolis for the 2004 NFL Scouting Combine. The combine is basically a four-day job interview for every college player who hopes to play professional football. All the top executives and coaches from all thirty-two teams, along with their player personnel departments and medical teams, are there. Just receiving one of the three hundred invitations to the combine is a big deal. However, being invited to the combine does not guarantee being taken in the April draft. That's where performances at the combine come into play. All the scouts and coaches have watched hours upon hours of game film on everyone in whom they have an interest. The combine gives them a chance to see every prospect up close. They time us in the forty-yard dash along with having us run pass routes, lift weights, do broad jumps and vertical leaps, and perform any other physical test they can think of. On top of the physical workouts, every prospect also has to take the Wonderlic test, which is supposed to measure our football IQs. We also undergo extensive medical and psychological evaluations.

Like I said, the combine is an intense four-day job interview. The better you do in the combine, the higher you might go in the draft. The difference between being taken in the first round, or even the second or third, as opposed to the sixth or seventh, is measured in millions of dollars. That made these four days potentially the biggest four days of my life career-wise.

Unfortunately, I still could not run or lift weights or do any physical activity more strenuous than walking across the room. When I received my invitation to the combine I almost declined going. However, I had hired an agent right after the Sun Bowl, a local Minnesota guy named Chris Murray. Chris recommended I go down to the combine and explain to teams why I could not work out. He put together a marketing packet promoting me as a player, including a highlight reel of my top plays in college. The whole thing reminded me of the VHS tapes my parents sent out to colleges in the hope that one of them might offer me a scholarship.

I soon discovered that highlight tapes did not impress scouts who wanted to see me work out in person. A couple of teams brought me in for interviews, but I could tell pretty quickly they wanted to see more than tape. The scouts needed to see me on the field. When I could not do that, the feeling I picked up on was "Well, why are you even here?" I asked myself that question a few times, but I always came back to my agent's advice. It was better for me to be at the combine and explain my situation in person rather than sit back in Minnesota and leave everyone to draw their own conclusions.

After I returned home, my agent and I arranged to hold a personal workout session at U of M for teams to come and get a close look at me. When I set the date I assumed I was going to get better. The pain in my abdomen and the weakness that spread down to my legs had to go away eventually, I thought. After all, twenty-two-year-old guys like me heal pretty fast. But, as the day of my personal workout drew near, I called Chris and asked him to contact the teams who had agreed to come and tell them I had to cancel. I still could not run. My mystery injury refused to go away. I started getting really frustrated.

About two months before the 2004 draft, Athletes in Action invited me to speak at one of their events on the University of Minnesota campus. Another U of M alum, Tony Dungy, was scheduled to speak right after me. I'd be lying if I said I wasn't excited to actually meet Tony for the first time. Not only was he coach of the Indianapolis Colts, but he had established himself as one of the greatest coaches in football. More than that, Tony was just as well known for how he lives out a very strong faith. He was the kind of man I strived to be. And he was also coach of Peyton Manning, one of the greatest quarterbacks, if not *the* greatest QB, to ever play the game. Any football player who catches passes for a living would absolutely die to play on the same team as Peyton Manning.

When it came time for me to speak, the first words out of my mouth were directed right at Coach Dungy. I said, "Hey, Coach, as a Golden Gopher alum, if you really care about the university, if you really care about the football program, I expect you to take me in the upcoming draft. Let's be honest, us Gophers stick together!" The seven hundred people in attendance at the McNamara Alumni Center all roared with laughter. Coach Dungy broke out in a huge smile and just shook his head. After the laughter and applause calmed down I had a chance to talk about the positive effect that Athletes in Action had on my faith journey in college. Athletes in Action is a discipleship program that focuses on one-on-one coaching and accountability. My Athletes in Action mentor was Tom Lamphere, ironically the same person who mentored Tony Dungy. It was an honor to share a stage and my testimony with such a man and coach of integrity.

I received a great reaction from the audience for my remarks. When Coach Dungy stood to speak, the first thing he said was, "You know, Ben, I know how talented you are. However, we drafted a tight end in the first round last year in Dallas Clark. Tight ends are not going to be high on our draft board this year, so we don't expect you to be available when we might get around to taking one."

Then he paused for a moment as if he were actually giving the question some thought. Then he added, "But, if for some reason you slip through the cracks and you are not drafted, which I can't see happening, I promise I will be the first person to call you."

The audience broke out in applause. I smiled and gave a nod of thanks. Honestly, I didn't think much of what he said. I knew the chances of me not being taken were very, very small. Chris, my agent, still felt I had a good chance of going on the first day, that is, in the first three rounds. If not, then I was a lock to go early on day two of the draft.

My family threw a party for me on draft day. For the NFL draft the only players that go out to New York are those who are most likely to go in the first round. Back in 2004 the draft took place over two days, a Saturday and a Sunday, which meant all of my family could come celebrate my dream coming true with me. My aunt Heidi (my mom's sister) and uncle Greg hosted the party. We chose their house because they lived in a central location, which allowed even more of my friends and family to attend. Of course my mom and dad were there, along with Karyn and her parents. The room was electric. Everyone was so excited to see where I was going to start my NFL career. A camera crew from one of the local television stations was there as well. After all, it's not every day that a local kid goes in the NFL draft, let alone on the first day.

Chris and I had a pretty good idea which teams were most likely to take me. Some teams, like the Colts, already had established or emerging stars at tight end. Like Coach Dungy told me at the Athletes in Action event, the odds of them taking another high-profile tight end were pretty slim. However, we knew the Cleveland Browns, Miami Dolphins, Washington Redskins, and Philadelphia Eagles all needed a quality tight end. Chris seemed to think one of these teams would select me.

When the draft broadcast came on ESPN, everyone gathered around the television, anxious and excited. To no one's surprise, Eli Manning, Peyton's younger brother, went number one overall. The first tight end came off the board five picks later. The Cleveland Browns, one of the teams Chris thought might be interested in me, took Kellen Winslow. While I would have loved to have been the first tight end taken, Kellen was the highest rated of the draft class. He played at a more passing-oriented college program at Miami, as opposed to the Golden Gophers, where running the ball was our first priority.

I sat anxiously during the entire first round. Karyn snuggled close to me. After every pick came and went without my name being called, my dad gave me a reassuring smile. "It's okay. It's still early," he said multiple times. When the New England Patriots made the final selection of the first round, they selected the second tight end to go in the first round. Unfortunately, it wasn't me. They selected Benjamin Watson from the University of Georgia. I was a little surprised. Watson and I had very comparable stats.

When the first round ended and my name had not been called,

I said, "That's all right. After my injury and playing hurt, my going in the first round was a long shot."

My dad added, "That's right. Don't worry. You probably won't have to wait long before your name is called."

Two tight ends were selected in the second round, neither of whom was named Ben Utecht. Two more went in the third round, including the Colts selecting Ben Hartsock from Ohio State early in the round. Ben and I had played against one another all through college. I didn't yet know him well, but I knew he was a good guy. I was happy for him going to a team like the Colts, but I would be lying if I said it didn't sting a little to see them take a tight end and it not be me. I tried to fight off thoughts like this, but sitting in my aunt and uncle's living room, packed with people, a fidgety news camera crew waiting for something to happen, I couldn't help but be disappointed.

After the Cincinnati Bengals took a linebacker from Purdue with the ninety-sixth overall pick of the day, the third round came to an end, as did the first day of the NFL draft. Everyone was very nice to me. "Don't worry, Ben," they said, "your time will come. You'll see." I smiled and thanked them and tried to be gracious, but I was very disappointed. Honestly, I was more embarrassed than anything.

We canceled the party on the second day of the draft. After what had happened the day before, I didn't really want a lot of people around. I watched the fourth and fifth rounds with my parents; my sister, Ashley; and Karyn. By the time the sixth round started I made an excuse about not feeling well and went upstairs to my room. I just needed to be alone for a while. In all, sixteen tight ends were selected in the draft, but my name was never called. For two years I had agents calling me, telling me I was a lock to go high in the draft. Two injuries later I found myself contemplating what I was going to do with my life now that professional football had been taken out of the picture. I couldn't believe no one took a chance on me in the sixth or seventh round. Teams take flyers on players in those rounds. No one expects a sixth- or seventh-round pick to be a star; most don't even make the team. Those that do become legends, which is why you hear so many stories of how Tom Brady was chosen in the sixth round and then set out to exact revenge against all the teams that passed on him. It looked like I wasn't going to have one of those stories. My professional football career appeared to be dead on arrival. I couldn't help but feel I had been in this place once before, as in exactly five years earlier when I got hurt in my senior year of high school football.

Once the seventh round came to a merciful end, my dad and I drove over to Chris's office to discuss what we might do next. It was one of the longest drives of my life. I sat and stared out the window through the whole trip, holding back tears full of fear. My dad and I must have talked about something. I know he probably tried to cheer me up, but I wasn't up for that. Not yet, at least.

When we finally made it to Chris's office my dad and I flopped down into chairs across from his desk. "So what happened?" I asked.

"I think you were red-flagged," Chris said.

"What?" I asked.

"The only reason I can think of for why you weren't taken is teams decided you were too much of an injury risk," Chris explained. "There is no other explanation. Based on your stats, I should be negotiating your first contract right now."

"So what are my options?" I wanted to know.

"Since you weren't drafted, you can sign with any team as soon as the college free agent signing period begins today. This gives you more flexibility as to where you end up," Chris said.

A college free agent is any undrafted college player who has completed his eligibility or has decided to leave school no less than three years after graduating from high school. Teams sign a ton of college free agents every year. Most just fill out the rosters for training camp and never make the team. However, there have been a few over the years who have made their mark, including Dallas Cowboys star quarterback Tony Romo, Hall of Famer Warren Moon, and future Hall of Famer Kurt Warner. Chris talked like I now had this incredible freedom to take my talents wherever I wanted and become the next Kurt Warner. I didn't share his confidence. In my mind, since no one drafted me, the odds of me getting picked up by anyone now were pretty remote.

At 5:00 p.m. on the Sunday of the draft, teams can start signing college free agents. Exactly twenty seconds after five, Chris's phone rang. He answered, spoke for just a moment, then handed the phone to me. "Ben," the voice on the other end said, "it's Tony Dungy. Our general manager, Bill Polian, is also on the call."

"Hi, Coach," I said, trying to hold back my excitement.

"I'll get right to the point. I never expected to make this phone call, because you are such a talented player and I knew someone was going to take you in the draft. Their loss is the Colts' gain. Bill and I have talked, and we would really like for you to become a part of the Indianapolis Colts. We feel very fortunate to be able to add such a talented tight end as yourself to our roster."

"That sounds really good to me," I said. I was almost bouncing in my chair. I looked over at my dad and gave him a thumbs-up. Chris mouthed to him, "Indianapolis." That put a big smile on my dad's face.

"Hi, Ben, this is Bill Polian. We know you are injured right now. Our medical staff has a pretty good idea what's wrong with you. They believe you have a sports hernia. We will take care of you getting that fixed. Now, the surgery will mean you probably won't get to play for a full season, but we're fine with that."

"That's right, Ben," Coach Dungy joined in. "We don't want

you to even worry about trying to play for the first year. Your job will be to get well and learn as much as you can about our system. We will commit to pay you through your first year, then have you come back strong next year and help us win some football games."

"So what do you think, Ben?" Bill Polian asked.

"I cannot think of a anyplace where I would rather play than Indianapolis. Thank you," I said.

"Bill and your agent can work out the details," Coach Dungy said. "Congratulations and welcome to the Colts."

I handed the phone back to Chris. The negotiations didn't take long. The Colts gave me a $20,000 signing bonus, which wasn't anything close to what I might have earned if I'd been taken in an early round, but I wasn't complaining. They also guaranteed my first-year contract at $230,000. The Colts were also going to pay for my surgery and take care of all the rehab that followed.

The drive home was a lot happier than the drive to Chris's office. The entire situation reminded me of my transition from high school to college. Then I worried that I might lose my scholarship because of my injury, but Coach Mason was a man of his word. And now I had worried that I might never get to play pro football. But Coach Dungy was also a man of his word. He promised to call if I slipped through the cracks. I did, and he did.

I looked over at my father as we drove toward home. "Can you believe it, Dad? I'm going to get to catch passes from Peyton Manning and play for a Super Bowl contender!"

"I never doubted it for a minute," my dad said.

I stared out the window again, thinking about what all this meant. That's when it hit me. If I had been healthy and had gone in one of the early rounds of the draft, I would not have the opportunity I now had. Not only was I given the freedom to get better before worrying about trying to make the team, but I had a full year to study under some of the best football minds in the world and learn all I could. I cannot describe to you the advantage that gave me when I went to my first training camp fighting for a spot on the roster. Once again I could hear my mother say, "Do you trust Jesus? He's in control. You will be okay." Her words just kept coming true in my life. I could not wait to see what was going to happen next.

CHAPTER 9

NEW BEGINNING

I HAVE TO START THIS CHAPTER with a disclaimer. I don't remember this part of my journey to the NFL. Most of what follows comes mainly from my agent and my dad. That's the real irony of this part of the story. I was so excited to sign with the Colts and start my career, and yet, as a result of my career I cannot even remember how it started.

According to my dad, right after my conversation with Bill Polian and Coach Dungy in my agent's office, I flew down to Indianapolis for the Colts' rookie minicamp. That is also when I signed my first NFL contract and received my $20,000 signing bonus. Twenty thousand is a far cry from what I could've had if I had stayed healthy through college, but I no longer cared. Just signing my name on the dotted line was a huge blessing.

After rookie minicamp, I returned home to get ready to fly out to St. Louis with my dad for my surgery. The team had decided to send me to Barnes-Jewish Hospital to see Dr. L. Michael Brunt. Dr. Brunt is one of the leading specialists in sports hernias, which is what the Colts suspected I might have. However, before I flew out I put my signing bonus to good use and purchased my very first car. Actually I bought an SUV, a Chevy

Tahoe. At six feet seven I don't fit into many vehicles, but in my Tahoe I felt like a king.

After I signed with the Colts my dad made the trip down to St. Louis with me. I was both nervous about what the doctor might find but relieved that I might actually get some relief. I'd lived with the pain since the beginning of the 2003 football season, and had experienced the major pop-pop-pop-popping in a game on November 8. I'd now lived with the results of that injury for six months with zero improvement. When Dr. Brunt met with us, he seemed confident that this was a sports hernia, but he needed to do an exploratory surgery to know the extent of the injury. At this time a sports hernia was still a new and hard-to-diagnose condition. Normally, a sports hernia consists of lots of microscopic tears in the oblique abdominal wall. Unlike with a regular hernia, sports hernia tears are so small that they do not result in a noticeable bulge. That's what makes them so hard to diagnose. Dr. Brunt's research has advanced the entire medical community's understanding and treatment of the condition.

When I first met with Dr. Brunt he seemed particularly concerned. "With the popping you experienced and the way this hasn't gotten better, something should show up on the MRI," he explained. "I'm anxious to get in there and find out what is going on."

The operation revealed more than a textbook sports hernia. Dr. Brunt found two significant bilateral tears across my lower abdominal wall. Each tear was about two inches in length. He also cleared up the mystery of why nothing showed up on the scans. "The tear is very low," he explained. "So low that I couldn't see it because of the white of the pelvic bones." He couldn't just sew up the wall. I now have two large sheets of mesh inside me holding my abdominal wall together. "This should fix you right up and I don't think you'll ever have a problem with this again," Dr. Brunt assured me. "Your recovery time is going to be longer than the typical sports hernia. If you had not aggravated the condition by continuing to play, I'd say you could be back out on the field in a couple of months. Now . . ." He paused to think. "It's probably going to be significantly longer. But, the good news is, you will be able to get back on the field and play just as well as you ever have. This will fix you up for good." Dr. Brunt was an answer to prayer. Again, I was so fortunate to have him as my surgeon. The Colts could not have sent me to a better doctor.

A day or two after my operation I flew back home to recuperate. Karyn and I spent as much time as we could together during my recovery time. We both knew that once I moved to Indianapolis we weren't going to see much of one another. I can't remember who brought it up first, probably me, but we talked about marriage a couple of times. I was pretty direct. Karyn knew how I felt about her. She knew I wanted to spend the rest of my life with her, and I was pretty certain she felt the same way about me. "But," I told her, "I really need to get my feet on the ground with the Colts before I can really think about anything else. I don't even know if I'm going to stick with the team. Nothing in my contract is guaranteed. I don't think it would be fair to you for us to get more serious until my future gets settled."

Of course, I was lying through my teeth.

I wasn't lying about the uncertainty about my future with the Colts. Even though I had signed a contract, and both Coach Dungy and General Manager Bill Polian had told me I was going to be paid while I recovered from my injury, contracts in the NFL are not guaranteed. Players can be released at any time, and many are. That's the harsh reality of life in the National Football League.

I moved to Indianapolis in late spring. Because of the uncertainty surrounding my long-term prospects with the team, my first home in Indianapolis was a shared suite at an extended-stay hotel near the team training facility. Eli Ward, one of my teammates from the Golden Gophers, became my roommate. Eli was also trying to make the Colts as an undrafted free agent. I felt like I was back in a dorm in college. We didn't spend a lot of time in the room. My days were filled with trying to soak up everything I could about the Colts' offense while Eli learned their defense.

I spent a month in Indy before I had my first break in the schedule that allowed me to go home for a short stay. In spite of what I had told Karyn before I left, I didn't want to wait to get married. I made my second major purchase after becoming a professional football player: a ring. Now I just needed to find the right way to give it to her.

Deep down I'm a hopeless romantic. I surprised Karyn when we shared our first kiss, and I surprised her when for the first time I told her I loved her. I guess I sort of surprised myself with the latter. Since I had told her I wanted to be serious with her right before the Music City Bowl at the end of my redshirt junior season, I knew I loved her. Telling her, and saying the words first, made me very nervous. Looking back, I think the two of us were sort of playing a waiting game to see who would speak the words first. I lost. Or maybe I won. Either way, I went first. The two of us were eating breakfast together at a Perkins Restaurant & Bakery. We talked about our relationship and all we'd been through in the past and where we were going to go in the future. Before I knew it the words "I love you" came out of my mouth. Thankfully, Karyn said, "I love you, too."

I was determined not to have the words "Will you marry me?" just come slipping out. For me, the timing had to be perfect, both for the moment and for where we both were in life. Even though I did not know if I was going to stick with the Colts, I did not want to wait to start our life together. Karyn was also in a transitional time, but she was in a place where whatever the future held, it would be better for us to face it together. She had graduated from U of M in December 2003, which meant we were both done with school at the same time. Her college golf career was over, but she stayed busy with the sport. She had a couple of national tournaments on the horizon with an eye toward playing professionally. Karyn also began pursuing a childhood dream of competing in pageants. Along with golf she spent a lot of time training for the local Miss Twin Cities pageant, which had been held a couple of months earlier, in February 2004. All of that meant that both of us were looking toward the future, and the future was now.

Memorial Day weekend I went home to Minnesota for the first time after my surgery. Early Saturday morning I crept to Karyn's room to wake her. The fact that I was there at 6:00 a.m. should have told her something was up. I'm not exactly a morning person, or at least I wasn't before I became a father. "I missed you so much that I want to spend as much of the day together as we can," I said. I tried to be as sweet as possible when waking her. "I'm sorry for waking you up so early, but it's time for us to leave." She looked at me suspiciously. "C'mon, my babe," I said. "You have to trust me. Let's go."

Thankfully she bought the line. Karyn smiled and gave me a big hug. "So what are you up to?" she asked.

"I don't know. All I know is that it's time for us to leave," I said.

Karyn got dressed and the two of us climbed into my truck and took off driving. She lived in the Twin Cities with her parents at the time, and there's a lot to do there, but I drove north right out of the city. "So where are we going?" Karyn asked.

"I don't know," I said. "I thought maybe we'd go see Terra and Jared." Jared was my teammate from the Golden Gophers and Terra was on the golf team with Karyn. The two had recently started dating. Jared lived north of the cities.

"Okay, that sounds like fun. I would love to see them," Karyn said.

When I passed the exit I needed to take to go to Jared's house, Karyn noticed. "I think we should have pulled off there," she said.

I played dumb. "Oh, shoot," I said, and I kept on driving. When I didn't take the next exit and circle back, she knew something was up, but I didn't say a word. I just kept driving.

After driving for about two and a half hours I pulled into the little, touristy town of Nisswa, Minnesota. I handed Karyn a ball cap and said, "You need to pull this down over your eyes. I don't want to see where we're going now."

Karyn gave me an open-mouth, "I'm not sure I trust you" smile, but went along with me anyway. She did add, "What are you doing, Ben?"

I just grinned. "You'll see. . . . But not until I tell you to take off the hat, okay?"

"Okay," Karyn said.

A few minutes later I pulled into the parking lot of the Deacon's Lodge Golf Course, which is her favorite place to play. "Okay, open your eyes," I said.

Karyn immediately recognized where we were. "What is this?" she said, surprised.

"Well, I know you have that big tourney coming up and need to practice, so I thought this was a way you could do that and we could still spend time together," I said.

She reached over and hugged me. "That's so thoughtful," she said.

You have no idea, I thought. "Your clubs are in the back," I said. "Your dad stashed them there while you were getting ready. I'm sorry but I can't pick them up for you because of the surgery."

"Oh, that's right, Ben. I'm sorry. You won't be able to play. We can go do something else if you want, something we can both do."

"Hey, this was my idea. I'll drive the cart and you practice. At least this time I won't get sunburned like I did in Iowa," I said. One year earlier I walked along with the group following Karyn during the Big 10 golf championship. I had buzzed my hair really close, and forgot to take a hat with me to the tournament. Karyn played thirty-six holes in one day. My scalp was burned to a crisp.

On this day the clouds filled the sky and occasionally spit a little rain. We didn't mind, and it kept other golfers off the course. The two of us practically had the entire place to ourselves. I knew she needed to concentrate to play well, but this wasn't a tournament, so we talked and laughed through the first seventeen holes.

We finally made it to the eighteenth hole, a long par five. Karyn hit a nice drive, then hit a long second shot to set up an easy approach shot into the green. I drove the cart. She climbed out and hit a short iron up onto the green. "Nice shot," I said. "I bet you can hole this out for a birdie. That will be a nice way to finish the round."

Karyn grinned. "Perfect way to end a perfect round. I hope I play this well next week," she said.

We drove along the cart path to the green. She grabbed her putter, and I stepped out of the cart to watch her putt. As she squatted down to line up her shot, she looked closer at the hole. "Wait a minute," she said. "The inside of the cup is painted pink, not white. What's going on?"

"Don't look at me. I have no idea. Someone must be playing some kind of prank," I replied.

Unconvinced, Karyn walked very suspiciously over to the hole. She leaned over, took one look, then snapped her head back toward me. "The cup is full of dried rose petals," she said. "You seriously don't know what this is?"

"Really," I said, raising my hands to protest my innocence. "The group in front of us must be playing some kind of practical joke. Is anything else in there?"

"I don't know," Karyn said. "Let me look." She reached into the cup and moved the petals around. Then she rose up with a small box in her hand. She turned back to me.

By this point I was right up close to her, down on one knee, my Bible open. "The Bible says a cord of three strands is not easily broken. That's my vision for us. You, me, and God. Karyn, will you marry me?"

Tears started flowing. "Yes, Ben, yes. Yes, I will marry you," Karyn said, her voice shaking. She threw her arms around me and we shared a kiss on the eighteenth green.

"*Hey!* What's going on here?" a voice called out.

Karyn and I both turned around. My dad came walking up out of the woods next to the green with a camcorder in his hand, videotaping the whole ordeal. Then my mom and her mom and dad came driving up in a golf cart, holding roses for us. The moment was magical, if I do say so myself.

The six of us stayed over that night in one of the hotels connected to the golf course. Karyn and I did not share a room because of our commitment to save ourselves for the wedding night. In my mind, that wasn't going to be too far away, so I was up for the challenge. After all, how long does it take to plan a wedding?

On the drive home to the Twin Cities, Karyn kept staring down at her ring. She seemed to have something on her mind, but I thought she was probably just thinking about the wedding. Finally she looked over at me and said, "So how would you feel if I gave one more local pageant a try?"

"What?"

"I took first runner-up at Miss Twin Cities. It was only my first attempt. My dream since I was a little girl has been to one day become Miss Minnesota, then compete in the Miss America contest."

"Karyn, you said this would be just a one-time thing. I thought the Miss Twin Cities was the end of it," I said.

"I know, but I've been thinking about this for a long time. I've already started looking into what it takes to really compete and be successful. I figured I had time since the last time we talked about marriage you said you wanted to get your feet on the ground in the NFL before you thought about getting married. But after this surprise, I figure if I am going to try this, now is the time," she explained.

"You know, Karyn, if this is important to you, it is important to me. I think it is great for you to try it," I said. I said this knowing full well that to be a *Miss* Minnesota meant you could not be a *Mrs*. Utecht. You could not be married and compete. Little did I know that by saying yes I had just signed up for a two-year engagement, two years that were going to test our faith, our commitment, and our self-control.

I really don't recommend two-year engagements.

CHAPTER 10

WELCOME TO THE NFL

I WENT TO MY FIRST NFL training camp when I was eleven. My dad took me down to Mankato to watch the Vikings' camp at Minnesota State University. I was a big Vikings fan growing up, so when my dad asked me if I wanted to go watch a few days of their training camp, I jumped at the chance. A ten-foot-tall chain-link fence surrounded the practice field, but I could see everything I wanted to see. As soon as the practice sessions ended, my dad and I ran over to the gate through which all the players had to pass to go to the locker room. Security tape kept us back enough to let the players pass, but we were close enough to get autographs. I really wanted star running back Herschel Walker's autograph, so I pushed my way to the front, hoping to get his attention.

On our second day at the camp my dad and I stood next to the fence waiting for Herschel Walker to pass by. Even though practice had ended, the kickers stayed out on the field practicing field goals. The gate was on the end of the field just past the goal-posts, which meant footballs from the kickers kept bouncing up close to us. As I watched the kickers boom footballs while I also kept an eye out for my favorite player, kicker Fuad Reveiz nailed one. The ball flew right up next to the fence, hit the ground, then bounced up and over the fence and landed on top of a utility shed that was maybe a yard beyond the fence. The moment I saw the ball go up on the shed, I ran over to the fence next to the shed and started climbing. By the time my dad realized what was happening I was nearly to the top. The security guard didn't even get a word out before I jumped from the top of the fence to the shed roof. I found the football, tucked it under my arm, and climbed back down to my dad. The security guard just sort of shook his head, then said, "I'm sorry, son, but I can't allow you to keep the ball."

I muttered something like "I understand" and handed the football back to him. The guard left with the ball. After he was gone my dad gave me a funny look and said, "What possessed you to do that?"

"I don't know," I said. "It just seemed like the thing to do."

My dad laughed. "Good thing your mother wasn't here to see it. She would have been worried sick." By this point my dad was used to me acting on impulse, and to me climbing things. When I was only four or five he hung a rope from a tree in the yard. I guess he expected me to swing on it. Instead I climbed to the top. That rope went higher than this fence.

Shortly after I handed the ball back to the security guard, an equipment manager came up to me and asked, "Are you the brave boy who got my kicker's ball back?"

"Yes, sir," I said.

"Follow me, son," he said.

I looked at my dad in shock. He stared back with the same expression. I followed the equipment manager over to the back of an equipment truck, where he handed me the ball that I retrieved. "Here you go, son. You earned it." Right at that moment Qadry Ismail, the star wide receiver, ran up and threw me his sweat towel. I was speechless. This was a dream come true. By the way, I still have that football.

•   •   •

My first camp with the Colts was a lot like that Vikings camp when I was a boy. Because I was physically unable to perform, I spent most of the camp fetching things for the veteran tight ends. At the end of practice I gathered their helmets and pads and lugged them back to the locker room. My duties didn't end once practice was over. One evening our number-one tight end, Marcus Pollard, came over to me and said, "Hey rook, make sure my rally run is in my room before I get there tonight. This is important, you got that?" Marcus had been in the league for ten years and carried a lot of weight in the locker room. Guys looked up to him.

With an unsure laugh I said, "Yeah, I got it," but I had no idea what he was talking about. I tried to figure out what a rally run could possibly be, but I finally decided it had to be some sort of hazing ritual for the new guys, like the proverbial snipe hunt.

The next day I realized how wrong I had been. Several of the veteran players came over to me and told me Marcus was not happy with me. "What did I do?" I asked.

"I don't know," I was told, "but you had better be prepared for what's coming."

As I finally entered the foyer of our team meeting room, there was Marcus, and boy, did he make his presence known.

"Hey, rook!" he shouted. "This is my time! Do you understand me? I put my time in, so when I ask for something you will do it!"

I was so nervous at this point, I could barely speak. "Marcus, what are you talking about?" I asked.

"You didn't make the rally run, that's what!" he responded, and walked off.

"What is a rally run? I've never heard of it," I replied but he didn't hear me.

One of the other players who watched the whole exchange

grabbed me. "Don't you get it? A rally run means you go to Rally's and buy him the burgers he wants."

"Rally's?" I asked.

"Yeah, the burger joint down the street!"

I winced. "Rally's. Oh man. Thanks." I turned and went off to find Marcus. "Marcus, man," I said when I found him, "I'm so sorry I didn't get your Rally run. I didn't know what you were talking about because we don't have Rally's in Minnesota and I had never heard of it, but I guarantee you that I will not miss another one. I promise you that. Whatever you need, you tell me, and I will make sure it happens."

Marcus seemed to calm down a little. "Okay, rook, I'll give you another chance."

Believe me, I never missed another Rally's run nor did I ever act annoyed at hauling helmets and pads or anything else I was asked to do. Marcus noticed. He was, in my opinion, one of the greats. Over the course of the season he became a fantastic mentor and friend to me.

My screwing up the Rally's run only made the apprehension I felt during camp that much worse, however. Because I was injured and unable to work out with the team, most of the time I felt very much like an outsider. There's something about the training camp experience that brings a team together. Everyone leaves their homes and moves into the dorms on the campus of Indiana State University, in Terre Haute.* There's nothing left to distract you as you set your focus completely on the upcoming season. Working out twice a day in near 100-degree heat and high humidity makes everyone equally miserable, but on the Colts everyone suffers together to prepare themselves to chase a much bigger

---

* The Colts' training camp has since been moved to Anderson University in Anderson, Indiana.

goal and that is a Super Bowl championship. For the coaches, camp shows them who needs to be on the roster. For the players, it's about becoming a team.

I may have been in Terre Haute, but I wasn't part of the team, not yet at least.

Every player hopes to make a good first impression when they step onto the field for a game. I first made my mark on the field of the home of the Colts, the RCA Dome, not as a football player but as a singer. Before the first home exhibition game of the 2004 season the public address system announced, "Please rise and remove your hats for the singing of the national anthem, which is performed tonight by rookie tight end Ben Utecht." I'm sure most people in the crowd went, "Who?" To be honest, most of the players and coaches probably went, "Who?" too.

And then I started singing. I felt a little nervous, but nothing like I did three years earlier when the University of Minnesota asked me and Dan Nystrom to sing the national anthem on our first home game after 9/11. Singing that day was one of the most emotional experiences of my life, and probably one of the high points of anything I will be asked to do as a singer. Nothing compares to the deep sense of honor, patriotism, and gratitude I felt singing before a packed house of hurting people after 9/11. By comparison, singing the anthem for the first exhibition game of my first season with the Colts was pretty routine. I just didn't want to screw it up.

By the time the crowd started cheering and clapping through ". . . and the home of the brave," I felt pretty good about how I'd done. Coach Dungy, Tom Moore, and Howard Mudd all told me, "Good job," which felt great. Since I wasn't going to be out on the field as a player anytime that season, this was one of the few times I was probably going to hear affirmation from these coaches. The

Colts strongly supported my singing passion and talents. None would prove more true than when Bill Polian and Coach Dungy allowed me to join Grammy winner Sandi Patty and the Indianapolis Symphony Orchestra for sixteen Christmas shows during the 2007 season. I will never forget how many of my teammates and coaches came to the shows to show their support. It's hard to explain what is was like catching passes from Peyton Manning and literally running straight from the game over to the concert hall to perform. One thing is for sure: it was a huge hit with the Indianapolis audience. If you're wondering about Sandi Patty, fear not—that story is coming.

The team headed back to Terre Haute after the first exhibition game. I worked as hard as I could to learn offensive coordinator Tom Moore's offense and all of offensive line coach Howard Mudd's blocking schemes. Coach Dungy had hinted that he hoped I might be available by the middle of the season. The normal recovery time for sports hernia surgery is four to six weeks. Because I had major tears, the doctor had no idea when I might be back at full strength. I had to learn everything I could to be ready.

Throughout training camp the roster is cut down from ninety players to fifty-three. By the time the final cuts were made I was not on the fifty-three-man roster. However, I was placed on the physically unable to perform, or PUP, list. That meant I remained a part of the team, still under contract, even though I did not take up an active roster spot.

Once camp was over I moved out of the extended-stay hotel and found a downtown apartment near the Central Canal, just across the street from the Circle Centre Mall. It was a perfect place to live for a single guy. Even though I did not play on Sundays, I stayed very busy. I spent my days at the Colts' facility going through rehab for my injury, as well as attending all the team meetings in preparation for games just like I was on the active roster. When Peyton Manning is your quarterback, the offensive schemes are more complex than for most teams. I had a lot to learn.

Karyn tried to come down to Indy once a month, but sometimes six or even eight weeks went by between visits. She worked part-time as a personal trainer at a Minneapolis athletic club. Most of her time went into preparing for the Miss Minnesota pageant. She'd won a local pageant, Miss Heart of the Lakes, which qualified her for the state competition. I soon discovered there was more to pageant training than just practicing a few numbers on the piano for the talent section. Most of her time was taken up with volunteer activities, speaking engagements, and all the other appearances she had to do as part of her preparation. That didn't leave a lot of time for her to come see me, and I couldn't leave the team during the season.

When Karyn did manage to come down to Indianapolis we had to spend the first few days together just getting reacquainted. The visits were also more than a little frustrating for both of us. Neither of us wanted a long engagement, but that's where we found ourselves. Long engagements and a commitment to purity don't normally go together. We made it work, and I took a lot of ice baths. This is also a difficult time for me to remember. To be honest with you, I struggle to remember many of Karyn's trips down to see me. It's embarrassing to have to ask your parents and wife what they remember about those trips because you can't.

Since I spent most of my time alone, I got into a routine as the season progressed. Thankfully, I wasn't the only injured player trying to work his way back onto the field. Another rookie, defensive back Bob Sanders, was in the same position as me. He starred at

Iowa in college, which meant the two of us had gone up against one another several times. Now that we were teammates we rehabbed together and worked out together. Once we both were deemed fit to run drills we went up against one another in practice. No one other than the trainer paid a lot of attention to what we were doing. I wish they had because I had some good days against a guy who was drafted in the second round and went on to become a Pro Bowler during his time with the Colts.*

Bob was cleared to play a little over halfway through the season. He ended up playing in six games, and started four. Coach Dungy hoped I might be ready around the same time, but it was not to be. About the time Bob was put on the active roster the team moved me from the PUP list to the injured reserve list, or IR. Landing on the IR meant I was done for the season. However, I kept working out, trying to regain my strength, speed, and training.

The Colts started slow in the 2004 season. At one point we had a 4-3 record, which is far below our expectations. However, the team went on an eight-game winning streak and won our division. By this point I was starting to feel like my old self again. My abs felt good and my speed was coming back. I kept working hard, trying to prove myself for the next season and to be strong going into the next year's organized team activities, or OTAs.

I was working out in the practice facility one day with one of the trainers, Erin Barill, when Peyton Manning and the offensive line came in for a photo session. I only worked out when the team was not using the practice field. The photographer asked if I minded waiting until they were finished before I started again. "Sure, no problem," I said. Then I pulled Erin over. "Okay, Erin, as soon as they're done with this thing, we're going to time it so

---

* The Pro Bowl is the NFL all-star game.

that when Peyton turns around to walk out and goes past us, you throw a huge post pattern for me."

"Sure, Ben. Whatever you want," Erin replied.

Erin and I kept busy doing a few things down in one of the end zones away from Peyton and the offensive line. I kept watching them, however. The moment the photo session ended I nodded toward Erin. "Let's do this," I said.

I lined up wide. Erin said, "Hike," and I took off down the field. I was burning it up. I got to the ten-yard mark, planted hard, and cut toward the post. I took maybe one more step when the proverbial turf monster came up out of the ground and grabbed hold of my cleat. Erin released the ball while I stumbled all over myself. My feet started flying in different directions and then boom, I fell flat on my face right in front of Peyton Manning as the ball soared over me. Thankfully, Peyton and the line just kept on walking. I wanted him to be anxious to add a weapon like me to his arsenal. That wasn't quite the first impression I made on him.

The 2004 Colts season ended like too many Colts seasons have ended: with a playoff loss in Foxborough, Massachusetts, to Tom Brady and the New England Patriots. Once the season was over the head of the Colts' scouting department, Chris Polian, had me come in for a workout session. Chris is Bill's son. He wanted to put me through the same drills I would have done the year before if I worked out at the combine. Now keep in mind that if I had worked out at the combine, I would have spent nearly two months doing nothing but practicing the combine drills. Instead, I went into them cold.

The first thing Chris had me do was run a forty-yard dash. The forty is pretty much the standard for measuring speed at every level of football. I took my mark, listened for the starter's pistol, then took off. I don't really remember my time that day. However,

I do remember turning around after I finished and seeing a huge smile on Chris's face. Mission accomplished.

Then Chris had me run what is known as the L drill. The L drill consists of running through a series of cones set up in the shape of an L. I hadn't run an L drill in a long time, if ever. Again, I do not know what my time was, or even what a good time on the L might be. However, after I ran it Chris called me over. "If you had run this time in the combine, you would have been in the top two or three percent of all receivers," he said.

"Receivers?" I asked.

"Right; not just tight ends but wide receivers as well," he said with a smile. "Great job, Ben."

Chris was so happy about my times because I showed him wide receiver speed even though I was six-seven and 250 pounds. Guys my size don't usually have that kind of speed. Those who do make an impact. And that's what I hoped to do in the off-season organized team activities and minicamps, then on into training camp in Terre Haute. Coach Dungy and Mr. Polian had taken a leap of faith with me by giving me a contract when I could not play. I was determined to show them their faith was well placed. The next season could not arrive soon enough for me.

CHAPTER 11

TRANSITIONS

W‍HEN THE CALENDAR SWITCHED FROM 2004 to 2005 everything in my life seemed up in the air. Karyn and I were engaged, but neither of us had any idea when we might get married. She was scheduled to compete in the Miss Minnesota pageant in June. If she lost, we planned on throwing together a quick wedding within the next month, possibly in her parents' backyard. The wedding and honeymoon all had to be over before the end of July and the start of the Colts' training camp. If she won, we'd have to push back those plans at least a year, possibly longer, depending on how she did in the Miss America pageant.

In the weeks leading up to the Miss Minnesota pageant, Karyn became even busier than she had been before, if that was even possible. Every candidate has a platform, and Karyn's was fighting childhood obesity. She couldn't just say this was her platform and wait to do something after the pageant. In the months between her winning the title of Miss Heart of the Lakes and the Miss Minnesota contest she became very involved with the American Heart Association's youth health initiatives, in- cluding the Jump Rope for Heart and Hoop for Heart programs. She also worked with the Food and Drug Administration and the U.S. Department of Agriculture to connect U of M student athletes with elementary schools to promote fitness. On top of that, she had to practice for the different aspects of the pageant and work a part-time job. In her spare time she continued working on her golf game, with the goal of possibly joining the LPGA tour someday. Needless to say, we didn't get to see a lot of each other.

By the time the Miss Minnesota pageant finally rolled around, I had mixed feelings. On the one hand, I wanted to see Karyn win. I knew she had it in her and I wanted to see her achieve her childhood goal. But I was also anxious, and ready for the two of us to start our life together. I hated living so far away from her. Only seeing one another maybe once a month was starting to take its toll on both of us. We talked on the phone every day, but it wasn't the same. Not knowing when we could actually get married was getting old. I don't like living with uncertainty. I was ready to get on with life.

However, I was going to have to wait at least a year longer. Karyn nailed her performance in the pageant. She showed poise when she answered the questions, and her piano solo brought down the house. By the time they got around to naming the winner, I knew it was going to be her. I was sitting with Karyn's family. Chris, my agent, sat right next to me. When the announcer said, "The winner, and Miss Minnesota for 2005, is Karyn Stordahl," Chris reached over, put his hand on my shoulder, and said, "Congratulations, buddy. Looks like you'll be taking a lot more cold showers."

I laughed. "Yeah, I guess so."

Then he added, "What are you going to do if she wins Miss America in January?"

"I don't even want to think about that right now," I said.

•   •   •

Our inability to set a wedding date wasn't the only part of my life
that was up in the air. Although the Colts kept me on the team
throughout the 2004 season, I didn't have a guaranteed spot on
the team going forward. My year of sitting back and learning
the offense gave me a leg up on any new players coming in, but
that only got me so far. I still had to go out and make the roster.
During the off-season Marcus Pollard moved on to the Detroit
Lions, which left Dallas Clark, the 2003 first-round draft choice
Tony Dungy mentioned at that Athletes in Action banquet, the
number-one tight end. Ben Hartsock also played a lot the year
I was hurt, and he was still with the team. Before training camp
the Colts brought in Bryan Fletcher as a free agent. Bryan had
bounced around between a few teams before joining the Colts. All
of these guys had a lot of talent. I wasn't sure if there was going to
be room on the roster for all of us.

Training camp opened a little over a month after the Miss Minnesota pageant. Since I was no longer a rookie I didn't have to lug
around anyone's helmet and pads, but it didn't take long for me
to look back at that time as the good old days. Within the first few
days of practice I realized that this game is all business. And when
you play for the Colts with Peyton Manning as your quarterback,
you aren't in the business of being average. This is the business
of becoming a champion. The expectations, the pressure, and the
stress were astronomical. We'd finished the previous year with a
12-4 record and won our division, but none of the veterans on the
team looked at the year as successful. The team fell short of our
own expectations, which made everyone in training camp even
more driven.

I struggled to keep up. Everything moved so much faster than
in college. Players were bigger and stronger, but they also had
moves and schemes I had never seen at Minnesota. As a tight

end, running routes and catching passes is only one small part of my responsibilities. On most plays I was called on to block and open holes for our running backs, Edgerrin James and Dominic Rhodes, or to protect Peyton Manning. In camp that meant I had to block our own defensive players, including the best defensive end in all of football, Dwight Freeney. In 2004 Freeney led the league in sacks with sixteen and was named first-team All-Pro. He had a spin move that made the best linemen in the game look foolish. When I tried to block him, he made me look like I had never played the game in my life. The coaches all noticed, and they let me hear about it. I never thought I was going to get it right. One night I called Karyn and told her, "I don't think I am going to make it."

"You can do this, Ben," she reassured me. "You have so much talent, and you're smart. You can pick this up. You'll see. Hang in there."

I needed that reassurance. All my life I've been a pretty sensitive guy. I really internalize criticism. One of my teammates even started calling me Sensi-techt because of the way I responded to criticism. I tried not to let things get to me, but when you are trying to pick up a whole new system and adjust from the college game to the pros after not having played a down of football in a year and a half, a lot of criticism comes your way.

From the start I worked hard to master the blocking techniques taught by Howard Mudd, our legendary offensive line coach. His approach was completely different than what I had done in college, and he wasn't shy about calling a player out when one of us didn't do things right. Mudd taught us to use our shoulders and forearms as weapons, to throw our bodies right into the chests of the guys we were trying to block. If we didn't, we heard about it. In the film room, going over tape from practices and games, I remember being singled out for my mistakes. "Utecht, what's the matter with you?" Then he unleashed a tirade of adjectives for my play that probably shouldn't be repeated, if you get my drift.

Mudd was tough and fair, but he wasn't the only one who got on me, either. Offensive coordinator Tom Moore was one of the most intense coaches I have ever been around. I enjoyed Tom. He and I shared a Minnesota connection because we were both originally from Rochester. On one play in practice I was supposed to get a clean release on the linebacker as I started my route. The linebacker in this case happened to be Gary Brackett. Gary was a really good player who had a great career with the Colts. On this particular play Gary anticipated my moves and hit me hard, throwing me completely off my route. All our passes built on precise timing between Peyton and the receivers. I blew that up on this play. The whistle blew and I went back to the huddle. The next thing I knew someone grabbed my arm, spun me around, then punched me square in the chest with his forearm as hard as he could. That's when I saw it was Tom Moore. "This is the way I want you to do it!" he boomed. Then he punched me again as he showed me how physical he wanted me to be with linebackers on my routes. The guy was sixty-six years old when he did this! The rest of practice I was angry and embarrassed and really pissed off that he did that in front of the entire team. But I also got his point.

He made another point later in a different practice. I had some sort of injury, I don't even remember what it was, and I had to sit out drills one day. While I was standing on the sidelines with some other players, Tom came over to us and said, "Utecht, you ever hear of a guy named Wally Pipp?"

"No, Coach," I replied.

Tom went on to say, "Wally Pipp played first base for the New York Yankees back in the twenties. He came to the ballpark after a night of too much socializing and told the manager he had a bad headache and couldn't play. So the manager takes him out and puts in a little-known guy named Lou Gehrig. Gehrig didn't miss a game for the next fifteen years and that was the end of Wally Pipp." Then Tom paused and let his words sink in before walking away without saying anything else.

I got his point. You stay on the field no matter what because once you come out, you may not get another chance. Playing hurt isn't optional. You do it if you want to have a career in the National Football League.

During my high school and college days I had already learned this lesson, but once I made it to the NFL "playing with pain" went to a whole different level. I always felt I had a pretty high tolerance to pain, but even I needed some help sometimes. And that help came in the form of painkillers and anti-inflammatories. Nearly all players have to take them.

My experience with medication to help manage pain started in high school. I've already described how I took maximum doses of ibuprofen to get me through my hip injury. The progression from weekly over-the-counter anti-inflammatories to prescription medications came about pretty quickly when I played college ball. In a couple of earlier chapters I wrote about the pain shots I received in my foot and my groin. I never really gave the shots a thought. They always felt like a normal part of the game. You do what you have to do to stay on the field and contribute to the team. Even before the major injuries forced me to turn to pain shots, I regularly took ibuprofen to deal with pain the game inflicts, until it didn't work any longer. I was then given Vioxx and Celebrex to keep me on the field. Vioxx was eventually taken off the market because of possible heart problems related to its use, and Celebrex had some warnings associated with its use, but that didn't worry me or my teammates. Late in my college career I received Toradol injections for the pain in my groin that was eventually diagnosed as a sports hernia. The shots kept me on the field, but, as I already wrote, they set me up for the more serious tear that came against Wisconsin.

In the NFL, weekly Toradol shots were as much a part of game-time preparation as film study. I did not yet know this when Tom Moore shared the Wally Pipp story with me, but I discovered it once I started getting hurt in games. While playing with an injury, I and any other player who needed some help with pain lined up for a Toradol shot right after our final team meeting the night before a game. As soon as the meeting was over I would grab a snack, then walk behind a divider that separated the dining hall. Lots of guys also lined up for their shots. I wanted my body to feel better so that I could stand up the punishment doled out on the field, so I did what I had to do. At the time I was thankful for them. I probably would have had to miss more games without them. And if you miss games, you stand the chance of being the next Wally Pipp. No one I ever played with wanted to earn that distinction.

Looking back on my career, from high school through college and the NFL, I cannot even begin to calculate the amount of pain and anti-inflammatory pills and shots I took. I don't think there was even one week where I didn't have to take something, even if it was as small as an Advil. However, I never knew, and would not discover until after my career was over, that anti-inflammatories don't just help hurting joints feel better. They also mask the symptoms and consequences of concussions, including the headaches incurred by hundreds of subconcussive hits that I took every year as a tight end doing my best to block defensive ends and linebackers. In the end, the drugs kept me on the field, and at the time, that's all that mattered.

Just in case you think my experience was unique, a former college teammate of mine who played in the NFL told me about his experiences with prescription drugs in the pros.

He played on one team where on the flight home after a road game, one of the flight attendants walked up and down the aisle handing out painkillers to players like they hand out sodas and peanuts on commercial flights. He also shared that there was a player on the team who collected as many pills as he could so that he could act as a pharmacist to his teammates during the week just in case anyone needed a little extra for pain management. My friend admitted that he frequently visited this player's locker to get a painkiller to help get through practice because he suffered so many injuries in his career. All of this was just a normal part of professional football culture. None of us thought twice about it.

Training camp gets pretty monotonous. Thankfully the endless parade of drills in 100-degree heat gets broken up by the exhibition games. The team starters don't play much in those games, but guys like me who are fighting to make the team do. The Colts opened the 2005 exhibition season in Tokyo against the Atlanta Falcons. I didn't play too much with the offense, but I did get a chance to play on specials teams. Believe me, I busted my butt on the punt and kickoff teams. On one punt return I lit a guy up with a huge hit. He came running down the field and I lowered my shoulder and knocked him off his feet completely. I got some huge props from the coaches when the team watched film of the game back at camp the next week. I have a hard time remembering any other specific details from that game but I do believe I had at least one reception on offense.

The rest of camp and the preseason games flew by. As we got closer to the final roster cuts I became more and more confident I was going to make the team. In our last preseason game, which is the last chance for guys like me to make an impression, starters don't play at all, which meant I got a lot of time on the field. Toward the end of the game I turned to our third-string quarterback, Tom Arth, and said, "I've been beating my guy all night. Get me the ball." The next play Tom arced a high, forty-yard bomb to me, which I caught easily. After the game Bill Polian came into the locker room and congratulated me on my great play that night. That's when I knew I had probably made the team. Coach Dungy confirmed my hopes the next day. I was now officially an Indianapolis Colt.

I scored a touchdown in my first regular-season NFL game. It came in the third quarter in the nationally televised Sunday night game against the Baltimore Ravens. Coach Dungy named me the starting tight end for the game when Dallas Clark had to sit out with a concussion. My touchdown came toward the end of the third quarter. We were on the Ravens' twenty-six-yard line. Peyton called a route combination where I ran a seam route. I took off down the field and the safety, future Hall of Famer Deion Sanders, should have been on me, but he wasn't. Peyton looked to his first read, that is, the first receiver to which he intended to throw, but the defender was all over him. Then he saw me running wide open. Peyton threw a beautiful spiral to my back shoulder. I adjusted to the ball, made the catch, then went over the safety into the end zone for my first professional touchdown. The next day the front page of my hometown paper, the *Minneapolis Star Tribune,* featured a photo of me in the end zone cradling the football. I still have that paper. And the ball.

After my performance against the Ravens, the coaching staff named me the starter for the second game. Since we ran a lot of two-tight-end sets, Dallas still played a lot. But, as the starter, I stayed in the game when we ran what is called the King's personnel package, that is, a one-tight-end formation. Basically, this meant the starting tight end spot was mine to lose.

I had a great week of practice the next week. My confidence was soaring at this point. I made great catches and great reads all week leading up to our second game, at home against the Jacksonville Jaguars.

On the second play of the game I fired off the line to block the defensive end. I shoved my hands into his chest and tried to steer him away from the play. All of the sudden, I felt him slipping away from me. As he started to get away I tried to go low and legally cut him at his knees. He moved faster than I could get down on the block. My body went low as he ran from me, and his heel came up and hit me hard in the ribs. Pain shot through my side as I felt something give. *This isn't good,* I told myself. When I went to pick myself up off the ground the pain grew worse. *Don't get Wally Pipped,* was all I could think, so I stayed in the game.

My form deteriorated throughout the rest of the game as the pain grew worse and worse. Somehow, I played through to the end. After the game the trainers took me in for an X-ray and discovered I'd fractured three ribs. The team doctor held me out of the next four games. Dallas reclaimed his spot as a starter and never let go. I came back in week seven but by then the rotations had been set and the offense was clicking. I went from being the game-one starter to a situation player. I didn't really play any significant time until the last game of the season, when Coach Dungy rested most of the starters to get ready for the playoffs. I had another good game and my second touchdown, but this one came from the backup quarterback, Jim Sorgi, not Peyton Manning.

We won the last game of the season and finished with a 14-2 record and home field advantage throughout the playoffs. However, the season was marked by a tragedy. The team had a 13-1 record (including a thirteen-game winning streak) when news came that Coach Dungy's eighteen-year-old son, James, had lost his life in Tampa. Suddenly, football didn't seem so important to any of us. The entire team was in shock. Coach Dungy was like a father to all of us. With his family in crisis he left the team for a few weeks. We lost the next game after the tragedy hit. The Arizona game was Coach Dungy's first game back. We dedicated the win to him and his family.

It is hard to say how much the tragedy carried over into the playoffs. As the number-one seed in the AFC, we had the first week off. Pittsburgh upset the Cincinnati Bengals when the Bengals' star quarterback, Carson Palmer, went down with a knee injury early in the game. The Steelers came to Indy the next week, a game in which we were heavy favorites. We didn't play like it. The offense never really clicked. Through three quarters we'd managed to score only one field goal and went into the fourth quarter behind 21–3. Then Peyton engineered one of his patented comebacks and we scored a couple of touchdowns and a two-point conversion to pull to within three, at 21–18. I thought we were going to pull the game out when Jerome Bettis, the Steelers' running back, fumbled the ball on our two-yard line. Nick Harper, one of our defensive backs and one of the fastest guys on the field, grabbed the ball and took off. It looked like he might go all the way when Steelers' quarterback Ben Roethlisberger dove at him from behind and managed to just trip him up.

Even so, that play gave us the ball on our own forty-two with a minute left. That's plenty of time for Peyton Manning in his prime. We quickly drove the ball to the Steelers' twenty-eight, but the drive stalled. Our kicker, Mike Vanderjagt, came in to kick the game-tying field goal and send the game into overtime. Vanderjagt was the league's most accurate kicker that season, having made 92 percent of his field goals for the year. But instead of sending the game into overtime, he pushed the kick way to the right. The ball landed somewhere up in the crowd and just like that, our season was over.

Even though my first season playing in the NFL didn't go exactly like I had hoped, due to the rib injuries, I felt confident that I could contribute to the team and make an impact as an NFL player. I was anxious for the next season to start. I had a lot to prove to the team and to myself.

CHAPTER 12

A SUPER YEAR

WHEN I FIRST STARTED SERIOUSLY CONSIDERING asking Karyn to marry me, I went to my father for advice. I asked him, "How do I know for certain that she is *the* one?" As I said before, I am a hopeless romantic. I also grew up in a home where my parents told me they started praying for my future wife from the day I was born. I knew I loved Karyn and I wanted to spend the rest of my life with her, but was that enough? Could I count on my feelings to know she was the one that God had ordained for me to marry?

"You know, Ben," my dad said, "you've always been one who believes in the idea of love at first sight, right? That there's only one soul mate for you, right?"

"Yes."

"To be honest with you, in reality the idea that there's only one right *one* out there for you is just not true. There are many women in this world that you're compatible with, and if you met them at the right time and in the right situation, you could very well spend the rest of your life with any one of them."

My father had just debunked every idea I had ever heard from all the movies I had watched in my life, going back to Disney movies and on up to all the romantic comedies I'd taken dates to see. "Really?" I said.

"Really. But to me, that's what makes marriage so beautiful. The Lord brings two people together, but then *you* have to make a choice. You fall in love with this person but there's always a choice. And that choice is that you choose this woman and she chooses you. For the rest of your life you choose every day to love her and to honor her in the covenant of marriage just like she chooses you. To me, that speaks so much more loudly than the idea that there's someone out there meant just for you and the choice is outside of your control. If you marry Karyn, you don't marry her because fate destined it but because you choose to love her and will choose to love her above all others every day for the rest of your life."

I didn't say anything for a while. Instead I let his words sink in.

"Does that help?" my dad asked.

"That's exactly what I needed to know," I said.

On July 15, 2006, Karyn and I were finally able to make that choice official and publicly commit ourselves to one another in marriage. We held the ceremony in the same church where my parents were married, as well as my aunt and uncle, and my grandma Joan, whom we affectionately call "Goldie Joan." For Karyn and me, holding our ceremony in this church was a way to honor our family while also declaring that our new home was really built on the love and commitment of those who came before us. Just as my mom and dad chose to love one another, Karyn and I were choosing each other as well.

On my wedding day I realized one of the greatest benefits of being a preacher's kid. When I walked out into the church and took my place at the front, my dad was right there with me. He wasn't my best man. No. This was even better. My father officiated our wedding. I cannot tell you how special it was to have my dad lead Karyn and me through our vows and the exchange of the rings and every other part of the ceremony. The moment I saw him there I went back to every special moment in my life, beginning with my first tackle in the backyard. My dad was always there for all of them. He's been my constant. More than that, he's been my example. When I said "I do" to Karyn in front of my father, I knew how to make this commitment last because he'd shown me.

And wow, the moment I saw Karyn walk down the aisle I knew that the long wait through our two-year engagement had been worth it. I have this image in my head of her coming down the aisle in her dress, the veil slightly covering her face. Wow. To think that this vision, this memory is also at risk, I just can't allow myself to go there. Karyn later told me that she wanted to run down the aisle. Both of us were very, very ready to start our life together.

The wedding itself wasn't too large. We had maybe two hundred guests. Ben Hartsock had become a close friend, so he and his wife came. So did Bryan Fletcher and kickers Dave Rayner and Rhys Lloyd. A lot of my college teammates attended as well, including my best man, Rian Melander, one of the best left tackles I ever played with. All in all, it was a great day.

Karyn's parents gave us a honeymoon trip to Puerto Vallarta, Mexico. The place was beautiful, but, looking back, we might have been better off saving the trip for after the upcoming season. Puerto Vallarta in late February sounds great, especially compared to how cold it gets in Indianapolis in the winter. However, going there in the middle of the summer made it difficult to spend much time outside. The place was hot. Very, very hot. We had to down a lot of cold drinks just to survive. Cold drinks meant ice, and apparently there was something in the ice in one of my drinks, because I got really sick. Not to go into too much disgusting detail, but my digestive system was a mess the rest of the trip and for a while after we returned home. A bad stomach presented a real problem because two days after we got home from Mexico I reported to Terre Haute for the Colts' training camp.

Going into my third camp with the Colts I still worried about making the club. I knew I could play in the league and I believed I had shown I belonged by how I produced when I got the chance. During our off-season OTAs and minicamps Peyton said more than once that the offense needed to find a way to get the ball to me more often. That made me feel pretty good. However, just as in college, injuries kept me off the field my first season. Images of Wally Pipp danced in my head every time the medical staff pulled me out of the lineup.

I arrived at camp still ailing from a messed-up digestive system. Throughout camp the team doctor gave me multiple IVs and had me tested for a parasite. Nothing showed up, and I eventually started to feel like myself again, but the first week or so was pretty rough. The heat and humidity of playing football in late July and early August is bad enough without already being dehydrated from never-ending bouts of diarrhea.

About the time I started to feel better from whatever bug I picked up in Mexico, I suffered another setback. During a routine scrimmage I caught a short pass, turned upfield, and had a massive collision with one of our linebackers. Today I cannot remember who it was but I do remember feeling my ribs pop and sharp pain shooting through my side. All I could think was, *NO! Not again!* It was the Jacksonville game from the year before, all over again. I kept on practicing but I could hardly breathe. *Four weeks, I can't miss four weeks of camp* kept running through my head. I'd missed four weeks when I broke my ribs the year before, and I never really got back into the lineup afterward. Missing four weeks now would be disastrous. I might well be cut as a result. I didn't tell anyone about my ribs. I had to try to play through this. There was only one place I could turn to.

That night I went back to my room and poured out my heart to God. I lay on my back because I could not roll to my side. I called out in pain, "Lord, I'm not going to accept this. I know You are a God Who heals and I call on Your Son's name to heal me." I had never prayed a prayer like this before, and I know better than to believe anyone can demand anything from God, but believe it or not, as soon as I prayed this prayer I felt a warm sensation spread from the top of my head down across my body. It felt like someone had put an electric blanket over me. Then I passed out asleep.

I'd forgotten all about the prayer and the rib injury when I woke up the next morning. For one thing, I slept like a baby all night, which is something I never did in training camp. I was always too nervous and keyed up to sleep well. Not that night. I passed out and woke up in the morning feeling better than I had in weeks. I sat up in bed and stretched, pushing my arms high up over my head. And that's when it hit me: nothing hurt. I could hardly believe it. My ribs felt perfectly fine. I didn't miss a day of practice, much less four weeks. This was the first time I ever experienced a healing miracle, but it wouldn't be the last.

By the time we broke camp I'd found my place in the offense. With Dallas Clark, Bryan Fletcher, and myself, we had a lethal tight end combination. (Ben Hartsock had signed with the Tennessee Titans during the off-season.) And we were only a small part of the arsenal of weapons at Peyton Manning's disposal. At wide receiver we had two of the best in Marvin Harrison and Reggie Wayne, who were complemented by Brandon Stokley and Aaron Moorehead. Then in the backfield we had the dynamic rookie Joseph Addai along with the workhorse Dominic Rhodes. On paper, at least, we had a potential Super Bowl offense. The defense, which was led by Dwight Freeney, Robert Mathis, Bob

Sanders, Cato June, and Gary Brackett, among others, looked strong as well. Everyone on the team believed this was going to be our year. Now we just had to go out on the field and prove it.

The opening game had a different feel to it than most regular-season games. We headed to New York to play the Giants at the New Jersey Meadowlands. But we weren't just playing the Giants. Their quarterback was Peyton's little brother, Eli. And Peyton wasn't going to lose to his brother.

The night before the game all of the offensive linemen, along with the tight ends and quarterbacks, went out to eat together at a really nice steak place in New York. We told the chef, "Give us your best. And keep it coming." The chef did not disappoint. Waiters brought out platters the size of a desk. One was filled with appetizers, including crab cakes and pasta and salads. Then came one covered with every kind of steak, from fillets and rib eyes to strips, along with racks of lamb and ribs and any other meat you can imagine. I'd never seen so much food, but it didn't go to waste. You have to keep in mind that I was one of the smaller guys at the table and I'm six-seven, 250 pounds.

At the end of the meal, someone pulled out a hat and every-one threw their credit cards into it. One of the guys then pulled out the cards, one at a time, and the last card left had to pick up the check for the entire meal. At the table were veterans who had been in the league for a while and were making millions per season. But none of them had to pay the bill. The last card in the hat that night was mine. When I saw it I felt sick. Karyn and I had just bought a house and I was making minimum league salary, which was good compared to what most people make two years removed from college, but it wasn't the kind of salary where you go out and drop a couple of thousand dollars on a single meal. A couple of the guys helped me with the bill, but I was still nervous when I called Karyn and told her about it. "Look, I understand," she said. "This is just part of being a team. I get it."

After the huge meal we went back to the team hotel and all the linemen and Peyton got on an elevator to go up to our rooms. We're all big guys and we were wedged into the elevator like sardines. I noticed Peyton was more quiet that night than usual. He's always an intense competitor, but on this night he took it to a whole new level with the game against his brother looming the next day. The rest of us laughed and made jokes when all of a sudden, about halfway up to our floor, the elevator just stopped. We were stuck. That brought out even more jokes, and guys started kidding around. Our quarterback was not amused. Finally the elevator started and we got to our rooms. The next night we went out and beat the Giants 26–21. Dallas Clark and I both had three catches apiece. I have to say, the mood on the plane ride home was a lot lighter than it was in the elevator the night before the game. Winning makes everyone feel better.

Of all the things that happened to me during the 2006 season, I never imagined that one hit I took in the second game of the year, against the Houston Texans, would have the greatest long-term impact on my life. I would not understand this fact for several more years.

The play came about halfway through the first quarter on our second drive of the game. We were up 7–0 and had the ball with a first down on the Texans' forty-nine-yard line. I went deep down the middle right in between the two safeties. Peyton arced a beautiful spiral to me, which I caught in stride for a twenty-six-yard gain. As I caught the ball, one of the safeties came in and hit me on my side right above my hip. It was a clean tackle. I held on to the ball and went to the ground. Just before my body landed on the turf, from out of nowhere the other safety came flying in on my left side and targeted my head, spearing me in the helmet with his helmet. My head violently snapped to the side as my helmet flew off. I thought I had broken my neck. A curtain slowly drew down into my field of vision in a circle like the end of an old movie. I blacked out.

But then, out in the fog in which I found myself, I heard the guy who speared me taunting me. I opened my eyes and saw him standing over me like Muhammad Ali standing over Sonny Liston after knocking him out in 1965. My mind was reeling, and my thoughts disoriented, but seeing this guy and hearing him taunting me made me so angry that my head cleared enough for me to jump to my feet and make the first-down sign right in the guy's face. The crowd in the RCA Dome went nuts.

I had to leave the field because my helmet had come off, but one play later I was back in the game. Two plays later Peyton found Joseph Addai over the middle for a twenty-one-yard touchdown pass, giving us a 14–0 lead. That was my last play of the day. Trainers kept coming over to me asking if I was all right. Of course I said I was, even though my head really hurt. Nor did I tell them that when I looked up toward the lights above the field I saw halos and the light pierced my eyes. I felt like a fog had descended onto the field even though we were inside a domed stadium. One of my teammates came over to me and started talking. I don't remember what he said, or what I said, but I remember him laughing and saying, "You're talking crazy, 'techt. That guy really rung your bell." The trainers noticed my crazy talk and took my helmet. My game was over. I had a very obvious concussion, my third documented concussion and my first as a pro. It was my first in three or four years. We also won the game, 43–24.

I don't remember much about that next week, but I know I made it back on the practice field in a day or two after passing some tests. I still had a headache and my eyes were still sensitive to light, but I didn't even think of missing practice or not playing in the next game. I'd been lit up, had my bell rung, that was all. If I knew then what I know now, I don't think I would have played again for weeks. That's easy for me to say six years after my career ended. If I am completely honest, I have to admit that I probably wouldn't do anything any differently. I'd been Wally Pipped the year before. That wasn't going to happen to me again.

Two weeks after the Texans game I suffered another injury that could well have cost me the rest of my season. We were back at the New Jersey Meadowlands, only this time we played the New York Jets. Late in the third quarter I caught a pass right next to the sidelines. The Jets defender hit me with his face mask right in the lower part of my back, knocking me out of bounds. Tremendous pain radiated through my back and shot down my legs. I could barely walk. The trainers took me off the field and took me to an X-ray room inside the stadium. "It looks like you broke three transverse process bones in your back, Ben," I was told. "You might be out for a while. Normally an injury like this takes at least six weeks to heal."

Visions of Wally Pipp danced in my head as I missed the next game. Our bye came the following week, which kept me from missing another game.

During the bye week Karyn and I had our dear friends Jeremy and Adie Camp over to visit. I could hardly enjoy their visit because I was so worried about missing time from the team. Missing four weeks the season before had relegated me to a minor role in the offense. I hated to think what six weeks might do. Jeremy approached the problem like he does most problems. "Let's pray over it," he said.

That's what we did. Jeremy, Adie, and Karyn gathered around me and started praying for my back. Moments later the doorbell rang. Jeremy and Karyn answered the door. There were two men from a local church standing outside. Jeremy asked, "Can I help you?"

What happened next is miraculous. Both men said they were at their church praying together when all of a sudden at the same time they felt prompted to come to our house and pray for me. Jeremy and Karyn were stunned, and invited them in. Together the six of us asked God once again to provide restoration. I think back on this event wondering how these two men whom none of us had ever met could've known that I was in need of prayer at that exact time. I cannot believe this was all just a coincidence.

The next day I went to the team facility and started walking on a treadmill. That's all the trainers would let me do at that point in my recovery. I was just supposed to walk. A funny thing happened as I walked on that treadmill. I felt a voice inside say, "Faster," so I started walking faster. "Faster," I felt inside, so I started going faster. "Faster," again came to me so I started running. Before I knew it I was running full speed without a trace of pain. In fact, the faster I ran, the better I felt. The trainers came over and examined me. They sent me to see the team doctor. Long story short: I was healing much faster than expected and I didn't miss another game. I was back in the lineup two weeks after fracturing three bones in my lower back, not six weeks.

We won our first seven games of the season. In week eight we went on the road to Foxborough to play the Patriots in prime time on the Sunday night game. Every game against the Patriots, at our place or theirs, was huge. We hadn't had a lot of success against them until the 2005 season, when we finally beat them in Foxborough. Coming into week eight in 2006 the two of us were once again the top two teams in the AFC. We were undefeated and they were 6-1. This game was also special to me because it was the first time for me to play against one of the greats of the game, a guy I grew up idolizing, Junior Seau. For years Seau played for the San Diego Chargers, where he put together a Hall of Fame résumé. I felt honored just to be on the same field with him.

On this night I had one of my best games of the season, especially in terms of blocking. I caught all four balls thrown my way on the day for forty-nine yards, which led all tight ends, but my work as a receiver was just the icing on the cake. Most of our blocking schemes had me go up against the same Patriots player, whom I will not mention by name. I blocked him really effectively all night long. Of course, I was also holding on to his jersey right up under his armpits most of the time, which the refs never saw, but that's beside the point. That's what you do, what you have to do, to block effectively in the NFL.

As the game went on I could tell this guy was getting more and more frustrated with me. At one point Peyton called a play where I zone-blocked this same Patriots player. I came up into his chest, got leverage, grabbed hold under his armpits again, and just shoved him right down the field. Our running back scampered out for about a five- or seven-yard gain behind my block. When the whistle blew I released my grip. All of a sudden the Patriot player punched me with a closed fist right into my face mask. The punch didn't hurt me, since it went into my face mask. It might have hurt his hand, I don't know. Instead of punching back, I walked up close to him, put my face right into his face, and said as calmly as anyone can talk in the middle of a football game, "Did you honestly just punch me in the face like a little girl?" Then I turned and walked back to our huddle.

The next play was another running play. I ended up blocking the same player again. When the whistle blew I released my block and again turned to go back to the huddle. As I turned to go I felt a tap on my shoulder. I turned around and here was the same player again, a look of conviction in his eyes. "Man, you're right," he said. "I'm sorry. I shouldn't have done that."

"No problem, man," I said. I grinned all the way back to the huddle.

The whole team was smiling all the way home because we came out of there with a 27–20 victory, our second in a row over the Patriots. We didn't then know it, but that win set us up for our biggest win of the season, but that's for the next chapter.

CHAPTER 13

THE ULTIMATE

AFTER WE DEFEATED THE PATRIOTS FOR our eighth straight win it looked like we had the inside track to gain home field advantage throughout the playoffs, just as we had the year before. But in the NFL, appearances change quickly. We beat the Bills the following week to go 9-0, but we then proceeded to lose four of our next six games. In a couple of those games we just looked flat, while we lost the other two on last-second field goals. In one of those games, the loss to Tennessee in Nashville, their kicker hit a sixty-yard field goal on the next-to-last play of the game. The NFL record is sixty-three yards, so, yeah, that loss hurt. I took that one really hard. Late in the fourth quarter I caught what should have been the winning touchdown. Instead I was flagged for offensive pass interference and we had to settle for a field goal. The four-point difference opened the door for the Titans. If not for that penalty, we would have gone home with a win. Believe me, I heard about my penalty the next week when we watched film of the game. Nine years later the play still bothers me.

We managed to pull out a win at home on the last week of the season against the Dolphins to finish the year with a 12-4 record.

The Patriots had the exact same record, but because we had beaten them that season, we were the number-three seed in the playoffs while the Patriots were number four. Both of us had to play games in the first round against the wild card teams.

We beat the Kansas City Chiefs 23–8 in the first round of the playoffs. I don't remember much from the game except one play where I threw a block against Jared Allen and opened a gaping hole for Joseph Addai, who basically walked into the end zone for a touchdown. The Patriots also took care of business against the New York Jets, 37–16.

Our game against the Chiefs should have been our last home game of the playoffs. The next week we went to Baltimore to play the number-two-seeded Ravens. Just like the year before, their fans hated us. Ray Lewis was still their middle linebacker and still as good as ever. Terrell Suggs had another year of experience and was becoming one of the top defensive players in the game. We had our work cut out for us. The whole game came down to a defensive struggle. Neither team scored a touchdown. However, we had a weapon few teams could match. Between the 2005 and 2006 seasons the Colts signed the Patriots kicker Adam Vinatieri, the same kicker who had kicked the game-winning field goal in their three Super Bowl championships in 2001, 2003, and 2004. Nothing can shake Adam. In the Baltimore game he kicked five field goals to give us a 15–6 victory.

That win should have sent us to San Diego to play the number-one-seeded Chargers. The whole time I played for the Colts we never played well against the Chargers. However, New England went down to San Diego in the second round of the playoffs and beat them 24–21. That meant we had to play the Patriots, with the winner earning a trip to the Super Bowl. This is where the week eight game becomes so important. Because we won the head-to-head battle against the Patriots, the AFC Championship Game was to be played at our house, the RCA Dome. We'd already proven we could win in Foxborough, but there's nothing like play-ing at home. Everyone on the team liked our chances.

And then the game started.

The first quarter went sort of like what one might expect from a game between such big rivals. They got the ball first and ended up having to punt. We didn't do much on our first possession and punted it back to them. Then they put together a drive and scored a touchdown. We answered with an Adam Vinatieri field goal. At the end of the first quarter we trailed 7–3. Sure, it would have been better to have been in the lead but there was still a lot of football to go.

New England scored another touchdown on their first posses-sion of the second quarter. Now we were down 14–3. Again, there was no need to panic. We just needed to take the ball down the field and answer. Instead, their cornerback Asante Samuel inter-cepted a pass intended for Marvin Harrison and ran it back for a touchdown. Now we were staring at a 21–3 deficit.

We got the ball back and did absolutely nothing with it. In three plays we ended up losing fourteen yards and had to punt from our own three-yard line. That gave them the ball at our forty-eight-yard line. If they scored another touchdown, the game would basically be over.

On their first couple of plays of that possession they tried running the ball, without success. Then their quarterback, Tom Brady, started tossing the ball around and they moved down to our twenty-eight. On the next play, Brady completed a pass to their tight end Ben Watson, which put the ball on our nineteen. Our crowd fell silent. Everyone seemed to be in shock at what was happening.

But then I saw a yellow flag on the field. The refs called offen-sive pass interference against the Patriots, which moved the ball back to our thirty-eight. One of their guys jumped offside before they snapped the ball again, moving the ball back to the forty-three. Now it was third and really long. Brady went back to pass, but one of our defensive ends, Raheem Brock, tackled him for a six-yard loss. They had to punt the ball back to us. We dodged a huge bullet on this sequence of plays.

We got the ball back on our own twelve-yard line with three minutes left in the half. We put together a good drive, taking the ball all the way down to their eight-yard line. The drive stalled out there and we ended up kicking another field goal, which made the score 21–6 at the half. Everything about this game so far made it look like our season was going to end short of our ultimate goal, again, at the hands of the Patriots, again.

A lot of the game is foggy to me. However, I clearly recall Tony Dungy's halftime talk to the team. Coach is not one of these fiery guys who yell and scream. If he were, this was the time to let us have it. Instead, he sat us all down and said to us, "We're going to get the ball to start off the second half. Okay. Terrence," he said to Terrence Wilkins, our return guy, "you're going to run the ball back to the twenty-five. Then Peyton, you're going to hand the ball off to Dominic on the first play. Then you're going to pass it to . . ." And Coach Dungy went on down the line of every play we were going to run and how it was going to turn out. Then he added, "And we will score a touch-down to pull within one score."

After talking to the offense he spoke to the defense. He said, "When they get the ball back, Dwight, Robert, Bob, and all you defensive players, we're going to hold them to a three-and-out and force them to punt the ball back to us.

"After the punt we're going to take the ball down the field and score again, then go for two and tie this game up. . . ."

He kept going from there until he had described exactly how we were going to pull off the greatest comeback in the history of the AFC Championship Game. What got me was how focused and confident Coach Dungy was as he said this. He didn't give off even a hint of panic or worry. Instead he told us how we were going to go out and win the game.

And that's exactly what happened. We scored a touchdown on our first drive. Our defense forced them to punt after three plays. We went down the field again and scored another touchdown and made the two-point conversion. The Patriots scored a touchdown on their next possession, but we answered with one of our own to tie the score at 28. We then traded field goals to make it 31–31. The Patriots retook the lead with a field goal late in the fourth quarter to go ahead 34–31. Peyton took over from there. We scored the go-ahead touchdown with a minute to go in the game. Marlin Jackson ended the Patriots' comeback attempt when he intercepted a Brady pass to cement the win.

With that we were on our way to the Super Bowl.

I only had one catch in the AFC Championship Game, but I still had a good game as a blocker. However, I hyperextended my knee late in the third quarter and had to come out of the game. Bryan Fletcher took my place. I was disappointed I got hurt, but the game wasn't about me. It was about the team. Everything at this point was about the team. We all did whatever it took to win. And it paid off. We were on our way to the ultimate game.

The Super Bowl is played two weeks after the conference championship games. Believe me, you need that extra week just to secure the tickets you need for family and friends and to arrange all their travel and lodging. I wanted everyone in my family and Karyn's to be there, along with our friends Jeremy and Adie. My mom and dad came down for the game, along with my sister and her boyfriend Doug (now husband). Karyn's parents made the trip, as did her brother and her sister and brother-in-law. Every player had a Cadillac Escalade for the week in Miami, so that was pretty cool.

I couldn't get everyone from our entourage in it, but we could get quite a few.

Everything about the Super Bowl is different than a normal game. For one thing, we spent an entire week in the host city. Normally on a road game, we fly down the day before and fly home right after the game. Because we had so much time in Miami, the team was going to allow our wives to stay with us in our rooms. Bill Polian explained this to the team in a meeting with all the team personnel, players, and our wives a couple of days after we beat the Patriots. He just sort of mentioned it, then moved on to the next item on his long list of things every player needed to know about the logistics of the week and game ahead. Before he could move on, however, Peyton raised his hand and said, "I think we should talk a little bit more about the wives staying with their husbands. We've never done that for any game. I think we should discuss it a little more before we decide to do it."

"Okay, Peyton, we will discuss it," Polian replied. "Now, the next item we need to talk about . . ." he said and kept going.

A few minutes later Peyton spoke up again with something like, "Excuse me, Mr. Polian."

"Yes, Peyton."

"I've decided that wives are not going to be allowed to stay with their husbands. We've come too far and this game is too big for us to deviate from the way we've done things all season long. I think if we are honest with ourselves and we really look at the magnitude of this game and what it means to all of us, we will all agree that we need to continue doing our game preparation the same way we have all year long. So we're not going to have wives stay in the same rooms as their husbands."

The funny thing is, no one disagreed with him. Well, some of the wives were not happy, but Peyton was right. We kept our normal game preparation and routine all the way down to room assignments. It was our way of trying to treat the biggest game any of us had ever played in as just another game.

However, you cannot treat the Super Bowl like another game. I've already written about my experience on media day and the craziness that surrounded our team the whole week we were in Miami. For me, the most important moment was the one I shared with my father before I ran out onto the field with our kickers and long snappers. That is the one Super Bowl memory I hope I never lose.

After that moment with my dad, I found myself in a surreal place. All the music and pageantry around the game were like nothing I had ever experienced. In the week before the game, our kicker, Adam Vinatieri, warned us not to blink at the start of the game. "Everything is going to happen so fast and it is easy to get lost in it," he warned, "so don't blink. Don't get caught up in it, or the game will get the best of you."

I thought about his words as I stood on the sidelines while Adam and the kicking team ran out onto the field for the opening kickoff. The referee held up his arm, blew his whistle, then dropped his arm. Adam started running toward the ball to kick it. As he did the entire stadium erupted in flashes of light as tens of thousands of cameras clicked at the same time to catch the moment. I wondered if Neil Armstrong would have been jealous of me standing in this sea of stars. I watched the ball fly high in the air as the flashes of light kept going. Then the ball landed in the Bears' all-star kick returner Devin Hester's hands. Ninety-two yards later Hester celebrated in the end zone after running the kick back for a touchdown. Just like that we were behind 7–0.

Having the other team run back the opening kickoff for a score in the ultimate game can knock some teams completely off-balance. They panic and never recover, especially on a night like this. It had rained all day and it rained all through the game.

Standing on the field, soaked to the skin, socks wet, losing, that's not any fun. I felt it. The moment it was clear Hester was going to score I felt sick to my stomach. Then I glanced over to my right. There stood Tony Dungy. He wasn't paying any attention to Hester or the Bears. Instead he was calmly talking to a couple of the other coaches with a play sheet in front of him, planning what we were going to do next. Then I looked to my left. There stood Peyton Manning talking strategy with our offensive coordinator, Tom Moore. Neither looked surprised or stunned that the Bears had scored.

The sick feeling in the pit of my stomach went away and a peace came over me. I knew that all we had to do was trust in our abilities and in one another and we were going to be okay. A Bible verse came to mind that says, "Whatever you do, work at it with all your heart, as working for the Lord."* That's how I approached this game. I knew if I went out on that field and gave every ounce of my ability, I was going to walk away a winner.

My biggest play in the game came in the second quarter. We were behind 14–9, but we had driven the ball all the way down to the Bears' one-yard line. Peyton called an inside zone run to the right. The ball snapped and I teed off on the defensive end, putting him flat on his back. Dominic Rhodes ran right through the hole on my side, squeezing in between the tackle and me. Somehow Dominic went under me and squirted right into the end zone for the go-ahead touchdown. We never trailed after that. After he scored, Dominic popped up and I ran over to him. I put both my hands on the sides of his helmet and he looked up at me with an electric grin. A *Sports Illustrated* photographer captured the moment. I never felt the cold or the rain after that.

I only had one catch in the game, but it, too, came at a big

---

* Colossians 3:23 (NIV).

moment in our first drive of the second half. We were up 16–14, which isn't much of a lead in a game like this. After starting out at our own thirty we moved the ball pretty well, but we now faced a third down and eight yards to go on the Bears' forty-six. If we didn't make it, we were too far to try a field goal and would have to punt. I lined up in the backfield alongside Peyton as the H-back. The Bears crowded the line like they were going to blitz, but they often faked the blitz in this formation and the linebackers dropped back into pass coverage. Peyton thought that's what they were going to do now. As he called out signals, right before the snap of the ball, he said to me, "Tech, this ball is coming to you. They're dropping into zone."

The ball snapped. The two linebackers did not blitz but dropped back into zone coverage, which opened up a spot under-neath for me. I took off down the field, ran out about five yards, planted my foot, and turned. The ball was already on its way to-ward me. Water sprayed off it as the ball spun in a tight spiral.

I cradled the ball in my arms, then turned upfield. I had to gain another five yards to get the first down. However, standing between me and the first down was the Bears' All-Pro middle linebacker, six-five, 265-pound Brian Urlacher. He was known as one of the most fierce competitors and hardest hitters in the game. This was a come-to-Jesus moment where I knew the hit I was about to take was going to hurt, but I had to have the first down. I ran toward him as hard as I could. As he drew close I lowered my shoulder and tried to get lower than him so that I could have leverage and barrel my way through to the first-down marker. I got low and he hit me hard. He caught me underneath my left shoulder pads on my back. Sharp pain shot through my rib cage, but I kept my legs churning and I got the first down.

After the hit I had trouble getting up. The trainer ran out onto the field to help me up. I knew what had happened. I'd cracked another rib. However, I wasn't coming out of the game. I popped some painkillers, either Vicodin or Percocet, on the sideline and continued to play.

That drive ended with a field goal, but the Bears only managed three more points the rest of the game and we went on to win 29–17. Hoisting the trophy hurt my ribs, but it was worth it. The pain is always worth it when you win, and we hadn't just won a game, we were Super Bowl champions. It was something I would carry with me for the rest of my life.

CHAPTER 14

NOT THE SAME

THE TEMPERATURE IN INDIANAPOLIS HOVERED AROUND minus 2 degrees when our team plane landed the day after our Super Bowl win. You wouldn't have known it from the reception we received. The city held a victory parade downtown, with huge crowds all around. All of us on the team rode on floats that did a short loop downtown, then headed into the RCA Dome, where another huge crowd waited for us. The place was electric. It felt like a game day. No one wanted the party to end.

And it didn't end, not really, at least not until the next season started. Everywhere Karyn and I went in the city for the next several months, people came over to congratulate me on the huge win. I don't think we paid for any meals in restaurants the entire off-season. It felt like we didn't just win the title for the team, but for the entire state of Indiana. For me that feeling even extended back to the Twin Cities. When Karyn and I went back home to Minnesota I was greeted like a hometown hero. I sang the national anthem for several Minneapolis teams, including the National Hockey League's Minnesota Wild, who gave me a jersey with my name on the back. That meant a lot to me, because my grandfather Bob Utecht was the longtime public address announcer for the Minnesota North Stars before the team moved to Dallas. Because of the family connection, singing for the Wild and receiving the jersey were two of the biggest honors I was given after becoming a Super Bowl champion.

Six weeks before the start of training camp, the team came together at the Indiana Roof Ballroom to receive our championship rings. Jim Irsay, the team owner, created an incredible event. The night felt like a Cirque du Soleil show. Literally. The room was filled with music, with dancers, and acrobats hanging from ropes from the ceiling. The Lombardi Trophy was front and center, stealing the show. The comic Sinbad made an appearance. A gospel choir came out and sang an incredible song about it being a time to praise the Lord. When the ring was presented to me, it came in a dark wooden box. I opened it to find what players play for their entire careers. In the center of the white gold ring was a blue horseshoe made of synthetic blue sapphires surrounded by more than fifty diamonds—fifty-seven, to be exact. "Faith" was engraved on one side of the ring, the only time that has been done on any team's championship ring. Including that word was a nod to Coach Dungy's leadership as well as, in Mr. Irsay's words, the faith that "gives you the strength to have the perseverance to move forward even after many disappointments." On the opposite were the words "Our Time," over a small horseshoe. On the players' rings on one of the horseshoe rivets there was a small red ruby that symbolized a drop of blood that came from us leaving it all on the field. The game score was carved on the side, as was my name.

I pulled the ring out of the box and put it on. Believe it or not, it was actually one size too small, but I was still able to get it on and later had it resized. The sad part for me in sharing this story with you is that I had to ask my wife for most of the details. I have little memory of Sinbad or even what my reaction was when I got the ring. To be honest, I hardly remember how the rings where distributed. I do remember each player had his picture taken holding the Lombardi Trophy. I know I had a turn with it. Actually taking the trophy in my hands, holding it, feeling its weight, this was the ultimate dream for every kid who ever put on a pair of cleats and played a down of football. This was the prize everyone hopes to hold but very few ever do. Only one team each season gets this honor. The other thirty-one end the season disappointed and dreaming of next year. For one season at least, our next year was now.

I just wish I could remember the night when we celebrated our victory.

We opened the 2007 season on a Thursday night prime-time game against the New Orleans Saints. The defending Super Bowl champion always gets the honor of opening the season with a spotlight game. The evening began with the unfurling of our world championship banner from high above the RCA Dome. There was no way we were going to lose after that. In the game itself I had one catch over the middle for a nineteen-yard gain early in the third quarter as part of a long drive to go up 24–10. I paid the price for the catch, as Nick Harper, a former Colt, absolutely drilled me. I held on to the ball, however. We ended up winning the game 41–10, but I felt that hit for days. Even with the pain, winning decisively set the tone we hoped to maintain throughout the season. After winning one Super Bowl, we were hungry for another.

Our next two games were on the road against division opponents. We beat a good Tennessee Titans team 22–20 in Nashville, then went down to Houston and defeated the Texans 30–24. I had a big game against the Titans, but my memories of the game are hazy. I also do not have a clear recollection of the Houston game. To be honest, the entire season is a little shaky in my mind because of a play in the first quarter of our next game, a week four showdown against the Denver Broncos.

• • •

After playing two road games in a row, it was nice being home in our dome for our game with the Broncos. We kicked off to start the game. Denver put together an eight-play drive and went from their own thirty-six down to our seventeen-yard line before the drive stalled out and they had to kick a field goal.

Our initial drive of the game started on our own thirty-yard line. On the first play Peyton hit Dallas Clark on a short pass to the right side that Dallas turned into a seventeen-yard gain. Peyton then called a running play where Joseph Addai took the ball over the left side, my side. At the snap of the ball I went to block the defensive end on what is known as a zone scheme. I lunged a bit and started falling toward the ground. All around me the other linemen were throwing blocks while the defense fought them off. In the mass of bodies you cannot see who has the ball or where the action is going as clearly as you can on television. In plays like this, the moment the defense catches a glimpse of who has the ball, they all fly at him. As this chaos unfolded around me, I lost my footing and fell. As I did, a defensive back leaped over me as he ran toward Addai. When he jumped, his foot clipped the back of my helmet. It was not a hard hit, not in comparison to the violent blow I took in the Texans' game the previous season. However, the foot hit me in just the right spot.

I crumpled to the ground. Everything went black as I lost all consciousness for about a count of ten. Then, just as quickly as the hit happened, I came back to life. My head cleared and I jumped up off the ground. I talked with some teammates, then sprinted to the sidelines.

One of the team doctors came over to me and asked series of questions. He might have asked what day it was, or who the president was. He could have asked me my name. I don't know what he said, but I gave the wrong answer because he pulled me from the game and didn't let me return.

My first memory of the game comes toward the end of half-time. I don't really recall being in the locker room. One of my teammates, it might have been Bryan Fletcher, I'm not sure, came up to me and said, "Man, you were messed up!"

"I was?" I asked.

"Oh man," he said with a laugh, "you had no idea where you were or what had happened. You kept asking me, 'What happened? What happened?'" He shook his head. "Wow. You really got hit."

I remember feeling really confused during the conversation. I had no idea what he was talking about. I just laughed it off. "Yeah, man, I guess I did," was all I could say in response.

I'd never experienced amnesia before. My only experience with it came from watching old sitcoms where someone gets hit on the head and forgets who they are. Later they take another blow on the head and all their memories come back. On television the whole thing is a big joke. That attitude is pretty much the way everyone thought of concussions and head injuries not long ago. Many still do.

I didn't understand the severity of the hit I had taken. Even after having several hours of my life cut out of my mind, I didn't really think this was going to be any kind of big deal. I'd had concussions before. This was my fourth. I'd always bounced right back. I thought I would this time as well.

By the time the game ended I didn't feel well at all. My head was pounding, but more than that, I just didn't feel right. My head, my stomach, everything just felt off. I just needed to go lie down. Unfortunately, that was easier said than done. The team medical staff would not allow me to drive home after the game. One of the doctors said, "I don't want you driving today, Ben. And I don't want you alone. You're married, right?"

"Yes, but my wife's out of the country right now," I said. Karyn had gone to Australia for a once-in-a-lifetime trip for the Golf Channel's *Golf with Style* television show. She had won a preliminary competition on the golf reality show and now she was headed "down under" to compete for the championship.

"I think you'd better spend the night with one of your teammates tonight, just in case," he said.

This should have been my warning that this little bell ringing might be more serious than I had first thought, but I didn't pick up on it. Again, I expected the symptoms to go away quickly. "Okay," I said. "I'm sure someone will let me bunk with them tonight."

I ended up going home with one of the offensive linemen, my good friend Dylan Gandy. Dylan and his wife, Melody, let me sleep in their guest room. It was one of the worst nights of my life up to that point. My head pounded, making sleep hard to find. All through the night the pounding just kept getting worse and worse. When I did manage to drift off to sleep I broke out in night sweats so severe I soaked the sheets. When I woke up, I was drenched. I'd never had a concussion do this to me before.

Even so, I thought my symptoms would clear within a day or two. The Colts, like every team in the NFL, had a concussion procedure that players had to go through before they were cleared to play. Also they had a neurosurgeon, Dr. Henry Feuer, on the team medical staff. I remember meeting with Dr. Feuer after the concussions I sustained with the Colts. Before the season started I and every other player took a cognitive assessment test that set a baseline for our brain function. All of this is part of the ImPACT process, which stands for Immediate Post-Concussion Assessment and Cognitive Testing. After being diagnosed with a concussion, I had to retake the test on a computer. Once I was able to hit my baseline scores, I would be cleared to return to play. I do not remember undergoing any other testing. Basically, all I had to do to get back to work was pass the ImPACT.

A couple of days after the Bronco game I went to the Colts' training facility to try to pass the test. I still had headaches and my eyes were still sensitive to light. I'd also noticed I had trouble pulling words out of my head during conversations. It was like I knew what I wanted to say but the words just wouldn't come. Once or twice I also noticed my speech was slurred. It worried me, but I figured it would clear right up. I don't think I shared any of this with the team medical staff when I went in to take my ImPACT.

My first attempt at the test was, in short, a disaster. I sat down at the computer and stared at the screen and nothing made sense. My brain felt sludgy, like I was trying to swim through quicksand. Questions popped up on the screen and nothing clicked in my brain. I had trouble even focusing my eyes. More questions popped up. I broke out in a sweat. Just like the night of the concussion, the sweat just poured off me. I felt lost and confused. I'd never experienced anything like it before in my life.

The trainer administering the test took one look at my score and said something like, "Looks like you're going to sit out this week, Ben. Don't worry. You'll be back sooner rather than later."

I thanked him and left the facility to return home. If I was not cleared to play, I could not participate in practice or drills. I tried sitting in on team meetings that week, but the fog in my head made it hard to concentrate. Working out was also difficult. Running hard enough to break a sweat made my head hurt. The team doctor told me to take it easy and get well. I followed his advice.

Looking back, in addition to Dr. Feuer I wished I would have consulted a sports neurologist, an expert in concussions. I also could have consulted a neuropsychologist and perhaps sought out the opinion of one of the experts in the growing field of research into football and concussions, a man like Dr. Robert Cantu or Dr.

Jeff Kutcher. But I didn't. I did not think such steps were necessary. The team medical staff seemed to think I would be back as good as new in a short time. I had no reason to doubt them. Nor did my coaches seem overly concerned. A football team is a lot like family, and the coaches fill a fatherly role for most players. They did for me. I believed the team had my best interests at heart. I gave my all for the team, and I believed the relationship was reciprocal.

When Karyn got home I told her what had happened, including experiencing a diagnosis of amnesia due to a concussion. I didn't make a big deal of it because, frankly, I didn't think it was a big deal. If I had given it more thought, or if I had done some research, I would have realized that the concussion I suffered in the Texans game the previous season made me more susceptible to a more severe concussion now, just as the two I suffered in college made me more susceptible to any kind of concussion both now and in the future. I still believed the *M* in MTBI, the official designation for a concussion, stood for *mild*. This fourth concussion was anything but mild, even though I was oblivious to that fact.

Another eerie experience regarding this concussion was watching it on film. The day after the game I found my way into the tight ends meeting room, where I could access the film by myself. I went right to the play when my concussion occurred. Sitting there by myself in a dark film room, I watched as my body went completely limp from what appeared to be a minor kick to my helmet. What happened next is hard to explain to anyone. I couldn't believe what I was seeing. I regained consciousness and got up talking to teammates, then sprinted to the sidelines, where I talked with many people. I stopped the tape, staring at a blank screen, wondering how in the world was I functioning yet having no memory of that experience.

A week after my concussion I still experienced headaches and sensitivity to light. My mood also changed, but I chalked it up to

the frustration of trying to get back on the field. I feared this lat-
est injury was going to give me the label of an injury-prone player.
That's kryptonite for an NFL player. My contract was up at the
end of this season and I hoped to sign a long-term deal that would
provide financial security for Karyn and me. Teams don't make
big, long-term investments in injury-prone players. I needed to
get back out on the field as soon as possible. I had to sit out our
week five game against the Tampa Bay Buccaneers. We had our
bye the week after that. I was determined to be back on the field
before we played our division rivals the Jacksonville Jaguars in
Florida in week seven.

I finally passed the ImPACT in time to practice for the Jaguars
game. In my mind, and in the eyes of the team medical staff, passing the test meant I was over the concussion, that I was back to
my old self. I wasn't. The sludge in my brain kept sloshing around.
As part of writing this chapter my coauthor asked me when I finally felt normal again. Honestly, looking back now, I don't think
I ever did. I have never been the same since the first quarter of
the fourth game of my fourth NFL season. Nine years later and
counting, I now realize the person I was before is never coming
back.

I don't think my play suffered on the field when I returned to the
lineup. I did not miss another game the rest of the season. We
went on the road and beat the Jaguars and followed that up with
a road win the next week against the Carolina Panthers in Char-
lotte. I had a really good day against the Panthers, with a couple
of catches, including one for thirty yards. We lost our first game of
the season the following week at home against the Patriots. The
game was close, and we even held a lead late in the fourth quarter, but the Patriots scored a touchdown with three minutes to go
in the game to take the lead. We tried to answer, but the Patriots

forced a fumble when they sacked Peyton at midfield. The Patriots beat us 24–20. They did not lose a game that season—that is, until the Super Bowl.

My memories of the first three games I played right after my concussion are cloudy. The fourth game, a road game against the Chargers in San Diego, is clearer in my mind. As a team, we looked awful in that game. We fell behind 23–0 before the second quarter was even half over. Our defense didn't give up another score, and we clawed our way back to within two points at 23–21. We had a chance to win late in the fourth quarter when we mounted a ninety-yard drive from our own two-yard line. But Adam Vinatieri missed a short field goal, and we went home with a loss. I had three catches in that game, but I also had a false-start penalty that pushed the failed field goal attempt back five yards. You never forget those kinds of mistakes, even when you want to.

The thing I remember most about that game is that it was the first time I ever saw Coach Dungy raise his voice at the team. He came in at halftime and just unloaded on us. His behavior was the exact opposite of how he normally addressed the team. To me, it was like watching Jesus flip the tables of the money changers over in the temple. We didn't quite complete the comeback against the Chargers, but coach lit a fire under us. That was our last loss of the regular season until the final game, when we rested most of the starters in a game that didn't matter in terms of the playoffs and our seeding.

I played just enough in the last game to hurt my shoulder. I'd hurt it the week before in a win over the Texans and finished it off when I landed hard on my side against the Titans. The injury was a severe acromioclavicular (AC) joint separation, but it wasn't enough to keep me from playing in our first playoff game, at home against the Chargers. I took some painkillers in addition to the usual Toradol shot and didn't miss a beat. The team, however, did. The Chargers ended our season when they scored late in the fourth quarter to take a 28–24 lead. We could not answer. Our season was over.

The playoff loss turned out to be my last game with the Colts. I became a restricted free agent during the off-season. That meant I was free to negotiate with other teams, but the Colts had the right to match any offer and keep me. The Bengals, against whom I always had big games, offered me a three-year contract worth $8.75 million. The Colts had signed Dallas Clark to a big contract the season before and did not have room under the NFL's salary cap to sign a second tight end to such a lucrative deal.

I talked to Coach Dungy about the situation before I made a decision and he told me I should accept the Bengals' offer. I respected his honesty. Like I said, an NFL coach is like a second father, and Coach Dungy certainly was to me. I took his advice and signed with Cincinnati. Karyn and I put our Indianapolis home up for sale and moved ninety miles down the road. I had high hopes that in Cincinnati I could become one of the top tight ends in the league. I was ready to get to work to reach my goal.

Where it all began, in the back-yard with Dad. That's a true NFL ball, by the way. Ironic . . .

Little me rocking a sport coat—dress to impress!

ABOVE: My sister, Ashley, and me in our Lindstrom, Minnesota, parsonage.

LEFT: Jeff and Lori Utecht (Dad and Mom)

Catch made versus the Tennessee Titans.

Pregame warm-ups before defeating the Kansas City Chiefs.

The family after a big win in Indianapolis. Left to right: Me, Karyn's sister Kristin, Braden (nephew), Larry and Sandy Stordahl (in-laws), Karyn, Ashley, Doug (brother-in-law), Jeff and Lori Utecht.

Doug and Ashley (Utecht) Goodmundson enjoying the pregame Super Bowl experience in Miami.

LEFT: Karyn and me during my first Nashville music photo shoot. What a babe she is!

BELOW: Me and my beautiful wife, Karyn, on our wedding day.

Walking my beautiful grandmothers down the aisle at my wedding. On the left is Grandma Joan Perschman; on the right is Grandma Donna Utecht.

Me, Karyn, and Larry and Sandy Stordahl in Austria.

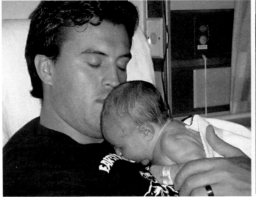

Elleora Grace Utecht, just hours old.

Daddy with Katriel and Amy.

Daddy and Elleora.

Mom and Dad after we won the Super Bowl.

Holding the Lombardi Trophy at the
Super Bowl after party.

Me and Karyn at the Super Bowl ring
celebration in Indianapolis.

Me and Coach Dungy at the Super Bowl
ring celebration.

My sister, Ashley, at her wedding.

My parents and Karyn, along with Erik (Karyn's brother) and Katy Stordahl, at my New Year's Eve performance with the Cincinnati Pops Orchestra.

My vocal performance at a Gaither Homecoming event. Bill and Gloria were wonderful mentors to me in Indiana.

Singing with the Cincinnati Pops Orchestra and the Mormon Tabernacle Choir.

Preseason football game against the New Orleans Saints at Paul Brown Stadium in Cincinnati.

Daddy-daughter guitar time with Katriel. She is rocking the Little Mermaid guitar and totally shredding it!

My professional speaking photo, taken at my second Nashville photo shoot.

Amy (left), Elleora (middle), and Katriel (right) with baby Haven.

Me, Karyn, and our four girls (left to right: Katriel, Amy, Haven, and Elleora).

A family trip to Mexico (left to right: Katriel, Amy, and Elleora; holding Haven).

CHAPTER 15

FRESH START

Leaving Indianapolis wasn't easy. In the four years I spent there it came to feel like home. Karyn and I spent a lot of time with teammates Dallas Clark, Bryan Fletcher, Ben Hartsock, Justin Snow, Hunter Smith, and Dylan Gandy. For much of the time Bryan was our token bachelor when all of us went out to places like St. Elmo Steak House. All of us were young with great-paying jobs and just starting out in life. These were some of the best days of my life.

I grieved leaving my friends behind, but that's life in the NFL. Dallas and Justin both stayed with the Colts for another four seasons, but none of the rest of my closest friends did. Ben Hartsock actually left before me to join the Titans. He later moved on to play for the Falcons, Jets, and Panthers. Bryan looked to gain an increased role in the offense after I left, but the team released him after they selected two tight ends in the 2008 draft. Dylan ended up moving on to the Detroit Lions after brief stops in Denver and Oakland. That's just life in the NFL. Team rosters are fluid. It is a business, after all.

Leaving my teammates wasn't the only difficult part of the move. During my four years with the team I had started working toward the life I hoped to have after football. Music has always been a key part of my life. Back when I sang the national anthem at ball games during college I wasn't just a singing football player. I felt I was a singer who happened to play football. Music started early in my life. I sang in my dad's church when I was a boy. Throughout high school I was in more choirs than I was sports teams and took vocal lessons from our choir teacher. In college I was part of the FCA worship team and sang in area churches. I did the same in Indianapolis. A "chance" meeting took this to a whole new level.

During my rookie season with the Colts, I was invited to speak to a youth event in Anderson, Indiana, about forty miles northeast of Indy. As I said earlier, the Colts now hold their training camp there. After I finished my speech, where I of course wore my Colts jersey since I had not yet made a name for myself with the team, a very energetic woman in a Peyton Manning jersey came running over to me. Jumping up and down she said, "I am the world's biggest Colts fan. I am so excited that you are here. I know everything about the team and I know all about you. May I have an autograph, please?"

How could I turn down such an enthusiastic fan? "Of course," I said. "Who should I make this out to?"

"Sandi Patty," she replied.

"Sandi Patty?" I asked, in shock. "Are you *the* Sandi Patty?" Through the 1980s and early '90s this Colts fan in front of me was the biggest star in all of Christian music. I grew up with her music filling our home. I did not realize she lived in Anderson.

"Yes, I am," she said.

"Oh my gosh," I gushed, "I want *YOUR* autograph."

Sandi was gracious and laughed. We talked for a while, and that might have been the end of it except a few weeks later I appeared at a school event and sang. Her husband, Don Peslis, happened to be there. Afterward he introduced himself to me and told me Sandi had mentioned me to him.

A friendship grew. Sandi and Don's home became a second home for me, especially when I was still single and living alone in the city. Sandi really encouraged me in terms of my singing. She even invited me to join her onstage for her Christmas performances with the Indianapolis Symphony Orchestra. Coach Dungy and several other staff members even came to hear me sing. During my time in Indianapolis, Sandi became a mentor to me in terms of music. She also told me that she believed I had what it took to have a career as a singer. These weren't just words. Her manager, Mike Atkins, came out of semiretirement to represent me.

The real highlight of my time in Indianapolis came in 2007 when Sandi and I sang "What Are You Doing New Year's Eve?" in front of more than one hundred thousand people on Monument Circle, outside in downtown Indianapolis during their annual Festival of Lights, which kicks off the holiday season in the city. Standing on that stage with one of the legends of the Christian music industry, singing in front of so many people, and of course wearing my Super Bowl ring, was a dream come true.

While Cincinnati was only ninety miles from Indianapolis, going there still meant leaving all of this behind. Sure, I stayed in contact with my teammates and with Sandi and others who mentored me in music, but it wasn't the same. I had new relationships that needed to be built. Before I signed the contract, Coach Dungy encouraged me, telling me that he felt God had a plan for me in Cincinnati. "God's going to use you as a light there, Ben, I'm sure of that," he said in one of our last conversations as player and coach. I felt confident Coach was right. Going to the Bengals meant leaving much behind, but it also meant a fresh start with new possibilities.

I actually signed my contract with the Bengals in my garage in my suburban Indianapolis home. I didn't have a fax machine, so

I went to a nearby church and faxed the contract from there. My $8.75 million contract included a $2 million signing bonus. Even after taking out my agent's fees and paying all the taxes, that still left me with a lot of money, especially for a twenty-six-year-old guy only four years removed from college. Karyn and I put our house up for sale. Since it was 2008, the year the real estate bubble burst in a big way, we lost a lot of money when we found a buyer. We chalked it up to experience and headed down Interstate 74 to the Queen City.

Initially, Karyn and I rented a downtown apartment a couple of minutes from the Bengals' facilities at Paul Brown Stadium. After losing money on our house in Indy, we were hesitant about buying another home in a second NFL city, especially with only a three-year contract. However, I saw the length of the contract as a blessing. I told Karyn, "I'm going to crush it these three years, then sign another three-year deal with the team. That will give me a ten-year career in the league and by then I'll be ready to really pursue a career in music."

I was so confident in my plan that we bought another house. We found a home tucked away in hidden development in the woods in Mount Carmel, Ohio. A golf membership came with the purchase of our new house and I know that excited Karyn. The house also had more amenities than our house in Indy. Going from a $250,000-a-year contract to one that averages just under $3 million a year will do that, even for two people determined to save as much as we could for the future.

We moved to Cincinnati right after I signed my contract. I needed to get to work right away learning offensive coordinator Bob Bratkowski's system. Both Coach Bratkowski and Head Coach Marvin Lewis showed a lot of faith in me, along with tight ends coach Jonathan Hayes, who in my opinion is one of the great tight ends ever to play and coach the game. My coaches' confidence motivated me even more. I wanted to make a good impression from the start. Unlike Indianapolis, I wasn't going to have a year to just sit and soak up everything. The team had a lot invested in me and expected me to contribute right away. I started spending time with my new quarterback, Carson Palmer, to develop a rapport with him. Few quarterbacks in the league could compare to the one I had in Indy, but Carson came close. Like Peyton Manning, Carson had been the overall number-one pick in the draft. Carson won the Heisman Trophy his last year at the University of Southern California and had been named to the Pro Bowl following both the 2005 and 2006 NFL seasons.

I came to the Bengals with a lot of enthusiasm, but I noticed a problem from the start. Even though the team's offensive schemes were not as intricate as those we ran in Indianapolis, I struggled picking them up. In OTAs and the first minicamp I felt like I was walking through a mental quicksand when trying to learn the new offense. At the time I chalked it up to my unfamiliarity with the system and all the new terminology I had to learn. *It will come. Be patient,* I told myself. I had to be very patient because it felt like nothing I read or studied stuck in my brain. I never associated my difficulty with the concussions I suffered in 2006 and 2007. I really had no reason to do so. Before I signed my contract with the Bengals I underwent all kinds of testing, including a close look at any lingering effects from the concussions in my past. The Bengals' doctors cleared me, just as the Colts' medical staff had before. I had no reason to suspect I might still suffer from lingering memory issues. Since not one but two sets of doctors had declared me fit, why would I?

A few weeks before my first training camp with the Bengals, Karyn and I went home to the Twin Cities to visit family and to celebrate my twenty-seventh birthday. The two of us went to the Downtowner Woodfire Grill in St. Paul, which is one of my favorite spots. We went through dinner, then she said, "Do you want your gift?"

"Of course," I said.

Karyn then took out a small package and handed it to me. It felt really, really light. I had no idea what it might be. Looking over at Karyn, she had a big grin on her face like this was something I really wanted. I couldn't imagine what she could have possibly bought that was so small and so light.

I tore through the wrapping paper and found a small box. Inside the small box was an infant-sized Minnesota Golden Gophers jersey, number 82 printed on the front and back, which was my number in college. My eyes got really big. I looked up at Karyn, who now had tears in her eyes. "Does this mean . . . ?" I asked.

"Yep. We're having a baby," she said.

"How did you get this?" I asked.

"I bought it before I graduated after we got really serious. I bought it for this day," she said.

I broke into tears. It was the greatest birthday present ever.

By the time training camp opened I had a great relationship with my new teammates, but I was still struggling to learn the offense. Karyn and I made friends quickly both on and off the field. It was a good thing my new quarterback, Carson Palmer, and I became friends because in the second preseason game of the year, I put our relationship to the test. Early in the first half Carson audibled to a play where I was supposed to stay in close to him and block. An audible is where the quarterback changes the play right before the ball is snapped based on the defensive alignment. Carson saw the safety creeping up close to the line to blitz, that is, rush him instead of dropping back in pass coverage. My job was simple: block the safety and protect the quarterback. I blew it. I didn't just miss the block. I completely misunderstood the audible. Instead of staying in and blocking I went out for a pass. The safety crushed Carson, driving his helmet up under Carson's face mask and breaking his nose. Neither of us knew it at the time, but that play was a harbinger of what awaited us in the 2008 season.

We opened the year on the road in Baltimore against the Ravens. Because they are in the same division, the Bengals play the Ravens twice every season. As a team we should have been up for the game, but we came out flat and stayed that way. It was a hot, humid day and we melted in it, myself included. I dropped a couple of balls I should have caught. I wasn't the only one. On the day, Carson only completed nine out of twenty-four passes, two of which were to me. The Ravens outgained us by two hundred yards and had twenty-one first downs to our eight. Even though they thoroughly outplayed us, we lost by only a touchdown, 17–10.

Losing the first game of the year was a new experience to me as a pro. In my three years playing for the Colts we started out 13-0, 9-0, and 7-0. The 2008 Bengals flipped that script upside down.

We played our second game in near-hurricane conditions against the Tennessee Titans. At game time the wind whipped through the stadium at 70 miles per hour. I don't know how the people in the upper deck of Paul Brown Stadium kept from blowing away. The wind certainly affected the football. On our first play of our first drive of the game, I went out for a short pass. The wind caught the ball and sent it up high. I jumped up to grab it but it was just out of reach. As the ball sailed over my outstretched arms, one of my former Colt teammates, David Thornton, plowed his helmet into my chest, driving me to the ground. I could not get up and I could barely breathe.

A stretcher carted me off the field and an ambulance took me directly to the hospital, where according to the doctor there, X-rays revealed I had possibly fractured my sternum. Later the team doctors looked at the same X-rays and said my sternum was merely badly bruised, not broken. Either way, I couldn't play again until week five, in a game on the road against the Dallas Cowboys at Texas Stadium, the stadium with a hole in the roof. Locals said the hole was there so that God could watch His team. (The stadium has since been replaced with AT&T Stadium, which also features a retractable roof.) I don't know about that. I do know that in 2008 the Bengals felt a little cursed. Going into the Cowboy game we were 0-4, losing not only the Titans game but also to the Giants and our cross-state rivals, the Cleveland Browns.

Looking back, I guess it sounds crazy to think that I came back from a bruised or broken sternum in only three weeks, but I did. I was able to play because I was wearing a special chest pad covering my sternum and I believe because I received anti-inflammatory injections before the game. Even with that I was not the same player. Carson threw my way five times. I only caught one of the passes and it wasn't because the passes were thrown poorly. Toward the end of the first quarter I went deep over the middle on a seam route. When you go across the middle of the field, you know you are going to get hit when you catch the ball, and get hit hard. As I watched the ball arcing toward me, out of the corner of my eye I caught a glimpse of one of the safeties bearing down on me. The ball, the safety, and I all arrived at the same place at about the same time. The pass was high but very catchable. However, instead of stretching up for the ball, I pulled my arms down and braced myself for the hit from the safety. I couldn't help myself. In that split second I reacted and did what most of us instinctively do: I protected myself from harm. The ball fell harmlessly on the turf, while the safety gave me an earful. To put it mildly, he questioned my manhood for letting a catchable pass go by out of fear of the hit he was going to lay on me.

I also heard about it in the film room the next week.

We lost to the Cowboys 31–22. If I had caught the pass, the game might have turned out differently. I didn't just let the pass sail. I also signaled my quarterback that he could not trust me to sacrifice myself to make a tough catch.

The following game, at the Meadowlands in New Jersey against the Jets, I set out to change that perception. Carson missed the game due to injury. Ryan Fitzpatrick took his place. We fell behind early but fought back. Right before the end of the first half we drove the ball down to the Jets' five-yard line. Ryan called a play where I ran an under route across the middle of the field right by the goal line. I caught the ball, but paid the price for it. One defender hit me in the legs, and another hit me squarely in the middle of my chest, right where I'd been hit four weeks earlier. I felt a pop. X-rays revealed a new break in one of my ribs in the upper left side of my chest. I played the rest of the game, but missed the next three. The team finally won our first game in the last of those three games. We held on for a 21–19 win over the Jaguars.

When I finally returned to practice we had a 1-8 record. The calendar said November 10, but for all intents and purposes our season was over. Teams who lose their first eight games don't make the playoffs, much less win a Super Bowl. Even so, I tried to maintain a positive attitude in the locker room. The team was pretty down. Our owner, Mike Brown, had canceled the team Halloween party because of our poor start. No one felt much like partying.

I came back strong my first week of practice as we prepared to play the Philadelphia Eagles at home. My chest still hurt, but that was nothing new. I followed the pain protocol, that is, painkillers and anti-inflammatories, and got back to work. In one of the first practices I lined up for a live blocking drill with one of our linebackers. The two of us crashed into one another, and as we did, our heads collided. I nearly blacked out. My vision went dark for just a moment and I felt a little woozy afterward. However, hits that make you see stars or go black and leave you with a headache are pretty common in blocking drills and games. I just ran back to my place in the line and didn't say a word to anyone, although the hit left me with a severe headache.

That night I woke up around 2:00 a.m. and found I had soaked the sheets with sweat. The next morning I still didn't feel right. When Karyn got up I told her, "I think I have another concussion."

"What are you going to do?" she asked.

"Nothing," I said. "I can't go out with another injury, not now, not after missing so much of the season already." I wasn't just being macho. I felt I owed my team and my teammates more than I had given them thus far. The Bengals gave me $2 million just to sign with the team and were paying me more than $2 million for this season. They hadn't paid me all that money to miss seven games and to go out with another injury now. In my mind, I had not lived up to my expectations. Just under half the season remained to be played. The playoffs were out of the question, but I could still play for pride and put myself in position to make a major contribution the following year.

Things didn't turn out the way I had planned. I didn't do much in the Eagles game, which ended in a tie. When the referee blew the whistle, ending the game, a lot of the players were confused as to what was going on. Most of us assumed we'd just keep playing until someone scored and won the game.

The following week, my first time to play in Pittsburgh against the Steelers, I had one of my best games of the season. I caught everything that came my way and ended the game with three catches for thirty-six yards. One of the catches was a seam route over the middle, the very same route where I pulled up short in the Dallas game. This time I caught the ball and absorbed a huge hit afterward. Believe it or not, I needed that hit to reassure me I still had what it took to be a receiver in this league. I trotted back to the huddle with renewed self-confidence.

But, since this was the cursed season, I got hurt the next week. I tore my plantar fascia in a game against the Ravens at home. I didn't play again until the last game of the season. We beat the Kansas City Chiefs to finish the year 4-11-1. In that single season I experienced more losses than all my years in Indianapolis combined. The Bengals canceled our team Christmas party. No one felt much like celebrating.

When the season ended I took a serious look at myself as a player. I made up my mind to sell myself out completely to fitness during the off-season. I was determined to come into camp in the best shape of my life. I changed my diet and cut out all empty carbs. No more desserts. No more pizza. Not even an occasional beer. I wanted to transform my body, and empty carbs weren't going to do that. I also changed my workout routine. I even bought a workout DVD that was supposed to produce amazing results.

The changes worked. By the time the 2009 training camp rolled around I had never been so cut, so athletically fit. My body felt better than it ever had before. I hoped it would translate into a career year on the field.

CHAPTER 16

ELLEORA

PREPARING FOR THE 2009 SEASON WAS far from the only thing on my mind after the 2008 season ended. It wasn't even the most important. Karyn's due date was February 21 and the season ended on December 28. That didn't leave us much time to get a lot done, beginning with the baby's room. I never knew someone so small required so much specialized equipment. You don't just buy a crib and some diapers and call it a day. We had a decorating theme for the room, plus video monitors and changing tables and a wide variety of special baby holders to carry her around in. Because we wanted to be surprised by the baby's gender we went with a light green color scheme with cute little frogs. In fact, Elleora still is fascinated with her little stuffed froggy and it goes with her everywhere. I hadn't been as engaged in this process as I would have liked during the season, which meant I had to make up for lost time now.

My other job was mastering the coaching skills our labor and delivery nurse told us I needed to have for Karyn to have a completely natural childbirth experience. A teammate of mine and his wife were also expecting at this time. Our due dates were about a week apart. Karyn and I might have been able to go to a regular birth class at our hospital, but instead we hired a nurse to come to their home and hold a couple of classes for just the four of us during the season. I would like to think that this setup was ideal because it gave me the freedom to ask more questions and to really focus on my role. Unfortunately, I have no memory of that experience with my wife, our friends, or the nurse. As my wife reminded me about this experience I could vaguely recall anything. I remember being over at their home for dinner one night, but beyond that is a fog. I wanted to do everything I could to help Karyn, especially as her due date grew closer and closer. I just feel sad that I don't have many clear memories from that time. I hope I lived up to her expectations.

February 21 came and went and still no baby. We had no idea whether we were going to have a boy or a girl. Karyn and I were excited to be surprised, but the suspense was starting to get to me. Whichever we were having, boy or girl, seemed to be in no hurry for his or her grand entrance.

A week passed and nothing happened. Both Karyn's mom and my mom had come down around Karyn's due date to help us in the event the baby's arrival was on time. Both sets of dads planned to come down to Cincinnati as soon as the baby arrived. They were anxious to meet their first grandchild. I stuck to my exercise and eating regimen. It gave me something to focus on instead of asking Karyn every five minutes if it was "time."

Karyn's doctor had told her that if she went one week over term, then they would have to induce labor. Both of us hoped that wouldn't be necessary. We wanted the full birth experience, complete with labor pains beginning at a random moment. That's exactly what happened. On February 28 we checked into Cincinnati's Good Samaritan Hospital after Karyn's contractions started on their own the night before. When the first labor pain hit I was right by Karyn's side, doing the whole coach thing. "Breathe," I said, and did the breathing exercises with her until the pain passed. Hours passed with little progress being made. Pains came and went and this baby still wasn't in a big hurry.

Finally, after ten hours of labor Karyn made a difficult choice. "Give me an epidural," she told the labor nurse. I agreed with her decision. She was exhausted and we still had a long way to go. I dozed off for a few moments, but it wasn't a deep sleep. Every little sound made me jump up and ask, "Are you okay?"

At long last the time came. Karyn's doctor came in, examined her, and told her it was time to push. Some men get squeamish in those situations. I'm not one of them. I was right there, holding on to Karyn's hand while watching for my baby's arrival. "One more big push," the doctor said. The next sound I heard was my baby crying and the doctor saying, "It's a girl." The doctor allowed me to cut the umbilical cord, then the nurses took my girl and cleaned her up. I watched how they handled her, and frankly, it surprised me. To me this baby girl was the most fragile thing in the entire world, but the nurses almost seemed rough with her. I watched them take the little suction bottle and suck the amniotic fluid out of my daughter's mouth and nose. It fascinated me how they did this. I couldn't look away.

Once they had my daughter cleaned up, the nurse placed my little girl in my arms for the first time. Tears flowed as I looked at my beautiful baby girl. It was the first time in my life I really understood John 3:16. I found myself praying, *"How could You give Your Son, Lord?"* Cradling my daughter in my arms I whispered, "I will never let you go."

"What are you going to name her?" the doctor asked.

"Elleora," I replied. "It means the Light of God."

"That's beautiful," the doctor said.

"Thank you."

Karyn and I spent a long time holding our daughter and enjoying her. I never felt more in love with my wife. At the right time I went out and brought our mothers into the room. Karyn's dad and brother arrived the day we brought Elleora home. My dad arrived the second day we were in the hospital with Elleora.

Even though God blessed us with a little girl, that did not change my plans for her homecoming. On the day the hospital released us to take Elleora home, I brought in a Superman onesie. My little Kryptonian princess was going to go home in style, not in some frilly little dress. This was going to be her first fashion statement to the world, and I was going to make sure it was the right one. Karyn laughed and said, "Sure, go ahead." I was so proud I think I flew home.

I didn't fly in the car, though. There's nothing like putting a baby into an infant seat to turn you into the world's safest driver. We had to make one stop on our way home. Sandi Patty was in town for a Women of Faith event, so we stopped to let my second mom hold the new baby. However, we didn't stay long. We were all anxious to get home.

Not long after we arrived home, Karyn's dad, Larry, and brother, Erik, arrived. They had driven straight through from Minnesota, which is nearly a twelve-hour drive. It was their first time seeing our new house so I gave them a quick tour. Karyn and her mom were upstairs giving the baby a bath. After the tour Erik, Larry, and I sat down in the living room and started talking. All of a sudden I heard a bloodcurdling shriek from Karyn's mom. I jumped up and ran up the stairs so fast that I ran right out of my shoes. When I got to the upstairs bathroom I found Karyn in a panic holding on to Elleora. "Ben!" she cried, unable to say anything else. She didn't have to. Our baby girl was turning purple and could not breathe.

I grabbed Elleora from Karyn. Flipping my baby girl over on her stomach, I took the suction bottle the hospital sent home with us and did exactly what I watched the nurses do. I jammed it into her nose and started sucking out all sorts of fluid. Then I put it down her throat and did the same thing. Elleora let out a little cry, then started breathing normally like nothing had happened. Saliva or mucus or something came out of her mouth, which also showed traces of blood. However, her color returned to normal. The baby seemed fine, but we still rushed her to the emergency room at Cincinnati Children's Hospital Medical Center, one of the best children's hospitals in the country.

By the time Karyn, her mom, and I arrived at the hospital it was around midnight. They admitted Elleora and started running tests. The resident doctor on call that night, Katy Clabo, guided us through the whole process. Both Karyn and I were in an absolute panic, but Dr. Clabo had such a calm, reassuring demeanor that we were able to gather ourselves. I told Karyn, "I wonder if she's a Christian. The way she handles herself and the words she chooses make me think she must be."

After about two hours Dr. Clabo came back out and said, "Your baby girl is fine. She had some fluid in her lungs that caused this, but you did exactly what needed to be done, Ben. Your quick thinking saved your daughter's life."

"What about the blood we sucked out?" Karyn asked.

"We didn't find anything. It might have been caused by the suction bottle," Dr. Clabo replied. "But she's fine. You can take her on home."

Karyn and I grabbed hold of one another and wept tears of joy. I turned to the doctor and said, "I want to thank you so much for how you handled everything tonight and just how you spoke to us. You helped the two of us so much." Then I said something that surprised me even as the words came out of my mouth, "Dr. Clabo, I don't know if I should do this or not, but I just feel like I am supposed to. Are you single?"

Dr. Clabo gave a very hesitant, "Yesss."

"Good. My brother-in-law is in town and I would just love to introduce you to him."

As Dr. Clabo tells the story, I brought it up at least three times before receiving her answer. In between my multiple pursuits, Dr. Clabo was embarrassed and nervous. She really enjoyed Karyn but also didn't want to get fired for giving out her personal information, especially for a potential date with a patient's family. Before giving me an answer she went over to another resident and told him what was happening. The resident said to her, "Do you have any idea who that person is? He won a Super Bowl with Peyton Manning. Now go back in there, say yes, and get me some tickets!"

In spite of the enthusiastic first piece of advice, the doctor consulted another colleague. He gave her a nod as if to say, "Go for it." A few minutes later, to my surprise and after some serious thought and obnoxious pursuit on my part, the doctor finally answered, "I don't usually do this but, sure. I will meet him." Dr. Katy Clabo made sure to give her information to Karyn, with whom she'd found a connection.

Today, Dr. Clabo is my sister-in-law. At the time of this writing she and Erik have been happily married for five years. The two of them live in Knoxville, Tennessee, where he's an engineer for a major automobile manufacturer and she's a pediatric ER doctor. I could write another book just about their story, but I won't. The two of them meeting and falling in love was just the topper to an already unbelievable experience.

My first football season in Cincinnati might have been a disaster, but welcoming my little girl into the world made all those bad feelings go away. The three of us settled into our new routines. Life was good. No, life was wonderful. I could not ask for more.

CHAPTER 17

THE FINAL BLOW

8/5/09—Concussion occurred at evening practice. Symptoms included 90 sec of unconsciousness, strong headache, dizziness, tingling in hands, soar neck, sweating, sleeplessness, loss of balance, blurry vision spots, and nausea.

—Concussion Symptoms Journal

When I first started keeping the journal I didn't have a book in mind. Doctors and my sports agent encouraged me to keep track of my symptoms and any changes I experienced with them. If I had thought of this book back then, I probably would have chosen stronger language for the first line. It sounds so innocuous, so minor. "A concussion occurred" doesn't really describe what happened during the first week of Bengals training camp in August 2009.

I spent the off-season getting my mind and body in the best shape of my life. The P90X workout routine and new diet paid off. I entered camp leaner and stronger with more muscle mass than at any time in my playing career. The disappointment of the previous season, in which we only won four games, drove a lot of my teammates to take the same approach to the off-season that I had. We knew we had a lot of talent on our squad. We were better than a 4-11-1 team and we were ready to prove it.

There was also a lot of excitement with the team because HBO's *Hard Knocks* was going to cover our camp. *Hard Knocks* is a reality show that gives viewers an unprecedented look inside the forming of a football team. Camera crews cover everything, from team meetings, practices, and the pre- and postgame locker room experience during the exhibition season, to the hard reality of the NFL whereby players get cut from the team and their dreams of an NFL career die. The *Hard Knocks* crews interview individual players and their families, because the business of football impacts every part of your life. All of us, including me, had to sign waivers giving HBO full access to whatever happened to us in camp. I guess we technically had a choice in the matter, but we really didn't. They did tell us if there was something that we did not feel comfortable with them filming or didn't want them to film, they would respect our wishes.

Some of the air came out of the team on either the first or second day of camp when our primary blocking tight end, Reggie Kelly, blew out his Achilles tendon. A hard hit did not cause the injury. Like the injuries I suffered in college, he was just running a route when all of the sudden he pulled up to a stop and started hopping on one leg, in obvious pain. Just like that his season was over. The team doctor broke the news to Reggie that he needed surgery that carried a six-to-eight-month recovery time. The Bengals placed him on the injured reserved (IR) list, which meant he remained a part of the team and was going to be paid for the rest of the season. However, once you are placed on IR you cannot return to the active roster that season.

After Reggie went down I knew I was going to have to fill his shoes. I was already a starter in our two-tight-end packages. But the team now needed me to do more than catch more passes. I had to step up and lead. To me, that's why they had signed me to such a big contract the year before. I felt I was ready for the challenge, even though no one was really going to take Reggie's place. He was a ten-year veteran, clubhouse leader, and one of the strongest men of God I have ever met. However, Carson made me feel better. He told the *Hard Knocks* crew, "We'll be okay. We have Ben Utecht and Ben has some of the best hands in the NFL."

The day after Reggie blew out his Achilles, I mean the very next day, we went through a routine offensive line blocking drill called half line. As the name implies, half of the offensive line goes up against half of the defensive line. I lined up on the right side. The play called for me to release and block the outside linebacker. I have little memory of the day, much less the play, so much of this information comes from the guys who were there and the practice film I later watched. Apparently I took on the linebacker in a run blocking scheme. When you block, you want to get low under them. At six feet seven, getting low can be a challenge. On this play, the linebacker got lower than me. As he did, his helmet came up under my face mask and hit me on the chin like a Muhammad Ali uppercut.

And just like Sonny Liston when he boxed against Ali, I was out.

Play suddenly stopped. Coaches and trainers and camera crews came running over to where I lay on the ground unconscious. On the opposite side of the field a camera focused in on Carson. He didn't know what had happened. When he saw someone on the ground he asked, "Is that Utecht? Is his wife here? Are his wife and daughter in the stands?"

I came to before the ambulance arrived. *Hard Knocks* showed several players come over at different times and put a hand on my leg, praying for me. Then the players moved back to give paramedics room. Wide receiver Chad Ochocinco, formerly Chad Johnson, kneeled down near me on one knee and prayed. Chad was one of the biggest characters in the NFL, but he also had a big heart and cared for his teammates.

Paramedics removed my face mask but left my helmet and pads on me out of fear of a neck or spinal injury. They strapped me onto a backboard, then lifted me onto a gurney and wheeled me into the ambulance. The emergency room doctors at George-town Community Hospital in Georgetown, Kentucky, where we held training camp, cut off my uniform and pads. I never wore a football uniform in competition again.

Someone from the team called Karyn. It might have been one of my coaches. She was at the Ivy Hills Country Club, near our home, practicing golf when they reached her on her cell. By the time they called it seemed pretty clear that I did not have a neck or spinal injury, only a concussion. She did not panic. When she heard them say it was another concussion she breathed a little sigh of relief. She still had the mind-set that concussions were *minor* traumatic brain injuries and nothing to be overly concerned about. For that matter, so did I. We'd been through a few already. Neither of us had any reason to think this one was going to be any different.

8/6/09—Strong headache, dizziness, sore neck, sleeplessness, night sweating, loss of balance, fatigue, blurry vision spots, nausea, hard time driving in car, forgetting sentences, hard to concentrate.

The hospital released me after just one night. I could not drive, so one of the young trainers on the team staff drove me back to Cincinnati, where I could access the team's full medical staff. We had a team neuropsychologist, but he was not in town. Instead, after this major concussion, the team sent me to see the Bengals' orthopedic surgeon, Angelo Colosimo. I had a lot of respect for Dr. Colosimo. I still do. He's a really good guy. However, looking back, I wondered if it was strange, even odd, that the team sent me to see an orthopedic surgeon rather than a neurologist for a head injury.

When I first went in to be evaluated by Dr. Colosimo, several people from the training staff were in the room, including the young trainer who drove me over from the hospital. The doctor went through the evaluation process, asking me about my symptoms. I honestly don't remember if any concussion tests were given to me, such as balance and memory tests.

Once he finished the overall evaluation, the doctor asked everyone else to leave the room. When we were finally alone, he asked me, "Ben, how are you really doing?"

I lost it. Tears started flowing and would not stop. Finally I gained my composure. "I'm scared," I confessed. "I don't know that I want to keep playing if this keeps happening to me." My outburst wasn't just caused by my fears. I remember feeling like I couldn't control my emotions, and that I also wasn't in the right state of mind to truly know or understand my feelings.

Dr. Colosimo listened. Then he said something that surprised me coming from a team doctor. "Ben, listen, I'm a dad whose son has suffered concussions. I've been on the other side of this conversation. I want to tell you, if you were my son, you'd be done. It's not worth it."

"Really?" I said.

"I'm just being as honest with you as I can. If you were my son, you would not play football again."

We talked a little while longer; it felt good to talk to a doctor who cared about my long-term health. When I left I thanked him for his honesty and support. "I'm going to talk this over with my wife. You've given me a lot to think about," I said. Leaving his office, I felt relieved. My fears weren't completely irrational. Five documented concussions and who knows how many more were enough. I'd battled injuries my entire football career, going back to my senior year of high school. I always battled back. I always got back on the field. I didn't think I wanted to do that again, not with a brain injury.

However, the relief I felt was short-lived. The moment I allowed myself to contemplate walking away from football at the ripe old age of twenty-nine another thought came crashing down on me: *And then what? What do I do now?*

8/9/09—Random headaches, dizziness, sleeplessness, night sweating, loss of balance, fatigue, nausea, hard time driving in car, forgetting sentences, hard to concentrate, irritability, sadness, snapping at wife.

My mother came down to Cincinnati because of my concussion. Now that my camp was over, she drove me back down to Georgetown to pick up all my belongings. I could not drive myself. Weeks passed before any doctor cleared me to drive again. I had a hard enough time just riding in a car for any time at all. The movement back and forth made me nauseous. But I had to go get my stuff. No one was going to pick it up for me.

I don't remember my mom driving me to Georgetown. She now tells me that I didn't say a word through the entire drive. I just sat and stared out the window, expressionless. When we got to Georgetown College, the guards waved us in. No one was around when I went in my room and stuffed all my things into a duffel bag. I took a final look around the room and said, "I just can't believe this is happening." It's the only thing I said the entire time we were there.

Once I finished packing my things I headed straight back to the car. Off toward the football field I heard the sounds of practice. I couldn't help but think that that's where I should have been. This was supposed to be my year. I'd played four years after sitting out my first season with the Colts. I knew the league. I knew the game. I was in the best shape of my life, and now I was packing up and heading home. By the time we got back to my car I was nearly in tears. My mom sensed it and reached over and took my hand. "Ben, let's pray." Then she started praying, "Lord, we need You to get us through this season of Ben's life. We don't know what Your plan is, but we trust You. We need Your help." Just like when I had my first football injury, my mom was there telling me to trust Jesus.

"Thanks, Mom," I said. "I really needed that."

"That's what moms are for," she replied.

When we pulled up to the gate to leave camp, the guard waved us through. He had a sort of smile on his face, but I could tell it was forced. He was trying to be cheerful, as if he were saying, "See you later," but he and I both knew he wouldn't. It had to be the same wave he gave guys when they were cut from the team.

It was a solemn ride home.

8/11/09—Head pressure/daze, dizziness from activity, sleeplessness, sweating, fatigue, nausea, hard time driving in car, forgetting sentences, hard to concentrate, irritability, impatient, sadness. Experienced hot flashes during movie, felt very loopy in car ride home, and had difficult time recalling recent past events.

8/14/09—Woke up with slight headache, tried doing more activities around the house but experienced increased dizziness. Still feeling as if I'm in a daze. Also still feeling impatient, and having trouble concentrating. I continue to struggle with forgetting what I was going to say, like my mind just goes blank.

8/16/09—Again woke up with pressure and a slight headache. Still experiencing a dazed feeling with trouble concentrating on things like reading or in-depth conversations. I also experienced two major head rushes today that took me back to the floor on my knees because I felt like I was going to black out. Both instances happened just from standing up from a sitting position on the couch. Still have trouble relaxing and falling asleep.

8/17/09—Met with Dr. Sullivan and Paul Sparling today. I did not pass my symptoms evaluation for the second time. They both were talking with me once again about where my stance is on my decision to keep playing. Again Dr. Sullivan supported his decision about not flying this last week to MA because it would have "hands down" made me worse, even though he told my agent that he couldn't say for sure if it would truly affect me. So I definitely experienced some mixed signals.

My symptoms are the same today. I woke up with pressure and a slight headache that comes and goes. I tried driving today and felt comfortable but still noticed that I would fall into dazes while driving. I am still forgetting my sentences; it happened twice today during my meeting with Dr. Sullivan. Concentration is still suffering. Also I have to try not to get into a sad or depressed state.

Thomas Sullivan, PhD, was the Bengals' neuropsychologist, while Paul Sparling was the head trainer. I met with Sullivan the first time on August 10. I went through all the battery of post-concussion tests and did terribly. Out of a possible twenty-one postconcussion symptoms, I had eighteen. Sullivan graded my concussion as a Grade 3, or severe. I remember him saying something along the lines of, "Honestly, Ben, I don't think you should play again. When you suffer a concussion it puts you at greater risk for another. This is your fifth and it is by far the most severe. You have a lot of life in front of you. I think the best thing for your future is for you not to play again."

I listened. Sullivan said basically the same thing Dr. Colosimo had told me. This time, Sullivan was fully on the record. He reported to the team that this was his recommendation for me.

However, I wasn't so sure I wanted to make that decision, not right then at least. Now, let me remind you that I was not in my right mind. I was severely concussed. I do not recommend making a major life decision in a fully concussed state. I contacted my agent instead and asked him what course we should take. At this point I did not know if I wanted to play again, or if I even could, but I knew I needed more information. I also needed time to heal more fully before I could make an informed decision.

I also wanted a second opinion, and I wanted to see someone who was an expert in concussions. My agent contacted Dr. Robert Cantu, whom I mentioned in earlier chapters. Dr. Cantu's office was more than happy to work my case into his schedule. Unfortunately, I had a problem. Dr. Cantu's office is in Boston. I lived in Cincinnati. Because of my concussed state, the Bengals wouldn't allow me to travel. Their refusal to let me get on an airplane made me very frustrated. Almost three weeks had passed since my concussion and I still had not seen a medical doctor who specialized in the brain. I had yet to see a neurologist or a neurosurgeon. I began to speculate that the Bengals were trying to keep me from consulting with an MD from outside the team. But why?

I called my agent, Chris, and shared my frustration. The two of us looked into every form of transportation possible to get me to Boston and meet with Dr. Cantu but the team denied every option. The Bengals would not allow me to fly. They would not allow someone to drive me to Boston. They wouldn't even let me get on a train for the trip. I know because I asked.

That's why I found myself back in an office with Tom Sullivan and Paul Sparling. They put me through the range of tests and once again, I did poorly. As you can see from the entries I included from my symptoms journal, I wasn't getting any better. Once again Sullivan brought up retirement. I do believe he was genuinely concerned. "I'm not ready to make that decision yet," I said. "If I can play again, that's what I want to do."

8/23/09—Still feeling pressure in my head. Did not sleep well last night. I just went on my first walk in eighteen days, only about a mile and a half. I got fatigued and lightheaded toward the end and started to get a headache.

8/24/09—The pressure and random headaches are still constant. I continue to struggle falling asleep. My mind continues to feel foggy and concentration still suffers. I am still struggling with my memory, forgetting sentences, and having difficulty drawing out information.

Met With Dr. Cantu today. He definitely seemed like an expert in this field. He shared information and research with me that I have never heard from any NFL doctor. One interesting thing I learned was about how specific blood alleles can be genetic markers that reveal people may be more predisposed to AD, Dementia, and even Concussions. I will be meeting with him again in a couple weeks.

After almost three weeks to the day the Bengals finally cleared me to fly out to Boston to meet with a nonbiased second opinion doctor. Dr. Robert Cantu was a leader in the field of concussions. Unfortunately I was meeting with him roughly twenty-one days after my injury occurred.

8/25/09—Met with Paul Sparling in the morning. Shared with him about my meeting with Dr. Cantu. I did share with Paul the research about the blood alleles and his response was he swept it aside by saying, "Well, there's a lot of research out there, but nothing conclusive."

I asked Paul what are the team's expectations for me as far as being around the facilities. He said there were none, and in fact encouraged me to go do something that would make me "happy" or bring some joy to my situation. So Karyn and I decided to visit some friends for a couple of days.

Still experienced the same symptoms that I have been this last week. There have been no improvements.

I was also asked by Hard Knocks *to do a follow-up.*

8/26–8/27/09—Spending time with friends in Nashville. I could not journal, due to being away from the computer. No changes or improvements with my symptoms. I did call both Jack Brennan at the Bengals and Alecia Zubikowski, who is in charge of setting up the Hard Knocks *"follow-up" interview to decline due to being emotionally uncomfortable and mentally incapable of interviewing or talking about my experience or about my future due to the effects of the concussion. Also my agent and I felt that because of my current injury and symptoms I should not be on camera talking about my situation until we are made aware what the team has planned for me this season.*

8/28/09—Still struggling with head pressure and headaches. Also I still experience some random dizziness whenever I have been moving more quickly. I am still having difficulty with my memory, especially with sentences, words, and even why I was doing something. Met with Dr. Sullivan today and failed the symptoms test again. He thought sleep medication could help with my sleeplessness.

8/30/09—Received a call from Marvin Lewis today asking me to come down to the stadium and talk with him about my injury situation. Everything went fine during the meeting until I noticed there was a camera in Coach's office on top of a cabinet pointing directly at the table. My first thought was that no way are they taping this after I specifically said no to an interview (with HBO's Hard Knocks). I came home afterward and shared my frustration with my wife and also called my agent.

Still experiencing the same symptoms from the previous day.

9/1/09—I received a call from Mr. Jim Lippincott informing me that the Bengals were placing me on IR for the season. He said that this season was done for me but that they would be paying me for the year and let me heal so that I could make a decision in the off-season whether or not I would return to play.

Still experiencing the same symptoms that I documented on the 28th.

I did a follow-up interview with *Hard Knocks* on the day I received the call from the Bengals telling me they had placed me on IR. The call came as a relief. Jim Lippincott, the team director of football operations, told me, "Your season is done, but you're still a part of the team. Take this year to heal and then evaluate what you want to do in the off-season."

Coach Lewis also called me and asked how I was doing. It felt good to have him check up on me. One of the dynamics of football that I've talked about before is how much the team is like a family, and the coaches are like second fathers to you. That's how Coach Dungy was, and the same was true of Coach Lewis.

Hard Knocks did their follow-up interview with me in my kitchen. Karyn came in at one point with Elleora and gave me the news every dad wants to hear: "She needs a diaper change."

"Oh boy," I said. So this was how I was going to spend my 2009 season, changing diapers. I didn't mind. I love being a dad. The camera crew filmed me taking care of my little girl. It was a sweet moment.

I can't remember the questions they asked, but when the

follow-up interview came I knew I had been placed on IR. I told the camera, "I consider it a blessing to be a part of an organization that cares so much about my health and well-being." And I meant it. I stopped keeping a concussion symptoms journal since I was now on IR and my season was done. There wasn't a reason to track my progress. At least not for two months.

11/18/09—I was let go by the Bengals today.

CHAPTER 18

WHAT NOW?

I COULD NOT BELIEVE MY EARS when I received the news that the Bengals had cut me on November 18. Ironically, I received the call while I drove home from the Bengals' facilities at Paul Brown Stadium, where I had just completed some light aerobic activity, including a "jog" diagonally across the field. I use the word *jog* loosely because the equipment guy picking up footballs was moving faster than me. This was my first time setting foot on a football field since the concussion. Drs. Cantu and Sullivan had only cleared me to do light aerobic exercise about a month earlier. My workouts consisted mainly of slow work on the elliptical machine in the Bengals' workout facility. Even though I had been cleared to do "light" aerobic activity, no one from the team's medical or training staff gave me any sort of workout plan to follow. Basically it was left to me to figure out. When I stepped onto the elliptical machine for the first time in mid-October, two and a half months had passed since I had done any physical activity beyond walking across the room. Some days even that left me dizzy.

By mid-October my headaches had subsided, although my head still did not feel right and I had memory issues where in midsentence I forgot what I was going to say. Even so, Sullivan cleared me to increase my workout to the moderate level. I consulted with Dr. Cantu a couple more times during this period (a common thing to do with a second-opinion doctor). He cautioned me. "Ben," he said, "the moment your head starts to hurt even a slight bit, shut it down. When you exercise and your heart rate increases, the pressure in your head increases, which will aggravate the concussion symptoms."

I followed Dr. Cantu's advice while continuing to meet weekly with Tom Sullivan. It seemed like every time I met with Tom he came back around to the subject of me continuing to play football. I know he felt strongly that I should not play again. At the same time, he cleared me to increase my workout intensity from light to moderate, which meant I was cleared to do some light weight lifting. Again, no one gave me a specific program as to what kind of weight-lifting regimen I should tackle. No one from the team even monitored me as I worked out. One of the first times I tried doing weights, I did some triceps extensions with a forty-five-pound free weight. I lifted the weight over my head, then suddenly my vision started to go black. The room spun around a couple of times and I dropped the weight. It landed on my forehead, cutting a pretty good gash, just as I fell to the floor. One of the weight room trainers happened to see what had happened and helped me up. I was taken to the training room and the cut on my forehead was sealed with butterfly strips. I didn't try lifting weights again for a few days.

On the day the team cut me, I tried some very light weights again. I don't remember exactly which weight exercises I did or exactly how much weight I used on each one, but I can tell you that the entire workout didn't even rise to the level of the warm-ups I did before the concussion. I also jogged a little on a treadmill, but I really wanted to go outside. That's why I put on a full sweatsuit and went out onto the field of Paul Brown Stadium. My workout consisted of that slow trot diagonally across the field I described above, which was followed by a walk along the goal line to the other side. I ran into a few of my teammates and a couple of coaches out on the field. They all seemed glad to see me.

After my jog, I went back into the locker room and started toward the weight room. Coach Lewis was walking through the locker room. "Ben!" he said when he saw me. "Hey, it's great to see you. How's the rehab going? How's your family?"

"Slow, Coach, but I'll get there eventually. The family's doing well," I replied.

"That's good to hear. Well, I'll let you get back to your workout. Keep up the good work and keep getting better," he said.

"Thanks, Coach."

Forty minutes later, as I pulled my truck out of Paul Brown Stadium, my phone rang. The voice on the other end of the line was not the general manager or team president. No, Coach Lewis called me. "Unfortunately, Ben, we're going to have to let you go," he said over the phone.

Three thoughts immediately came to mind. First, I thought, but did not say, *Wait a minute. I thought you guys were going to keep me!* The second thought was, *How can you cut me? Who cleared me to play?* And the third was a question I really wanted to ask but didn't: *Why didn't you tell me this to my face a half hour ago when I saw you in the locker room?* The last one left me with an empty feeling. All of my life coaches had been like second parental figures to me. Now he was just a boss cutting me loose. Any illusions of "family" bonds were now ebbing away.

I hung up the phone and turned my truck around to go clean out my locker. My ties to the Bengals were now over. Coach Lewis might as well have said, "You're fired," because that's what I was. Cut means out, as in out of a job and out on the street and out of luck if you are injured and unable to seek a job with another team. It also means you have to remove all your belongings and get out. After this day I was no longer welcome in the Bengals' facilities.

On my way back into the stadium parking lot I called Karyn and told her what had happened. She was as shocked as I was. Then I called my agent, Chis Murray. "What?!" he said. "They can't do that. You're on IR. This isn't right. They can't cut you when you're hurt!"

"That's what I thought," I said, "but they did."

When I walked back into the locker room an equipment manager was waiting for me at the door. He handed me a large black garbage bag for all of my stuff in my locker. No one else was anywhere to be found. I stuffed my pads and jerseys and anything else I could take home into the bag, told the equipment guy "Thanks," and that was that. I may be naïve but this was the first time I realized what kind of business football really is. It's a great place to be when things are going well and you can perform. But when you can't, you're done. I guess I was one of the lucky ones. The average NFL career lasts about three years. I played five and had a Super Bowl ring to show for it. Most guys never get that.

When I walked into my house, my conversation with Karyn was sad and awkward and something I'm glad I don't remember. Losing a job is never fun, but I had lost more than that. I was now damaged goods. I couldn't just go out and catch on with another team, because, in spite of what the Bengals said, I had not been cleared to play by a physician, specifically a neurologist.

At the time of my termination, I still had a year and a half remaining on the three-year contract I signed in the spring of 2008.

That didn't matter. My contract was not guaranteed. For me, that meant the nearly $1 million I was to be paid for the rest of the 2009 season was gone, to say nothing of the more than $2 million I was to receive in 2010 if I remained with the team.

I'll be honest. Having that much money stripped out of my hands upset me. But what really made me mad was my conviction that under the collective bargaining agreement (CBA) signed by the NFL and the NFL Players Association (NFLPA), the Bengals had no right to cut me because I had not been properly cleared to resume football activities.

When I was cut on November 18, I had not even seen a physician in a few weeks, much less been cleared by one to resume playing. I had only begun to try certain moderate exercises when the call came. Something was wrong here.

I called my agent again. The realization that I suddenly had no job and no paychecks to look forward to was starting to set in. "What can we do, Chris?" I asked, desperate.

"Let me contact the players association and start the process of filing a grievance," Chris said. He then put me in contact with Tim English, one of the attorneys for the NFLPA who handles cases like mine.

Tim was just as shocked as Chris. "The CBA is really clear on this," Tim said. "Paragraph nine of the NFL Player Contract states that any player injured in the performance of his services 'will continue to receive his yearly salary for so long, during the season of injury only.' If that's not you, I don't know what is."

I felt a little less panicked. "So you think this should be pretty much an open-and-shut case?" I asked.

"There's precedent, Ben," Tim explained. "For three decades the standard for these cases requires a player to be sufficiently recovered so as to be able to perform *all* the usual moves and actions required of his playing position before he can be cleared to play. And you can't be cut from the team if you aren't cleared to play. That's called the Bohannon standard. The Bengals can't just ignore a standard the entire league has had to live by for thirty years."

"Okay. So let's get the ball rolling to file a grievance," I said.

I called Chris again to let him know how my conversation with Tim had gone. "I know the players association attorneys will handle the actual grievance," Chris said, "but I think it would be a really good idea if you had an attorney of your own to walk through this process with you. I have someone I think you should meet: Scott Hillstrom."

"Do you really think I need my own attorney?" I asked. "Shouldn't the NFLPA be enough?"

"Talk to Scott," Chris said, "then you'll understand."

Chris set up a time for me to meet with Scott. I would soon discover this was one of the best things my agent ever did for me.

After I hung up the phone with Chris I called Dr. Cantu's office. When I told him what had happened he was nearly speechless. "Who cleared you to play?" he asked.

"I don't know," I replied. "The only doctor I have seen of late was Tom Sullivan, I met with him a week ago."

"But he's not a medical doctor. He shouldn't be able to make that call," Dr. Cantu said.

"There's a lot that's happened that seems a little unusual," I said.

Five days later, on November 23, 2009, I was reexamined by Dr. Cantu. He told me flat out, "Ben, there's no way you can return to football anytime soon. I think you can increase the intensity of your workouts, and if you don't have any symptoms, then we can move you up to stage four; then, perhaps, stage five. But you aren't anywhere near football shape. If everything went perfect and you had no returning concussion symptoms whatsoever, you are still four to six weeks, minimum, away from being declared fit to return to play. That's if everything goes in a best-case scenario, and that's a big *if*."

"Then how could the Bengals declare me ready to go?" I asked.

"That's a good question," Dr. Cantu replied. "However, in my opinion, I cannot clear you to play. And, honestly, Ben, you should think long and hard about ever playing again. There's just too much risk of long-term complications if you do. And you have too many other things you can go and do. You're a young man with a lot of gifts. It's probably time for you to pursue them."

"I appreciate that, Dr. Cantu. Right now I just don't know what I am going to do. Even though I knew this day was going to come, I never expected it to come so soon. I mean, how many people find themselves at the end of their career at the age of twenty-nine?"

Unlike the Bengals, Dr. Cantu gave me a specific exercise program to follow. He also suggested I resume using my concussion symptoms journal, especially since I had filed a grievance against the Bengals. A week later I made my first entry:

12/2/09—As I have been increasing my workout intensity I have started experiencing some symptoms again. I have noticed some short-term memory losses. One in particular was completely forgetting that I had a conversation with my agent about my injury situation and also setting up the time of an important conference call. After a few days I called my agent asking him when and what time are we going to set up that conference call, whereby he responded with concern that I had completely forgotten our in-depth, detailed conversation.

Along with the short-term memory problems I have begun to experience headaches and increased pressure (11/26, 28, 30, and 12/1) after some of the more intense workouts. I have also been waking up with light headaches. All of this being unusual for me because I have never struggled with headaches until this last concussion.

I will be calling Dr. Cantu to ask about these symptoms.

When I called Dr. Cantu he told me to take a day off and back off a little on the workouts. I did. On December 4 I tried doing a light version of the P90X workout I'd used during the off-season. I only did the chest and back exercises, and even then I went at a much slower speed than I had six months earlier. The slower pace didn't help. About three-fourths of the way through the session I experienced a dizzy spell. I stopped the workout. Even so, pressure built up in my head. By now it was obvious to me that I was not going to have a best-case outcome in my rehab process.

I did not work out the next day. Karyn's good friend Melody Gandy stopped by the house to see us. I stayed with Melody and her husband, Dylan, my teammate, the night after I was kicked in the head in the Broncos game back in 2007. Dylan now played for the Detroit Lions, who were in town for a game against the Bengals. Melody, Karyn, and I sat down for lunch and Melody started talking about how nice it was to be back in our home. I sort of nodded my head. It was nice to have her back. This was her first time seeing our house in Cincinnati— at least I thought so. She and Dylan spent a lot of time in our house in Indy.

"You've done a lot since I was here last fall," Melody said to Karyn.

Karyn then started talking about decorating and things like that, but I couldn't follow it. Instead, all I could think was, *Last fall? You weren't here last fall.* The conversation went on. The two of them talked about this phantom visit until finally I had to say something. "Melody, when were you here before?" I asked.

"October, or maybe it was early November. Somewhere right in there," she replied.

"In this house?"

"Yes. You two had just moved in."

"Both of you were here?"

"Yes. Why?"

I didn't say anything because the look on my face said it all. "Ben, honey," Karyn said, "don't you remember Melody and Dylan coming to see us?"

"No." I paused for a moment and scanned every corner of my mind. The memories were gone, completely erased as though they had never been there. It scared me. I've always had a remarkable memory. Back in 2005, before Karyn and I got married, she came down to visit me one weekend in Indianapolis. She noticed all my bills were laid out on a table, almost in random order. "How do you keep track of them all?" she asked. "Don't worry," I told her. "It's all right here," I said, tapping my forehead. Now "right here" wasn't there. I'd had some short-term memory issues since the last concussion, but this was the first embedded memory that had suddenly disappeared. I wasn't sure what to make of it.

In confirming this story with Melody and Dylan for this book, Melody shared with me that after leaving our home that weekend she called Dylan, concerned. She told him, "That's not the same Ben, that's not our friend anymore. Something is wrong." That truth was hard for me to hear.

Back to that weekend: Once Melody left, Karyn came over to me and wrapped her arm around me. "Ben, are you okay?"

"No," I said. "Karyn, I'm scared. I think I made a big mistake playing after my last concussion with the Colts. I noticed some changes after that, but I didn't pay that much attention to them."

"Maybe Dr. Cantu can help," she said.

"I hope so." I paused for a moment, then said, "You know, if any of my team doctors had given me the information Dr. Cantu has given me, I would have strongly considered ending my career right after that hit in the Denver game. I just hope I haven't done permanent damage to myself by playing last year and into camp this year."

"Everything will be all right," Karyn said.

"I hope so," I said, but I wasn't so sure it could be.

CHAPTER 19

SEARCHING FOR DIRECTION, LOOKING FOR ANSWERS

LOOKING BACK I NOW REALIZE HOW much I should have known about concussions before I was knocked out on the practice field at the beginning of training camp in August 2009. Concussions had been a hot-button issue for the NFL for fifteen years by the time I suffered my final blow. The league set up a committee to study the subject back in 1994 after a rash of concussions to star players made the problem front-page news. Perhaps the most visible of all came when Hall of Fame quarterback Troy Aikman took a knee to the head during the 1993 NFC Championship Game. His team, the Dallas Cowboys, won the game, but Aikman had no memory of the day. Afterward he didn't even know where he was.

Yes, the league set up a concussion committee in 1994; however—and this is something I also should have known—the first chairman of the NFL's Mild Traumatic Brain Injury Committee was not a neurologist or a neuropsychologist. He was a rheumatologist. (In light of this, perhaps it wasn't surprising that the Bengals sent me to see an orthopedic specialist for my brain injury and not a neurologist.) Not surprisingly, the NFL MTBI committee produced multiple papers that concluded concussions were rare in football, and that they were not a serious problem. Dr. Ira Casson even appeared on HBO's *Real Sports* in May 2007 and declared that there was no evidence of long-term problems associated with head injuries in football players. When asked, "Is there any evidence as of today that links multiple head injuries with *any* long-term problem," Casson replied, "In NFL players? No."*

The same year, 2007, the NFL published a pamphlet for all NFL players on concussions. I really don't remember seeing one. The pamphlet states, "Q: Am I at risk for further injury if I have had a concussion? A: Current research with professional athletes has shown that you should not be at greater risk of further injury once you receive proper medical care for concussion and are free of symptoms." The same pamphlet says that current research has not shown a link between more than one or two concussions and any permanent problems. All of this has been documented in the book *League of Denial,* by Mark Fainaru-Wada and his brother, Steve Fainaru.

Two thousand seven was also the year I took a blow to the head in the Broncos game. Thanks to the bye week I missed only one game. When the Colts' neurosurgeon cleared me to play, I went back on the field without reservations. I did not think I was putting my future at risk. Why should I have? The NFL told me that I was not at greater risk of further injury, and that the concussions I had thus far shouldn't lead to any permanent problems. All of this came exactly five years after Dr. Bennet Omalu discovered chronic traumatic encephalopathy (CTE) in the brain of Hall of Famer Mike Webster, who played for seventeen years and won four Super Bowls with the Steelers. Iron Mike pretty much lost

---

* Dr. Casson's response can be viewed at https://www.youtube.com/watch?v=R4NbU_HaB3Y.

his mind, and the NFL itself admitted that he suffered brain damage from football.* I didn't know any of that when I returned to play in 2007. I just knew what the team doctors told me.

And now I discovered that, unbeknownst to me, the Bengals' neuropsychologist, Tom Sullivan (who is a PhD, not a medical doctor), said I was medically fit to return to play, which opened the door for the Bengals to cut me. Yet it was Sullivan who told me repeatedly that I should consider never playing football again. He warned me that there might be a connection between multiple concussions and a tendency to develop dementia later in life, even though at that time the NFL officially said there was no such connection.† "You should consider retiring," Sullivan told me multiple times. But the NFL did not consider this threat to my future health to be relevant to my fitness to play. So Sullivan cleared me to resume football activities despite what he had told me. To me, this decision certainly didn't make any sense.

In the months after I was cut from the Bengals I continued consulting with Dr. Cantu, one of the leading concussion doctors in the country. Even a month after the 2009 season ended he still had not cleared me to play. That's why my agent and I filed a grievance with the NFLPA.

As part of the grievance process, I went to see a neutral neuropsychologist, one with no ties to the Bengals or me. The NFL chose this doctor. I had another appointment a few weeks later with a neurosurgeon selected by the NFLPA. My first visit was on January 25, 2010, with Ruben Echemendia, PhD, the chairman of the National Hockey League's Concussion Working Group, the

---

* http://espn.go.com/espn/otl/story/_/page/OTL-Mixed-Messages/nfl-disability-board-concluded-playing-football-caused-brain-injuries-even-officials-issued-denials-years.

† The NFL reversed itself in December 2009 and admitted that concussions do have lasting consequences. However, this came one month after the Bengals cut me. http://www.nytimes.com/2009/12/21/sports/football/21concussions.html?pagewanted=all&_r=0.

NHL's equivalent of the NFL's MTBI Committee. Prior to going I talked to Tim English, the NFLPA attorney handling my grievance. Tim fought incredibly hard for justice for me. I also sought advice from Scott Hillstrom, my attorney. Scott helped me be more aware of what to expect during this process, as well as advising me on some questions I should ask the doctors.

I traveled to Penn State to meet with Echemendia. He put me through a full day of testing, which included tests to determine whether or not I was exaggerating my symptoms. After testing me himself, as well as reviewing my records provided by Drs. Cantu and Sullivan, Echemendia found them all to be consistent. After the day of testing, he called me into his office and told me, "I wouldn't clear you to play right now."

"How much longer do you think it will take for me to recover from this?" I asked. Keep in mind, my concussion happened on August 5, 2009. Nearly seven months had passed by this point.

From what I can recall, he said, "Best-case scenario, I would say you still need at least another eight to twelve weeks."

I asked Echemendia more questions about concussions in general and about my situation. Unfortunately, he couldn't give me any specific answers for what my future might hold. Even so, I felt pretty good after going to see him. During the two weeks prior to going to see him I felt like I had improved. I backed down the intensity of my workouts, keeping my maximum heartbeat below 150 beats per minute. That seemed to be working. I'd only had a little random dizziness, but nothing like I had earlier.

My fears returned a week later, however. I called one of my best friends back home in Minnesota, Brandon, to talk about his daughter's baptism. He'd asked me about my dad performing the service and I wanted to talk to him about the details of when all that was going to happen. When I told Brandon why I had called he sort of stuttered on the other end. "What's wrong?" I asked. "Did you change your mind about my dad doing the service?"

"No, Ben," Brandon replied. "It's not that. It's just that . . . uh . . ."

"What?" I asked.

"We had this exact same conversation a week ago."

"We did?" I asked. I searched hard in my brain. Nothing came up. Even after Brandon recounted the earlier conversation nearly word for word, nothing rang a bell. I had, and still have to this day, absolutely no recollection of that conversation. The first time I experienced a memory gap I thought it odd. Now I was starting to see a pattern. I was scared. For the first time I started to wonder how many of my memories now had an expiration date.

I also experienced a setback with my workouts. When I increased my intensity, headaches returned. My head felt fine during the workouts themselves. However, either late that night or when I woke up in the morning, my head was pounding. I started getting very frustrated.

In March, four months after filing my grievance, I went to see the doctor the NFLPA had arranged to examine me as part of the grievance process, Dr. Marc Mayberg in Seattle. He too was "neutral," that is, he had no previous connections to me or to the NFL. Like the others who had examined me, Dr. Mayberg put me through a series of tests and examined all the records compiled by Sullivan and Dr. Cantu. Thankfully, even though I had recovered from most of my postconcussion symptoms, he came to the same conclusion as all the other doctors. He told me I should not have been cleared to play at the time of my release. Dr. Mayberg also informed the league that I could not return to play "without undue risk of further aggravation of the injury." The alarming thing to me was that he reached this conclusion a full seven months after my injury.

After meeting with Dr. Mayberg I called Tim English. "Now that the tests are over, how long should it take before we get a decision?" I asked.

"Normally, in arbitration cases like this, once both sides have assembled their briefs, the arbitrator will hold a hearing. After that, you should hear something in a few months," Tim told me. "However, it could take longer. You never know."

Now I had two things hanging over my head that frightened me. First, every time I forgot what I was going to say in midsentence or had a memory gap like I had with my friends Melody and Brandon, I wondered if this was just the tip of the iceberg. I honestly had to start wrestling with the question, Will my mind slip away? That was frightening enough, but then I also had the added pressure of wondering how on earth I was going to provide for my family moving forward. When I signed my last contract with the Bengals, I thought I could play until I was thirty-four or thirty-five and then retire financially secure. Not only did that not happen, but I also now found myself fighting to get the nearly $1 million the Bengals refused to pay me.

From the time I started playing with the Colts, I always planned on pursuing a career in music when my playing days were over. I got my start while I was still in Indianapolis. In addition to getting to know Sandi Patty and being mentored by her in the business, I also became friends with Bill and Gloria Gaither. In the world of Christian and gospel music, the Gaithers are royalty. They taught me so much about the music industry. Sandi's manager, Mike Atkins, agreed to represent me as well. I've already written about how I sang with the Indianapolis Symphony while I was with the Colts. When I arrived in Cincinnati I appeared with the Cincinnati Pops Orchestra a few times. In fact, one of the highlights of my life came during one of my appearances with the Pops. I was scheduled to sing the national anthem and "God Bless America" with the Mormon Tabernacle Choir. When I arrived at the arena and found my dressing room I discovered that I was sharing it with none other than Neil Armstrong. His name was on the door right beside mine! When I walked into the room I introduced myself and he shook hands with me. We didn't talk much, but we didn't have to. How many people have shaken hands with the first man to walk on the moon? Just being in the same room with him was thrill enough for me.

Not long after I moved from Indianapolis to Cincinnati, I recorded my first, self-titled album for Sandi Patty's label, Stylos Records. Word distributed it while the William Morris Agency handled my bookings. The album came out in April 2009. Unfortunately, due to my obligations to the Bengals I could not tour with the album, which is what you normally do when your first album comes out. Most of the reviews of my music were very positive, and I made a handful of appearances, but I had to turn down most of the invitations that came my way. As a result, the album just did okay commercially. However, I at least had an album on a label. That was the first step.

Now that my football playing days were over I decided to plunge full bore into music. I don't remember exactly how the conversation went, but one day I just sort of announced to Karyn, "We need to move to Nashville." Karyn and I had been in our house less than two years, and we moved into it after losing a lot of money on our house in Indianapolis. Even so, Karyn told me, "Okay. Whatever we have to do, I'm on board." I called my friend Jeremy and a couple of other people I knew in Nashville, and we started packing. I did not have any doubts about what we were doing. I fully expected to get to Nashville and carve out a successful career as a singer. Again, I had already done one album with a label. That alone set me apart from so many others who go to Music City with dreams of breaking into the music industry. I had already broken in. Now I hoped to break out.

•　　•　　•

However, before we moved to Tennessee I made one last attempt to resurrect my football career. In April I finally passed all five stages of the return-to-play protocol. Nearly nine months after my concussion I was able to go through strenuous workouts without recurring concussion symptoms. Officially, Dr. Cantu cleared me to play, although he and every doctor I had seen since August 5, 2009, told me I should never play again (although none of them told me I *couldn't* play). When my head pounded and my brain felt like sludge, I agreed with the doctors. But once the symptoms went away I had second thoughts about hanging it up. I also looked around at my life and I thought back to all my football dreams going back to college. Injuries always kept me from reaching my potential. I was healthy now after sitting out an entire year. *What if . . .* I wondered. I contacted my agent, Chris. "I still want to play," I told him.

"Are you sure, Ben?" he replied.

"I just can't walk away from the game like this," I said.

"Okay. I'll see what I can do," Chris said.

A couple of weeks later, right before the NFL draft, I flew back to Boston. This time, instead of visiting Dr. Cantu, I went out to Foxborough and tried out for the New England Patriots. Their team doctors put me through a physical, then they went through a long list of questions about my injury history, with, not surprisingly, a lot of questions about my concussions. Then I went out on the field and ran pass routes and went through agility drills and blocking drills and all the other drills teams use to evaluate talent. I felt like I killed the workout. I caught every ball they threw at me and my speed was right where it had always been. Afterward I met with their head of scouting and he was really encouraging.

That was the last I heard from the New England Patriots. If they had wanted to sign me, they would have called. They don't call when they don't want you. Ultimately, my concussion history proved to be too much for them. Instead of signing me, the Patriots drafted Rob Gronkowski, who developed into one of their most productive players. I think they made the right choice, for both of us. If I had sustained another concussion, who knows where I might be today. Yet at the time I was incredibly disappointed. I knew the end had come, but it was a hard pill to swallow. Just as injuries had kept me from really fulfilling my potential going back to my senior year of high school, an injury had now ended my career.

With my football career now officially over, I faced the daunting journey of redefining myself. I had played football at some level for nearly twenty years, and while I never thought of myself purely in terms of the game, it was always a huge part of who I was. When my family moved to Hastings when I was only ten, most of my new friendships started on the football field. In middle school and high school I played in the band and sang in school choirs and acted in nearly every school play, but my doing so stood out even more because I was one of the school's star athletes. Starting in college, football and my future went hand in hand. The game paid for my education and was my first job out of school. I was a Colt and a Super Bowl champ, then I became a Bengal.

And now . . . Who was I now?

I thought I might find the answer in Nashville. As soon as my tryout with the Patriots ended poorly, Karyn and I loaded up our stuff and headed south. We left Cincinnati so quickly we didn't have a place to stay. Thankfully our friends Jeremy and Adie opened up their home to us for a few months as we began looking for a rental house to call home. We learned our lesson in Indy and Cincinnati. Rather than buy, we planned on renting for a while to see how our life there might shake out.

A couple of months after our move to Nashville, Karyn and I were still staying with our friends. I stayed busy with demo tapes and making the rounds in town. Karyn wasn't feeling well. When she noticed the nausea felt a lot worse in the mornings, she bought a pregnancy test. All the bad feelings I had about my time in Cincinnati evaporated the moment she told me, "We're having another baby." I cannot tell you how excited I was to become a father again.

Shortly after we discovered Karyn was pregnant, she went to see her doctor. I was on the couch in the basement of our friends' home when she called.

"Hey, Karyn," I said.

"We're having two," Karyn said.

I sat there on the couch, my phone in my hand, unable to speak.

"Ben?" Karyn said. "Are you there?"

I was speechless. Finally, after more awkward silence I managed to say, "Two?"

"Yes, two as in twins," Karyn said.

More stunned silence followed on my end. "Twins?" I said at long last. "How is that scientifically possible? We have zero history of twins on either side of our family."

"I don't know," Karyn replied. "The doctor didn't explain how it happened. She just said we have twins on the way."

"Wow," I said. It wasn't that I wasn't excited by the news. I was. I was just in shock. However, once the shock wore off and the reality settled in that we were going to go from man-to-man to zone coverage in one pregnancy, we both became very excited. We felt like these two little babies were a special gift from God, a confirmation that the timing of our pregnancy was ordained. Both Karyn and I believed that this news signaled a true fresh start for us.

I had felt such a huge weight on my shoulders when we moved to Nashville. I didn't know if the transition from football to music was going to work out. I didn't know if or when the grievance I filed might be settled. The future looked so unsettled. And yet, God had decided to bless us with two new babies. That gift told us that God didn't feel apprehensive about our future. Like my mother had told me so many years before, when I suffered my first injury in a football game, I just needed to trust the Lord. He was going to take care of the rest.

CHAPTER 20

BACK INTO THE JUNGLE

KARYN AND I MOVED TO NASHVILLE to get a fresh start. I was trying to find myself, to redefine myself, find my identity. All of my life I had been a standout athlete. That life was over. It was time to start anew.

However, a few months after diving into my new life I had to return to Cincinnati to try to bring closure to my old. The grievance I had filed against the Bengals had yet to be resolved. Since the day we filed the grievance on December 1, 2009, I spoke daily either to Tim English, the NFLPA attorney in charge of my case, or Scott Hillstrom, my personal attorney, or my agent, Chris Murray. A lot of days I called all three. I was very nervous about how this was going to play out. When I was first cut I thought my case could be resolved very quickly. The way Tim English explained it to me, the CBA left little room for interpretation. Hurt players on the IR who have not recovered to the point where they can perform all the usual moves and actions required of their playing positions cannot be cut. End of story. But now, nearly one year after my injury and seven and a half months after filing my grievance, we were no closer to a resolution.

I hoped the grievance hearing in Cincinnati might finally settle this thing once and for all. I drove up to Cincinnati the day before the hearing and spent the night in a hotel. The next morning, July 13, 2010, I got up early and met Tim for breakfast. When the two of us sat down, his first question was, "How are you doing, Ben?"

"I'm nervous," I said.

Tim smiled. "I understand that. You don't need to be." He then gave me a rundown of how the hearing was going to play out and what I could expect from both the NFL's attorneys and from the arbitrator. "The arbitrator's name is Richard Kasher. He's from Pennsylvania. He has a strong résumé. He's even been appointed to serve on boards by more than one president."

I was impressed, but still nervous.

We left breakfast together and headed over to Paul Brown Stadium, where the hearing was to be held. Pulling up in front of the stadium for the first time as a non–football player felt very strange. Not only was I not a Bengal, I was going up against the team. I didn't know how I might be received. In my time in Cincinnati I had enjoyed a good relationship with everyone in the Bengals' organization, or at least I did until November 18, 2009. As I wrote before, football teams have a family feel to them. From the coaching staff to the general manager's office, all the way up to the owner, the entire organization tries to create a sense of oneness, like we are all working toward a common goal and have one another's best interests at heart. That relationship extends to the players' and coaches' families. Karyn had developed a friendship with owner Mike Brown's daughter, Katie Blackburn. Karyn and Katie played golf together while I was with the team. All the "family" connections gave the grievance hearing the feel of a divorce proceeding. No wonder I felt so uncomfortable walking through the main doors of the stadium office area.

The NFL's lawyer greeted Tim and me as soon as we walked in. Katie Blackburn also came over and said hello and asked about my family. I saw one or two other Bengals staff members who asked about my health in a way that seemed to suggest they were genuinely concerned about me. Everyone seemed so cordial and kind. I started to think my apprehensions were misguided.

And then the hearing started.

The conference room where the hearing took place looked and felt like a miniature *Law & Order* set. The arbitrator sat at the end of a large conference table, while the lawyers from the two sides sat opposite each other. A courtroom stenographer sat off to one side, typing out everything that was said.

I was one of the first witnesses called to testify. I do not remember the specific questions the NFL attorneys fired at me, but I clearly recall the overall direction of their questioning. Specifically, they asked about my return-to-play workout and rehabilitation program. Their questions and the way they asked them implied I was able to do much more than I let on. They also seized on my concussion symptoms journal. One of the lawyers read specific passages out of it, then asked questions about why I wrote what I did. They challenged the accuracy of my record and suggested that I exaggerated my symptoms. In short, they all but accused me of lying about being hurt. All my life I've tried to live with honesty and integrity. To have that challenged, well, it ticked me off. However, I didn't lash out. I answered every question and simply told the truth.

I didn't have to defend myself because even the members of the Bengals staff testified at depositions verifying my character. The team's sport psychologist, Peter Ganshirt, had testified that I was "absolutely truthful and honest." Even Tom Sullivan, the team's neuropsychologist, who had cleared me to play (without telling me, I might add), had testified, "I can't imagine Ben Utecht lying. . . . Ben is a very credible person." I don't think the team lawyer asking the questions appreciated those answers since part of the team's defense hung on their trying to prove that I did not give an accurate account of my condition. I guess they believed I was faking my headaches and sensitivity to light and memory lapses and all the rest.

Both the team attorney and Tim English called a variety of witnesses, either at the hearing or by using their deposition testimony, who were connected to the team. Of all of them, I found Sullivan's testimony to be the most interesting. After all, he was the one who cleared me to return to full football activities, which opened the door for the team to cut me. Keep in mind, he is not a medical doctor. Nor did we believe he should have been the one to make the decision about my returning to play. The NFL issued a memo on November 24, 2009, less than one week after my release, where they said any player diagnosed with a concussion could not return to play until they had been evaluated and cleared by the team physician and by an independent physician who would be an "outstanding local neurosurgeon or neurologist." Maybe that's why the team moved so quickly in cutting me when they did. Maybe they knew a change was coming and they wanted to get me out before the new guidelines were adopted. I don't know this to be true. It's merely a guess on my part, but the timing sure looks suspicious.

During his cross-examination of Sullivan at his deposition, Tim English focused his questions on how and why Sullivan cleared me to play. In his last evaluation of me, Sullivan wrote in his official report that I "should no longer be excluded from typical activities as a professional football player." However, in the very same report Sullivan wrote that it would be ill-advised for me to return to playing competitive football. Those two statements certainly seemed inconsistent, which is why Tim English went right to the heart of what Sullivan meant by "typical activities as a professional football player." He asked, "Let's take a player in Ben's situation. If instead of releasing Ben . . . you said, okay, Ben is ready to begin participating in routine football activities—"

"He *was* doing routine football activities," Sullivan interrupted.

"Like what?"

"Doing weights and aerobic activities," Sullivan replied.

When Tim pressed the questions, Sullivan admitted that he had no idea what kind of "weights and aerobic activities" football players even did. He said it was "[n]ot my thing." What was confusing to me was the question of how I could be cleared to perform "football activities" when the person clearing me didn't even know what those "activities" were. Even though Sullivan's decision was confusing to me, I do believe he operated in his own personal good faith.

The real issue behind my case, and this only became clear with time, was the nature of my injury. If I had blown out my knee, an MRI would have revealed the extent of the damage. A surgeon could then have gone in and fixed it. Because knee injuries are so common in football, teams know how long it takes someone to come back. Again, you can take another MRI to see how the healing process is coming along.

But concussions are not like that. They often don't show up on MRIs or X-rays or CT scans. In spite of the years of research that had been done into this field, the NFL still calls this an emerging science with much to be learned. Through 2004 and 2005 the NFL's concussion committee churned out one paper after another that said concussed players could safely return to play in the same game in which the injury took place, even if they had lost consciousness.* For years they also claimed that the link between blows to the head and long-term brain problems is not conclusively established.

In the midst of all of this, I found myself on IR with a concussion whose symptoms refused to go away. My case challenged everything the NFL had said about concussions prior to the No-

---

* Fainaru-Wada and Fainaru, *League of Denial,* Kindle ed., locs. 3150–51.

vember 24, 2009, memo. Even with that, the league did not want to admit the seriousness of injuries like mine, or their long-term implications both for players like me and the league as a whole. I believe that is why my case was moving so slowly. I was on the leading edge of a massive shift in the way football deals with head injuries.

When the one-day hearing ended, I thanked Tim for fighting so hard for me and asked how long he thought it might be before the arbitrator rendered his decision. "That's hard to say," Tim cautioned me. "We still have several more people to question through depositions, including Dr. Cantu and the neutral doctors who examined you. That's going to take a few months. Once we have all the testimonies in, both sides will file briefs arguing for our sides of the question. Once all of that is in it will still probably take three to six months to get a decision."

"So it's going to take a while," I said with a sigh.

"Hang in there, Ben," Tim said with a smile. "You're not in this alone. The players association is going to do everything we can to get justice for you."

All of the testimony from the hearing ran through my head throughout the three-hundred-mile drive back to Nashville. Once I arrived at our home in Franklin, Tennessee, just south of the city, I had to try to focus on more than the grievance. Karyn and I had found the perfect rental home, but we had a lot of work to do before our twins arrived. We thought for sure the twins would be fraternal and we hoped for a boy and a girl. But, with all the work involved with preparing for twins, we had an ultrasound that showed we were having two little girls. I couldn't have been more excited. With one baby girl already, I felt confident I knew what to expect with more daughters.

Finally having a place of our own after spending three months in our friends' basement gave us a sense of belonging in our new hometown. Karyn immediately connected with our neighbors Winston and Rachel, who became lifelong friends. Between preparing for twins, which was going to give us three children under the age of two, and laying the groundwork for a life in music, I stayed really busy. The grievance was never far from my mind, especially late at night, but life kept me so busy that I could not obsess on it. During this period I did not notice any new memory gaps, although I continued to have some short-term memory issues. Most of these I chalked up to the unfamiliarity of a new city. Soon I had something much bigger to worry about.

During Karyn's twenty-week OB appointment, an ultrasound revealed a problem with our twins. The doctor diagnosed them with twin-to-twin transfusion syndrome. The condition only affects identical twins, and even then it is quite rare. Identical twins share a common placenta. However, in cases of TTTS, the blood vessels become intertwined, causing blood to be transfused disproportionally from one twin to the other. In some cases the condition causes the death of both babies. When Karyn told me what the doctor had said, she included his warning. "She told me not to go home and research it," she told me. "I don't know what to do."

"Why can't we research it?" I asked.

"She said the treatments are all risky and that researching it will only make me more worried than I should be."

Both of us felt completely out of control. The fact that we were having twins already made Karyn's pregnancy high risk. The TTTS took the risk to an even higher level. I noticed over the next few weeks that the diagnosis had an impact on my wife's spirit. I tried very hard to stay positive and encouraging for her, but it wasn't working. About all I could do was pray for her and our babies.

A few weeks after the diagnosis Karyn felt almost overwhelmed by what we faced. One afternoon she placed her hands on her stomach and started pouring out her heart to God. "Please,

God, protect my precious babies," she pleaded. All of a sudden a blanket of peace settled over her, so much so that she drifted off to sleep in the middle of the day. About an hour later she was suddenly awakened by a literal popping in her stomach. I wasn't home at the time. Later she told me she could both feel and hear the sensation, yet she knew it wasn't a bad thing. Nothing was going wrong inside her. Instead she felt an overwhelming reassurance that her prayers had been answered.

Karyn managed to carry our twins to one day short of thirty-six weeks, which was a miracle in itself. The typical gestation period for TTTS babies is between eighteen and thirty weeks. Every day the girls stayed in utero increased their chances of coming into the world without complications. We spent those weeks getting their room ready and picking out the perfect names. After much back-and-forth, we first picked the name Katriel, a Hebrew name that means "God is my crown." For our second, we decided to name the smaller of the two babies after my aunt Amy, who was never able to have children of her own due to a battle with breast cancer, a battle she won. The doctors warned us ahead of time that the smaller twin might have a harder time initially, so it just seemed right to name our little girl after a fighter like Aunt Amy. Her full name is Amy Joan. Joan is my grandmother's name. The feminine of John and means "Gift of God."

Karyn's doctors kept a very close eye on the twins. When we got to thirty-five weeks they informed us it was time. On November 9, 2010, we checked into the hospital and they induced labor. Even with twins Karyn hoped to deliver the girls naturally. However, for the second time the fetal monitor lost one of the girls' heartbeats during a contraction. Our room filled up with every doctor and nurse in the hospital, or at least it felt like it. In a flash they had Karyn disconnected from the monitors and sprinted her bed down the hallway to the operating room for an emergency C-section. I ran alongside her, saying over and over, "It's going to be okay. Our girls will be fine. You will see."

Once we reached the doors of the OR, the staff rushed Karyn through and the doors slammed in my face. Standing alone in the hallway, my thoughts went where I guess everyone's go in a moment like that. I could not help but see the worst-case scenario coming true. The high-risk pregnancy, the TTTS, and now no heartbeat, I couldn't help myself.

A few minutes later a nurse came out. "Come with me," she said. She escorted me into the OR, where she positioned me directly behind Karyn's head. A medical blanket kept me from seeing what the doctors were doing. All through the procedure I looked down into my wife's eyes. Tears streamed down her face. She was heartbroken that she could not have the girls naturally and scared to death of what might happen. I stroked her hair and whispered softly, "The girls will be okay. They need to get the girls out fast and this is the best way. Let's just trust the Lord on this. He will carry us through." I then told her how beautiful she was and how much I loved her.

A baby's cry filled the room. Karyn and I locked eyes. Both of us were so excited, yet we held our breath, waiting for the second cry. When it came I leaned down and kissed Karyn softly on the forehead. We were both so relieved.

I did not get to hold either of my daughters in the operating room. Katriel had a minor breathing issue and they whisked her away very quickly. It did not take them long to resolve it. I held both girls for the first time in the viewing room. They seemed so tiny and fragile, although, for twins born at thirty-six weeks, their sizes were actually very good. Katriel entered the world at six pounds, seven ounces, while Amy Joan was a whopping four pounds, eleven ounces. They looked very, very small in my arms.

• • •

It didn't take us long to figure out life with twin baby girls and another daughter under the age of two was not for the faint of heart. Between the sleepless nights and constant drain on Karyn of breastfeeding two babies at the same time, we adopted a rule in the house that whatever is said between midnight and 6:00 a.m. doesn't count. The twins had different schedules, which pushed us to the limit. Okay, if I am being completely honest, they first pushed Karyn to her limit, because I thought I could sit back and help from a distance.

One night the twins were wide awake, crying, each demanding different things. "Ben," Karyn said to me, "I need some help."

"Okay," I said, half-awake, from the bed. Then I did the most helpful thing I could think of. I raised up slightly and shushed the girls from the bed. After accomplishing such an important job, I fell back down and nodded back off to sleep.

"Ben! Don't you hear the girls? I need your help."

Startled, I sat back up. "Okay, okay, okay." Then I shushed the girls again.

Finally Karyn looked over at me and dropped a verbal bomb with words I had never heard come out of my wife's mouth before or since. I shot out of bed, grabbed a twin, and then looked over at Karyn as if to say, "Whatever you need, I'll do it." She looked back at me and just started laughing, as did I.

The next morning, neither of us said a word about the incident. After all, when you have twin babies, whatever is said between midnight and 6:00 a.m. doesn't count.

CHAPTER 21

"WHY WASN'T I INVITED?"

MY POSTFOOTBALL IDENTITY CRISIS DID NOT resolve itself when we moved to Nashville. Yes, we moved to Music City for me to pursue a full-time career in music. However, when I declared myself a musician and singer as opposed to a football player, I faced another question: Who am I as an artist? As I transitioned from Indianapolis to Cincinnati I recorded my first album for the contemporary Christian market. It had more of a pop-worship style. While I was in Cincinnati I got to know Paul McCready from the Cincinnati Music Academy. Paul became my vocal coach and really transformed my voice to a level I had never achieved before. The training also revived my passion for the classical side of my training. Yet that wasn't the style of music on the album I recorded and released. All of that brought me back to the question of who I was as an artist.

Right before we moved to Nashville I thought I had my answer. I had a vision of creating a pop-classical style where I incorporated my big voice with string instrumentation. In a way, I really saw myself in the vein of Josh Groban. I believed this was a way I could carve out a niche for myself while also moving into the mainstream music market.

The first few months after we moved to Nashville I started

working to make my vision a reality. I sat down and started writing songs. Then I invested more than I should have into creating a four-song demo album. I hired actual string musicians, as opposed to creating something on a keyboard, and also brought in one of the best string arrangers in Nashville, David Hamilton. Because this EP was basically my demo CD for all the labels in town, I hired some of the best mixers available, and produced what I felt like was an incredible set of music. I loved the finished product. The songs hit exactly the target at which I aimed.

Then I started taking the songs around town to all the labels. I didn't have much trouble getting people to listen to them. However, the response was not what I had expected. Every single label came back and said, "Great voice. Big voice. I don't get it." I quickly learned how little I knew about the music industry. Everything, no matter what the genre, is driven by radio. The pop-classical style I hoped to master isn't exactly burning up the airwaves. The whole thing blew up in my face. I thought I could become the next Josh Groban, only to discover that one Groban is enough.

However, the story does not end there.

In early spring of 2011, I flew out to New York for a gig at a jazz club. While in town I reconnected with my good friend Steven Reineke, the music director and conductor for the New York Pops. The two of us had gotten to know one another when Steven was with the Cincinnati Pops. I brought one of my EPs for Steven. By this point I was handing them out to anyone and everyone.

Steven had invited me over for drinks. He also said, "I have someone in town I want you to meet."

"Okay," I said, "who?"

"Jim Brickman," Steven replied.

"The piano player?" I asked. That's an understatement. Jim Brickman is one of the most accomplished adult contemporary musicians of all time, with multiple gold and platinum albums to his credit.

"That's him," Steven said.

Later that evening Jim came over to Steven's apartment. Steven had more in mind than simply introducing me to one of his friends. He had me play Jim the demo EP I had created. When the music first started the look on Jim's face told me he had trouble believing this sound came out of a football player. "This is really good," Jim said. "I like it a lot."

"Would you like for me to sing something live for you now?" I asked. Steven had a beautiful piano in his apartment just for moments like this.

"Sure. What do you know?" Jim replied.

"'What about that Italian song you've been doing on tour with your current male vocalist? The song 'Caruso'?"

"But that's in Italian," Jim said.

"That's all right. If you will play it, I'll sing it for you."

He did and I did. This impromptu audition resulted in a phone call a week or so later from Jim, inviting me to come to his studio in Cleveland for a formal tryout. Even though it was early spring, he was already finalizing plans for his next Christmas tour. While in Cleveland I was introduced to his longtime female vocalist, Anne Cochran. If I landed a spot on his tour, Anne and I would sing together.

The audition went better than I could have ever dreamed. Not only did Jim hire me to tour with him on his next holiday tour; I also got to cut a holiday album for the tour. I stuck with the pop-classical style for the album, even going so far as to release it under my full name, Benjamin Utecht. "Benjamin" has a more classical sound than "Ben." A side note on the album: it received a Dove Award nomination for holiday album of the year. I was very proud of how it turned out.

Preparation for the tour hit high gear that summer. Karyn and I talked about what it was going to be like for me to go out and perform thirty-two shows in thirty cities during the holiday season. The prospect of her trying to hold the household together, alone, with three very small daughters did not thrill her. However, she was very supportive of me. "I think it's a great idea that you do the tour. But we need help with the girls, Ben," she said to me one night. "We should move home."

By home, she meant Minneapolis. We'd always talked about moving back close to our families, but up until this point the two of us had moved around chasing my career. "But what about my music?" I said.

"You don't have to be here to be successful. I talked to Jeremy and Adie about it. A lot of successful artists do not live in Nashville. Sandi doesn't," Karyn said.

I thought about the upcoming tour and what was going to be best for the family while I was away. I also thought about where I wanted our daughters to grow up. Both Karyn and I had always wanted our children to have a close relationship with their grandparents. That's hard to do when you live more than nine hundred miles away. "Okay. I think you're right," I said.

That summer, the summer of 2011, Karyn and I packed up all our things once again and bought a home just outside the Twin Cities. The move came in the midst of my recording my album and preparing for the upcoming tour. Looking back, that summer, like much of our time in Nashville, is a blur. I think that's why I didn't panic when I had trouble learning all the songs I was to sing on tour. We had so much going on that I couldn't really concentrate and focus. At least that's what I told myself. Everything would be better once we got in the new house and got settled.

Not long after we moved back to Minnesota, Karyn, the girls, and I went to see our good friends Matt and Kim Anderle. Matt and I were teammates and roommates at Minnesota. We hadn't been able to spend much time with Matt and Kim since we graduated, but they're the kind of friends where you can go ten years without seeing them and when you get back together it's like you have never been apart. We had so much fun that evening. All of us sat in Matt and Kim's kitchen, sharing stories and laughing.

The night, however, turned when during our conversation Matt said something about their wedding. "Oh my gosh, I want to hear all about it," Karyn said. Matt started telling stories, with Kim giving commentary. With each one Karyn laughed and smiled. The conversation kept going, with Matt and Kim going back and forth, adding little details to which the other replied, "Oh that was great," or "I almost forgot that!"

I sat there in shock. With each story I kept wondering why I had not been a part of it. Matt and I have been close for years, and yet he didn't think enough of me to invite me to his own wedding? I invited him to my wedding. How could he not return the favor? I know my schedule can get a little crazy, but Matt and I are close. I don't care what I had going on, I would have certainly made time to be there.

As I listened to the conversation I went from being annoyed to downright angry. Finally I'd had enough. I stopped Matt in the middle of one of his stories and asked, "Why didn't you invite me?"

He looked at me awkwardly, paused for a moment to acknowledge my sarcasm, then went back to telling his story.

"No, Matt, I mean it," I interrupted again. "I don't care what I had going on, I would have found a way to be there. How could you not have invited me to your wedding after all we've been through together?"

Matt, Kim, and Karyn stopped talking and stared at me as if they were waiting for me to bust out laughing. I didn't feel like laughing. This was no joke. "When was it? Surely I wasn't busy," I said.

No one said a word. After more awkward silence Kim got

up, walked over to a table, and picked up their wedding album. "You're right there, Ben," she said, pointing to a photo of Matt and his groomsmen. She was right. There I was, right in the middle of them all, wearing a matching tux. "And there . . . and there . . . and there," she said, turning page after page.

"You weren't just a groomsman," Matt said. "You sang for us. Don't you remember?"

I didn't know what to say. I scoured the farthest reaches of my mind and nothing came up. I had absolutely no memory of the day. None. Seeing the photos didn't nudge faint recollections of the wedding. I didn't have an "Oh, yeah, now I remember" moment. I felt like an excavator had come in, dug up every trace of the memory, filled in the hole, and planted grass on top to make it appear as though it had never been there. For me, it never had. The face in the photos looked like me, but it might as well have been someone else, someone long gone.

This little episode pretty much put an end to our fun that night. Matt and Kim and even Karyn looked at me a little differently, like I was somehow now fragile and broken. They hesitated to share any stories not only about their wedding but also about any of the good times we had had together. No one wanted a repeat of what had just happened. Neither did I.

The ride home was more than a little awkward. This was the first time that the realization hit both Karyn and me that something was wrong with me. Up until this moment I did not share a lot of what was going on with my memory problems with her. I didn't want to burden her with it. Now we both had no choice. I wasn't just a little bit forgetful. My brain had changed. Memories had been erased and weren't coming back. I was frightened. I wondered how many more might be gone.

A couple of weeks later I had another episode. I had a business breakfast meeting planned, which I was going to host. On the day of the event I got the girls up and rushed them around getting ready. Karyn and I ran around getting all the food ready, cleaning the house, and everything else you have to do to get a home with three very young children ready to host guests. I thought the meeting was going to start at nine. We had the girls dressed in their Sunday best, ready to make a good impression.

Nine o'clock came and went, and no one pulled into the driveway. Nine fifteen passed. Nine thirty came and went. Karyn finally said to me, "Double-check your email. Maybe we have the wrong time written down."

I pulled up my email. At the top of the list was one from the day before. It read, "Writing to confirm our conversation from earlier today that we are cancelling tomorrow's meeting." I'd read the email. I'd had the conversation. But I had no memory of either. Like Matt's wedding, every memory of what I imagine was a long conversation had completely disappeared. I could not ignore this any longer.

In late fall I had to leave home for six weeks for the Jim Brickman tour. We dove headlong into rehearsals, but I quickly noticed another problem. I could not remember the song lyrics. I'd worked on learning them all summer long, and some of the songs were old, familiar Christmas songs I'd sung my whole life. Yet in the middle of a verse I found words suddenly escaped me. You might be able to fake it by mouthing "Watermelon, watermelon" when you are in a large choir, but that wasn't going to work onstage, alone or in a duet, in front of thousands of people.

I doubled my efforts to learn the song lyrics, but gaps kept showing up. Jim and Anne were both gracious with me, but I could tell it was concerning at times. Finally, I wrote out large-print copies of some of the lyrics and taped them to the stage floor. I did this in rehearsals and for many of the shows I performed on the tour. It was the only way I could get through them.

In spite of my frustrations with the song lyrics, I loved being on tour. We hit a city a few hours before the show, ran through a quick rehearsal, then geared up for the night's performance. Every night before I went out onstage I went through a set of "pregame" warm-ups. Believe it or not, I did many of the same warm-ups I did before a football game. I jumped up and down and kicked my legs in the air. I may have even let out a primordial grunt or two. To me, the adrenaline rush and excitement felt the same. I went out onstage ready to compete. If a linebacker had cut in front of the drums, I would have plowed right into him. Concert night felt like game day. I felt I could have hit somebody with a football move.

As soon as the show was over we all piled on the bus and hung out for a bit before heading to the next city. Everyone slept on the bus as we traveled through the night from Syracuse, New York, to Burlington, Vermont, or from Burlington down to Washington, D.C. Tour buses have small, built-in sleeping quarters, which are basically three-sided coffins in the sides of the bus. From end to end the bunk is six feet, six inches long. Cramming my six-foot-seven frame into that space wasn't easy, but I never minded. I slept like a baby on the bus. All my life I had dreamed of becoming a professional musician. Now I was living my dream.

As part of the promotion of the tour, I hired my own public relations firm to set up press opportunities in each city ahead of us. They passed out press releases to the local media and tried to create a buzz for the show and for the artists performing. Keep in mind that at this point I was looking at making this a career. The holiday tour was, I hoped, just the first step into this life full-time. In D.C. the PR firm connected me with a reporter from *USA Today*, Erik Brady. The story of the singing Super Bowl champion intrigued Erik, which brought him out to interview me. However, the story soon stopped being merely about the singing Super Bowl champion. I opened up to Erik about my concussion story and my battles with memory loss. It resonated with him. He also interviewed Jim and Anne and others connected with the tour as part of writing the story. On December 21, 2011, Erik's feature article about me appeared on the front page of the *USA Today* sports section. I had now gone public in a really big way with my story. I did not yet know it, but the *USA Today* feature would prove to be the launch of something much bigger than I ever imagined possible.

The tour continued through the holidays. I loved it. I invited Karyn and the girls to come join me for a few days toward the end of the tour. Having them there was, to put it mildly, a disaster. Tour buses and jumping from city to city don't really work with twin one-year-olds and a not-yet three-year-old. Karyn was miserable, which made me miserable. I had hoped they could come and share the joy of this new stage in my career. Instead, Karyn and I had one of the worst fights of our marriage. "I can't believe you would choose this over us," she said to me.

"I'm not. I'm doing this for us."

"Are you sure, Ben? Are you sure?"

There was more said than just that, but that gives you an idea of the point of it. Singing for a living may have been the life I had dreamed of since I was a teenage boy singing in the high school choir, but this wasn't the life my wife imagined when we started a family of our own. Clearly, something was going to have to give.

CHAPTER 22

SURRENDER

I WOKE UP LATE ONE MORNING. The sound of little girls laughing and squealing echoed up from downstairs. I didn't move. I couldn't. The Brickman tour had ended a few months earlier, after which I came home to Minnesota. Karyn, the girls, and I settled into our dream home. Both sets of grandparents lived fairly close by, which meant the girls got to see them whenever they wanted. That's what Karyn and I had always wanted. This house was what we had always wanted as well. I should have been up and happy.

Instead I couldn't get out of bed.

I thought the Brickman tour might open new doors, and I almost landed a contract with a label soon after, but the deal fell through. A career in music now felt a long ways away—around nine hundred miles away. Rightly or wrongly, I felt like when I left Nashville I left my dream behind. When we lived there I kept myself busy working on my EP, then trying to sell it to every label in town. About the time I gave up on the EP, Jim Brickman had entered the picture. I spent my last few months in Tennessee in the studio, working on my album *Christmas Hope*, which was followed by breakneck preparation for the tour.

But all that was over now. I was label-less.

Jobless.

Worthless.

I rolled over and stared out the window. *What's the point?*
I asked myself. *What's the point of getting out of bed, of doing
anything beyond lying here hoping it all goes away?* I heard my
now three-year-old yelling something at her little sisters. Sounds
of "Mooooommmmm" filled the air below. I just lay where I was.
Karyn probably needed some reinforcements. I should have been
the cavalry riding down the stairs to the rescue. Instead I stared
out the window.

Part of me screamed, "Get up!" I'd never been this guy before. I'd never battled emptiness and hopelessness. Now they
defined me. Maybe what I felt was the normal letdown from the
end of the tour. Thirty-two shows in thirty cities with only one day
off through it all. That much adrenaline can be addictive. Yeah,
maybe that's why I couldn't force myself out of bed.

Or maybe it was the disappointment of not landing the deal
with the new label. The negotiations had gone very well. I thought
for sure we were going to sign. My dream felt right there, only to
fall away. Anyone would be depressed after seeing their dream
escape their grasp. Yeah, maybe that's why I spent so much time
in bed in a fog.

Or maybe it was the fact that nearly two and a half years had
passed since I filed my grievance against the Bengals and I was
still no closer to getting the nearly $1 million the team owed me.
After the hearing, which was a year ago, Tim English told me
they still had to take depositions of other witnesses before the
arbitrator could make his decision. All of the depositions were
completed by late fall 2010. Tim filed our brief with the arbitrator
in late February 2011. The brief summarized all the evidence in
my case in my favor as well as offered counterarguments to the
evidence presented by the team and the NFL. In the letter that
accompanied the copy Tim sent me, he told me to expect a deci-

sion in three to six months. More than a year had passed and still no ruling had been given. About three months after I received the brief I started calling Tim to ask if he'd heard anything. The calls continued on a weekly basis. Twice we were told the arbitrator had suffered different medical emergencies, which was the official explanation for the delay. Nothing could explain why it was now taking so long. I started to think that I was never going to see a dime of that money I had counted on for my family's future. Football had taken my memories and now it was going to take away my family's financial security. Yeah, that's why I was depressed. Who could blame me?

Or maybe the reason I didn't get out of bed was that I didn't want to. I had no energy, no purpose, no sense of anything mattering much right at that moment. I just wanted to lie there and hope the world disappeared.

Karyn came upstairs and stuck her head in the door, very quietly. "Are you awake?" she said in a near whisper.

"Yeah," I said.

"Are you going to come downstairs soon? The girls want you."

"I don't know. Maybe. I don't know." I kept staring out the window. My daughters' voices echoed into the room. I tried to muster up the energy to move. Eventually I did, but not before I lay in my bed for another hour, maybe longer, just staring out the window, trying to pull myself together.

I had never struggled with depression in my life other than a brief period in October and November 2009. Back then doctors told me concussions might be connected to depression and changes in behavior. After we settled into life back in Minnesota I found myself struggling again. I couldn't help but wonder, *Is this going to be the new normal? Did the concussions also do this to me?*

I knew other former NFL players battled debilitating depression along with memory loss and mood and personality changes, all caused by concussive and nonconcussive blows to the head. Not long after my grievance hearing in July 2010 I started researching the effects of concussions on other players. I googled CTE, the brain disease Dr. Bennet Omalu discovered in former players who died young, many by suicide. I watched former Pittsburgh Steelers legend Mike Webster's rambling, nearly incoherent interviews on YouTube. His story ended with him dying at the age of fifty after living in his pickup truck because of the mental haze in which he lived. I also read stories of Andre Waters, Terry Long, and Justin Strzelczyk, former players whose stories were later a key part of the movie *Concussion*. They all died young and tragically after suffering with memory problems and alarming behavior changes. One died in a fiery car crash when he drove his truck the wrong way down an interstate highway and collided with a tanker truck. Another took his own life by shooting himself in the chest. He did not shoot himself in the head, so that his brain could be tested for CTE. Another died by downing a gallon of antifreeze. As I read their stories, all I could think was, *Is that going to be me? Am I doomed to the same fate as all these other players?*

On one of these dark days I managed to force myself downstairs and started engaging with my daughters. I felt better. The fog cleared somewhat. I felt more like the old Ben. At the time we were trying to potty-train Elleora, which, as any parent will tell you, can be a frustrating experience for both parent and child. Elleora was nearly four and a little behind schedule because she had some digestive issues that made going number two painful. Karyn asked me to take Elleora to the bathroom and see if she would do anything. "Sure," I said. Reaching down, I took my daughter by the hand, "Come on, sweetheart. Let's go potty." Yes, we parents are reduced to saying words like *potty*.

I put Elleora on the toilet while I sat down on the edge of the bathtub. After a couple of seconds she announced, "I'm done."

"Did you do anything?" I asked.

"I don't need to go potty," she said.

"You need to try. Sit there until you do," I said.

"I can't," she said with a frown.

"Yeah, you can, honey. You need to try a little longer."

"I don't need to go. I can't go." Elleora's voice was almost a cry by this point.

"I don't care," I said, anger rising in my voice. I stood up, stretching my entire six-seven frame above her. "You are going to sit here until you go. DO YOU UNDERSTAND ME?!"

Elleora started to cry but I wasn't moved. Anger took over. It's hard to remember but I think for the next forty-five minutes I stood there, towering over her, waiting for her to do what she was supposed to do.

"Please, Daddy!" she finally cried. "Please! I don't need to go!"

I yelled back, "Don't you cry! YOU DO WHAT I TOLD YOU TO DO!"

At that moment I happened to glance toward the mirror. There I caught a glimpse of the angry monster I had become. All I could think was, *Is this who I am destined to be? Is this the man my daughter will remember all her life?* I immediately left the room even more frightened than my little girl.

Oh, God, help me. What is happening to me?

Shortly after the bathroom scene, Karyn took Elleora to see a doctor about her digestive issues. She asked Elleora, "What are you feeling when you have to go potty?"

Elleora responded, "Scared of Daddy."

When Karyn told me this I was crushed and broke down. From that moment I vowed that that monster would never return, and it hasn't. I've committed to try to never allow the effects of concussions to change my behavior. Even now as I look back at what happened, I think the thing that scares me most is how out of control I felt. It was as though I could not help myself. Something took over and I just went along for the ride. I wondered if this was the result of concussions. Was the outburst a symptom of potential CTE growing in my brain? Or was it simply the end result of all my frustrations, with Elleora unfortunately being at the wrong place when they all came pouring out? I still don't know. And it frightens me.

Something else happened that scared me as well. One night I was sitting down in my man cave in the basement of my house, watching ESPN *SportsCenter,* when a story broke from San Diego. Junior Seau, a legend of the game, a man I played against in the wars the Colts fought against the Patriots, had shot himself in the chest and died. The way he killed himself fit a growing pattern in former players. He shot himself in the chest so that his brain could be tested for CTE. According to the news reports, Junior Seau's behavior had changed over the previous few years. He separated himself from those who had known and loved him while also engaging in more and more risky behaviors. He'd always been a man who found great joy in life. Now he was dead by his own hand at the age of forty-three.

I sat and watched the story in stunned silence. I could still see him across from me in a game. For me, it was a huge honor just being on the same field as him. Everyone in the game had the greatest respect for him, not only because he was so talented but also because he played football with a youthful enthusiasm that marked his entire career. He played like he loved the game. Now he was dead. *Forty-three, he was only forty-three,* I repeated to myself over and over. *Is this me in ten years?* I wondered. *But he played twenty years,* I reminded myself. I now found myself hoping the injuries that cut my career short might have protected me from even greater brain damage. Even so, the story of Junior's death shook me. It shook everyone connected to the NFL. The thinking was, if it can happen to him, it can happen to any of us.

And of course, I discovered more missing memories. The story of Matt's wedding was the big turning point, but moving back to Minnesota, my land of memories, brought so much more to light. Writing this book has been one discovery of loss after another. Many of the most important stories you've read, including some key moments that shaped me as a man and in my faith, came from my mom and dad and Karyn, not me. I don't remember catching passes from my dad in the backyard when I was a boy. I also don't remember my mother running down on the field when I had my first injury and asking me, "Do you trust Jesus?" That question shaped this entire book, it has shaped my life, but I don't remember her asking it. I can't believe I don't. There have been more. It seems like with every chapter I call my coauthor and ask him, "Did that really happen? Was I there?" Now, I do not mean to imply that my entire mind has been wiped clean or that I remember nothing. I still have a vast treasure of memories to which I cling. But I don't know how many I have lost. Let's be real: how do you know when you have lost a memory? You can't.

In the months after the Brickman tour the new reality in which I now lived became very clear to me, along with growing fears about my future. I found myself in fear of losing all my memories, of waking up one day and not recognizing Karyn or Elleora or Katriel or Amy. The fear fed my depression, which fueled my frustration and my anger, and I knew I had to do something to break this cycle before I snapped. I had to decide how I was going to live with this.

Honestly, the easiest thing for me to do would have been to get really angry at football and the NFL and let that anger consume me. Some days that's exactly what happened to me, but at the end of the day getting mad didn't solve anything. Anger only made me more distant from my wife and daughters, and that's the last thing I wanted.

I also could have easily fallen into a victim's mind-set and found a way to blame every poor decision I made going forward on my brain injury and on football and on the doctors who let me keep playing when I probably shouldn't have. Nothing would be my fault. Playing the victim also meant I could feel sorry for myself without guilt. Poor, poor me. Why did this have to happen to me? Again, some days I feel like this, but I try to snap myself out of it as quickly as possible. Self-pity doesn't accomplish a thing.

Another option for me was to shrink back and try to hide and deny my problems. Few things are as uncomfortable as the looks I get from people when my memory fails me. When I played football, especially with my size, fans looked up at me in awe. Now I found people staring at me with a mixture of fear and pity. Honestly, hiding my problem sounded much better than enduring those looks.

As I wrestled with all these thoughts, I kept coming back to the question: Do you trust Jesus? As I seriously considered this question, my mind went back to the parade of injuries I suffered playing football, all the way back to that broken pelvis in high school. I've bruised or broken or somehow injured every part of my body, from the top of my head to the bottom of my feet. Every injury, every single one, always came at a time where my faith was put to the test. Now I found myself living with the lasting effects of the most serious of my injuries. If all the injuries leading up to this one were tests of my faith, why did I think God had any other purpose for this one as well?

Do I trust Him? I had to decide. The question is not do I trust Him to take my problems away. Both Karyn and I experienced what we can only describe as miracles, but those were rare and not something we believed we should expect God to deliver anytime we asked. Yes, I believe He can heal my brain, and believe me, I've asked Him to do so. But the real question I had to come to grips with was whether I will continue to trust Him even if my mind gets worse, not better. Am I willing to surrender my condition to Him and allow Him to use it however He thinks is best?

In the end I realized I had no other choice. No other option led me anywhere except back to my bedroom, huddled under the sheets, staring out the window, unable to move. *I surrender, Lord,* I prayed, *I give my brain injury over to You. Do with it whatever You think best.*

Something changed when I first prayed that prayer. I do not mean to imply I never struggled again and never had another day where I had trouble pulling myself out of bed. But when I surrendered my condition to God and gave Him permission to use it for His purposes, He set me free from the anger and self-pity that threatened to drown me. He also opened my eyes to the people and moments around me. I could not take anything for granted again. From that moment forward, every time I take my wife's hand I grab hold of the memory and treasure it. Every time I read a bedtime story to my girls or wrestle on the floor with them, I savor the moment. Yes, I might one day forget all of it. But, until I do, I will hold on to the memory as my greatest treasure.

I started forcing myself out of bed in the morning. I made a choice to start getting up before Karyn and the girls. Early in the morning I got up and went down into my office, which sits just off our living room. There I sat down in a big, comfortable chair, opened my Bible, and spent time alone with God. Not long after I got back into this habit, my door opened one morning. A little face peered around the corner. "Daddy?"

"Yes, Elleora."

"What are you doing?"

"Reading my Bible."

"Can I come in?"

"Of course."

The door opened a little wider. Elleora walked slowly in, still dressed in her pajamas. Her hair looked like she had just crawled out of bed. She came over close and I reached down and pulled her up on my lap. She laid her head on my chest and snuggled close. "After you finish reading the Bible would you read to me, too?" she asked.

"I sure will," I said as I wrapped my arms around her. "Do you want to pray with me first?"

"Okay," she said in that soft, little girl voice.

After we prayed I read a story to her. Then another. And another. Neither one of us was in a hurry to move. At one point she raised herself up and said, "Are you going to be in here tomorrow morning?"

"I sure am."

"Can I come back then and we do this again?"

Tears filled my eyes. "You sure can."

This is now our daily routine. I never take even one moment of it for granted. These are the memories I will treasure as long as I can.

CHAPTER 23

AT LONG LAST

In the spring of 2013 I laced up my cleats for the first time since my last play with the Bengals. The agent for MarQueis Gray, a star quarterback and wide receiver for the University of Minnesota Golden Gophers, called me and asked if I might be willing to work with MarQueis. Although he played wide receiver in college, all the scouts thought moving to tight end gave him his best chance to play in the NFL. "Would you come over, work out with him, and teach him the position?" they asked.

"I would love it," I said. I'd stayed in really good shape. The thought of going out on a football field again excited me.

However, the first time I put the cleats on and walked out on the U of M practice field, I got surprisingly emotional. I flashed back to when I was the star receiver with dreams of playing in the NFL. But I pulled myself out of that place when one of the coaches introduced me to MarQueis. "I grew up in Indianapolis," MarQueis said. "Man, I remember when you played for the Colts. Super Bowl champion. Wow. I really appreciate you coming out here and helping me out."

"My pleasure," I said. "Where in Indy did you go to high school?"

"Ben Davis," MarQueis said.

"Ben Davis. They always have great teams," I said.

"I was a quarterback then. Halfway through my time here they made me a wide receiver. Now I guess I'm going to become a tight end," he said with a laugh.

"I made the move from wide receiver to tight end," I said. "The biggest difference, besides the types of routes you run, is going to be the blocking. Let's get to work on that."

Over the next couple of months I worked with MarQueis several times a week. We focused primarily on the fundamentals of blocking. Throughout my career, both in college and the pros, I had some great teachers, especially in Indy with Howard Mudd. MarQueis caught on quickly because he's such a great athlete. I also went over some of the routes that tight ends run and wide receivers don't. He picked those up quickly, too. I didn't just tell him the routes. I ran them with him. Working with him got my competitive juices flowing, so we ended every workout with a catching competition. I never lost. Not even once. The coaches out on the field with us noticed. "Wow, Tech, you haven't lost a step," one said. "You still have those great hands. Man. You can catch anything," another said. I just grinned and took it all in. Honestly, it just felt good to be on the football field again.

After about a month of running routes and catching passes again, I started to wonder if I could still play at a high level. I was still only thirty-two. I hadn't played in four years, but I'd kept myself in great shape. *I wonder . . .* I kept thinking.

Then one evening I turned on *SportsCenter* and saw images of Patriots star tight end Aaron Hernandez being led away in handcuffs. The scroll across the bottom of the screen said, "Hernandez charged with murder." Aaron Hernandez was one of the two tight ends the Patriots drafted after I tried out for them in the spring of 2010. It was now June 2013. The draft had already passed. Most of the impact free agents on the market had already signed with other teams. That meant the Patriots were going to have to find another tight end, and fast.

The next morning I called my sports agent, Chris Murray. He hadn't heard from me since I retired except for the occasional call asking if he'd heard anything on my still-unresolved grievance. "Hey, Chris, Ben. Listen, I wonder if you would do me a favor. I just saw where Hernandez was arrested for murder. That means the Patriots need a tight end. Would you contact them for me and see if they are interested in having me come in for a tryout?"

A long pause followed. "Are you sure about this, Ben?" Chris asked with a very hesitant tone of voice.

"I think it's worth a phone call," I said.

"Okay," Chris said with the tone of a man being forced to do something against his will. "I don't want to put any time into this if you're going to change your mind. But if you are serious about it, I'll call."

"Great. Thanks," I said. After I hung up the phone I was immediately gripped with second thoughts. I knew the risks, but I also kept thinking about how I had never really reached my potential. Besides, the Patriots already had one star tight end. I wouldn't be the main guy. And the thought of catching balls from Tom Brady excited me. *Well, let's see if they're even interested before getting too worked up over it,* I told myself.

A week or two later Chris called. "I put out a feeler to the Patriots and a few other teams," he said. "The Patriots didn't show any interest, but the Seahawks did. They want to bring you out for a tryout if you are really interested."

"Seriously?" I said, surprised. "Okay, uh, let me talk to Karyn, then I'll let you know."

When I went to Karyn, I explained to her what was on my heart. "I think I will always be haunted by the fact that I never really reached my potential. Maybe this is my chance to do something about it," I said. Believe it or not, Karyn was open to my playing again because she never wanted to keep me from my pursuing my dreams. "But we should talk to your parents, too," she suggested.

I thought it a good idea. I called my mom and dad and they came over later that evening. Karyn and I sat them down and I told them the whole story. I explained how I had been working out with MarQueis Gray and how I still had the speed and the hands that made me successful the first time around. "The Seahawks are interested in me coming out for a workout," I said. "Pete Carroll seems to really be a players' coach, and they have an exciting young quarterback in Russell Wilson. I think it could be a good fit. So what do you think?"

My parents sat there without saying a word for several moments. They exchanged a glance, then my dad spoke up. "Ben, you are a grown-up man and I'm not going to try to tell you what to do. But, if you do this, because of your concussions, I will never watch you play. I will not watch a single game."

His response settled it. I called Chris. "Thanks for going to so much trouble, but I'm going to stay retired," I said. Football began with me and my dad in the backyard. His words that night ended any thoughts I had of making a comeback.

When I tell people this story they always ask how I could possibly even consider playing again after the toll concussions had already taken on me. I really cannot explain it. Sitting here, right now, typing this chapter, I can tell you that I am very glad I did not try to play again, even though if I had made the team, I would now have a second Super Bowl ring, since the Seahawks won it all that year. Even so, I know without a shadow of a doubt that I should never play again. I wish I had not played as long as I did. However, there's something about this game that just gets a hold of you and does not let go. It is violent and dangerous and takes an unbelievable toll on your body, but it is also a beautiful game that I love. Even with all it has cost me, I still love it, although I would probably never let my son play it, if I had a son. My girls better not even think about playing.

Around the time training camps opened in the summer of 2013, I went to a different kind of training camp, in Mount Laurel, New Jersey, just outside of Philadelphia. Every year the NFL holds a four-day broadcasting boot camp for players and former players interested in making the jump from the field to the broadcast booth. I signed up. What did I have to lose?

After the second or third day I went back to my hotel for the night. My cell phone rang. Tim English's name showed up on the caller ID. I let out a sigh before answering. Tim and I talked on a regular basis and the conversations always revolved around why the arbitrator in my grievance still had not delivered a decision. "Hey, Tim," I said without much enthusiasm.

"We won," he replied.

I could not believe my ears. "What?" I asked.

"We won, Ben. The arbitrator ruled in your favor. The Bengals have to pay you the rest of your contract for the 2009 season, with interest."

Tears filled my eyes. I could hardly hold myself together. "I can't believe it," I said.

"Believe it, buddy. This is a huge win. Enjoy it."

"Thank you so much, Tim. Thank you for fighting so hard for me. This never could have happened without you and the NFLPA," I said.

"That's why I do what I do," Tim replied. "This is a great moment for me, too. Congratulations, Ben."

I hung up the phone and lay back on the bed in shock. I'd waited for this day for three and a half years, and now that it was here I didn't know what I felt. After what seemed like hours but was probably only a few minutes, I called Karyn. "Tim called," I said. "We won."

Karyn reacted exactly the way I did when she called me to tell me we were having twins. After complete silence for a few moments I asked, "Are you there?"

"Yeah, I'm here. I just . . . I can't believe it."

"Believe it because we won!" The two of us then burst out laughing. "We actually won! It only took three years when it was supposed to take three months, but we won."

A check from the Cincinnati Bengals arrived in the mail soon after. The teller at my small Wells Fargo bank branch did a double take when I went in to deposit it. I should have told her I wanted to cash it, just to see her reaction.

My grievance settlement wasn't quite the victory it at first seemed, at least according to my personal attorney, Scott Hillstrom. According to Scott, my case posed a simple question: Can a player who has been taken out of play due to concussions be forced to choose between returning to play or being fired by his team when return to play might aggravate his brain injury or result in more severe brain injury due to past concussions? In other types of injuries a player cannot be "cleared" to return to play if play might aggravate his existing injury or result in a more severe one. Most injuries, like orthopedic injuries, for example, can be judged based on objective symptoms; there is not much room for disagreement when CT scans tell the story. But the existence or severity of a concussion, or the risk of aggravating one, or having a more severe one, cannot be judged objectively. Diagnostic and predictive tools are not very useful because concussions cannot be as easily seen as joint injuries or broken bones.

With that as the main question, several times in the years that I waited for a decision Scott explained that the arbitrator could decide in my favor, that I could not be forced to return to play, and would therefore win the grievance. Like a player with a shredded knee, I would then be entitled to remain on the injured reserve list and collect the balance of my contract without ever playing again. In this case, concussions would be viewed like any other severe injury, even though the diagnosis depended on more subjective symptoms.

Or, the second option was that the arbitrator could rule against me. That is, the arbitrator might say that I could be forced to return to play even though I ran a risk of aggravating the existing brain injury or putting myself at risk for a more severe injury. This would set a precedent that even in the presence of these risks a player could be forced to choose either his brain or his pay.

However, when Scott read the actual decision he realized the arbitrator in my case did not choose either of these options. Instead the arbitrator ruled that the Bengals should not have cleared me to play when they did because I "had not been sufficiently tested" both in my aerobic and strength reconditioning program. Nor had I been tested in sports-specific activities, which, according to the arbitrator, would have been a more accurate means of determining whether the damage caused by the concussion had been cleared. Scott believed that the NFL didn't want to get into the bigger and far more important question of whether a player susceptible to more concussions with even more severe consequences can be denied payment of his contract if he declines to take this risk.

Scott tried to make this final point clear when he drafted a joint statement for us to release with the NFLPA, announcing the settlement of our grievance. He included a line that said the arbitrator did not reach this ultimate question. That line did not appear in the final draft that was released to the press.

Less than a month after my case was settled, the NFL announced it had reached a settlement in the billion-dollar class action lawsuit thousands of former players had filed against the league regarding concussions. I wondered if the timing was just a coincidence.

With the grievance settled, and any doubts about my playing football again laid to rest, I turned my attention to going forward with life. New opportunities had opened up to me where I was able to speak out about brain injuries. Not long after the Jim Brickman holiday tour ended, a representative from the Minnesota Brain Injury Alliance called me. "Ben, we read the story about you in *USA Today* and we were touched by it. We're a group that advocates for people with brain injuries. We want to raise awareness about them and enhance the quality of life for all people affected by brain injury."

"I'm so glad you called. How can I help you?" I said.

"We would love it if you would consider becoming an ambassador for us, someone who can be a voice for others and help raise awareness of the seriousness of traumatic brain injury," the representative said.

I didn't even have to give the question a thought. "I'll do whatever I can," I said. That phone call started a relationship that lasted for the next two years. That fall I helped with their Walk for Thought, the organization's biggest fund-raiser of the year. They also had me do some speaking. One of the things I really wanted to get across to people was that traumatic brain injuries can happen to anyone, not just football players. "I never thought I would be in this position," I said in most of my speeches, "which is the exact same thing every person with a brain injury thinks."

I also continued pursuing music. A year before my grievance was settled, music gave me a once-in-a-lifetime musical opportunity. While we lived in Nashville, Karyn and I got to know Bob S. Castellini, the son of the owner of the Cincinnati Reds. Bob invited me to Sanctuary on Camelback Mountain Spa & Resort, a golf resort he owned in Arizona, for a fund-raiser for the foundation Athletes for Hope. But this wasn't just any fund-raiser. Sports legends were there, including Tony Hawk, Alonzo Mourning, Andre Agassi, and Johnny Bench. The highlight for me, though, was when they asked me to sing for Muhammad Ali for his sixtieth birthday celebration. I sang the song "What You'd Call a Dream." I changed one verse and sang, "It's the final round, just before the bell, when Frazier says no more. The champ is crowned and the crowd erupts with Ali as the roar. And he's what you'd call a dream."

Would you believe that what followed was a standing ovation started by none other than Andre Agassi? *Are you kidding me right now? Is this happening to me?* is all I could think. Then the champ raised his hand toward me, to show me how much he appreciated the song. I have to tell you that that memory is one I will treasure forever. There are a lot of ways to define a successful music career. This was it for me.

The event in Arizona was only one weekend. And while it is something I hope to never forget, it wasn't the kind of event that pushed my career closer to where I hoped it would go. From time to time Jim Brickman called and asked me to make appearances with him, which I happily accepted. Anne Cochran and I had worked well together on the holiday tour, so we tried to capitalize on our work by recording an album of love songs that was released in 2013. That album marked the official end of my pop-classical days. I had pretty much come to the realization that I was not going to create a demand for something the public clearly did not want.

Now that I had given up on pop-classical, I once again had to ask myself, *Who am I as an artist?* I had recorded a pop-worship album, and I had recorded a pop-classical Christmas album as well as a collection of love songs. Neither one really caught on. So who was I as an artist? I wasn't just trying to figure myself out; I was also trying to find a niche that both worked for me *and* would actually sell some records, leading to a real career in music.

Early in 2013 I met a record producer in Minneapolis, Rick Barron, and the two of us became friends. I asked Rick one day, "Why can't I seem to break out in music? What do I need to do to give myself the best chance to make it?"

He asked me, "So what genre of music do you fit into? You are a big, strong, athletic, churchgoing, God-fearing guy with a big voice. What genre of music embraces guys like you?"

"I have no idea," I said.

"Pop-country," Rick replied.

At this time I had never really gotten into any country music outside of maybe Garth Brooks back in the day. However, in my never-ending quest to find a way to break into music in a big way, I dropped the name Benjamin Utecht, grew my hair out, and started sporting a beard. I was now pop-country.

Rick and I also went to work writing songs for a new album. A couple of other writers—Tommy Barbarella, Dave Barry, and Terry Foss—also came on board. I decided to make this a very personal album with songs that spoke of the struggles in which I found myself because of my brain injury. When people first hear the songs they may not know that's what the songs are about, although the titles of a couple of them, "Collide" and "Oblivion," should be strong hints.

I felt renewed with an album to work on. Rick and I put together a set of really good songs. However, something seemed to be missing from what we had written. "You're holding back," Rick said to me one day.

"What are you talking about?" I asked.

"You've put a lot of yourself into these songs, but you haven't put in the most important thing," he said.

"What are you talking about?" I asked.

"Have you ever really thought about what the future may hold in terms of you and your family?"

"Of course I have," I said. I didn't like where he was going with these questions. He was starting to make me mad.

"Have you ever considered telling them what you want them to know if the worst-case scenario takes place?" Rick asked. He was thinking about more than our album.

"I think they know," I said.

"Do they?" Rick asked. "Have you written it out for them?"

"No." I did not want to go there.

"Don't you think you should?" Rick asked in a tone that totally disarmed me.

"Yeah," I said.

"So what are you waiting for?"

CHAPTER 24

"YOU WILL ALWAYS
BE MY GIRLS"

I DON'T RECOMMEND HAVING AN EMOTIONAL conversation right before you board an airplane. Nor do I recommend sitting down on
a plane and writing a letter that expresses everything you want
your family to know about how you feel about them just in case a
day comes when you can't tell them yourself. But that's what I did.
Rick and I had the conversation about the fact that something that
was missing from our collection of songs right before I boarded a
Delta flight for home. "It would be really special for your family to
have a song that told them exactly how you feel," Rick said to me.
I knew he was right. I'd thought about writing something like this,
but I had not been able to force myself to do it. I knew the reason
why. I did not know if I could confront that reason right now, but
I also know that if I didn't now, I might never do it. That's why I
chose such a public place to write such an intimate, personal letter. I had to do it. And I had to do it right now.

I settled into my seat and pulled out my iPad. *Okay, what do
I say?* I stared at the screen for a few minutes. Across the aisle
from me a man tried to sleep. A woman in the next row worked on

her laptop. The flight attendants had not yet started handing out small plastic cups of Coca-Cola products. I typed, "My Love Letter." I paused. The cursor blinked at me. I laid my fingers on the screen and paused. Could I really type out words that expressed my single greatest fear? Part of me knew that the moment I typed them on the page I would cross a barrier into a place from which I could not turn back. It's funny. We can know things deep in the recesses of our soul, but we find ways to convince ourselves that they are not real, even when we know they are. But when they come out of that deep place within us and we put them down on paper, or in my case, on a Pages document on my iPad, then suddenly they become real.

I let out a long sigh, then typed, "I'm afraid to forget you, to wake up and open my eyes and not know you anymore, to be unable to recognize the greatest loves of my life by face or name." I reread the sentence. Tears welled up in my eyes. I wiped them away and continued: "I fear being lost in an abyss without any of you. All alone, left with whatever remains of my former self. I don't want to die inside, please God, don't let it take me. . . . I want to stay home. I need to stay home."

Tears now flowed. I pulled my ball cap down over my face, trying to hide from a planeful of people. I don't know if anyone noticed me. Around me a couple of people slept while others read and one guy played video games on his phone.

"To my sweet ones," I continued, "I promise no matter how bad it gets, I will never give up my grip on you. I will fight desperately for you in my mind. The physical may take me apart, but my spirit will always battle for you. My heart will always remember your smiles, and the way you laughed. It will hold on to every moment I was with you, and every way I was in love with you. Nothing can take you away from my heart. Please know that if I ever lose you in this world, I will always have you in another. I will always be your daddy, and . . ." I punched both the italics and bold buttons before typing, "**you will always be my girls**." I went back to normal text and kept typing: "No matter the circumstance please keep smiling knowing that deep inside my blank stare is a place where we are all together, living and loving. I will always meet you there in that place my sweet ones. I love you. . . ."

Oh God, I hope my girls never have to read this, I prayed. Then I thought, *But if I am taken away from them, I want them to know. They have to know.*

I stopped typing and looked out the window at the passing clouds. "Excuse me, sir. Would you like something to drink?" a flight attendant asked.

I looked up at her cart, with all the varieties of soft drinks. "Just some water," I said. "Thanks."

The letter isn't finished, I told myself. *It's not just your little girls who need to know how you feel.* I knew she knew, and will always know how I feel. I've never been shy about expressing my feelings to my wife. But I wasn't writing this letter to say all the things I could never bring myself to say in person. No, this was to be a lasting voice, a message she could hold and read over and over if and when that day came when my voice fell silent.

I opened my iPad again and typed, "Oh to my beloved Karyn, how I ache to lose you. How I weep at the thought of missing your face. I'm so sorry if I leave you, if my mind lets you down. The last thing I ever wanted was this. To be trapped in a cave where you are outside but I don't recognize your voice calling out . . . calling me home. My sweet love, how beautiful you are to me and forever will be. My love for you is stronger than the restriction of my body. Nothing can remove it from me. I assure you I will always be thinking of you, always longing for you. You are forever imprinted upon my soul. You are my shadow that can never escape my presence. My sweet babe, please smile when you see me, surely that will have the power to save me, to lift me out of the coffin of my mind. As I told our girls, find peace knowing that I will always find you in the special place where memory meets the heart, a place out of darkness' reach. Oh my love, thank you for the greatest years of my life. Thank you for the privilege of your hand, and the gift of your heart. My lips will always remember yours and my hands your face as I long to touch it now. Every day when you close your eyes come meet me there where memory meets the heart and we will dance once again. I love you my sweetest one. . . . Ben."

I read and reread the three paragraphs. I corrected a couple of grammatical errors I noticed and then I saved the document and put my iPad away. When I got home I printed it and sealed it in an envelope. At the time I never planned on anyone reading it until the time came, and I hoped that time never came.

The next time I talked to Rick I told him, "I wrote them a letter."

"Can I read it?" he asked.

"No," I said.

"How can we write a song that expresses how you feel to your family if I don't read the letter?" he asked.

"Yeah . . . I guess you're right," I said.

Rick cried when he read the letter the first time. Once we pulled ourselves together emotionally, we sat down with Tommy Barbarella on the piano and wrote a very powerful song. We recorded it a short time later in Nashville, then went through all the production and postproduction steps that have to be done to a song to get the song just right. We knew we had written a special song when none of us could get through it without crying. I just don't think we knew how much it would impact people.

I didn't know how Karyn would react the first time I played her the song. The two of us were in the car driving somewhere and I popped it in for her. She smiled when she heard the opening notes on a piano. Then as the words started and the rest of the instrumentation kicked in, she started bobbing her head. "Yeah, this is good," she said. I liked the sound of that. But then the words began to sink in and tears began streaming out from behind her sunglasses. "Never mind," she said, "I don't think I'm going to like it." All I could do was hold her hand.

She had an even stronger reaction the second time she heard the song. The two of us were in Chicago visiting my uncle Paul and aunt Beth for a long weekend getaway, just Karyn and me. The girls spent the weekend with Grandma and Grandpa. Paul and Beth and Karyn and I were in the car driving home from dinner when Uncle Paul asked, "What are you up to these days, Ben? Anything new?"

"I have some brand-new music I'm really excited about," I said. "Do you want to hear it?"

"Sure. I'd love it," Uncle Paul said. He and I were in the front seats of the car, while Karyn and Beth were in back. I put in the working copy of my new CD and played him a couple of songs. I think I played "Oblivion" and the title track, "Standing Strong." "Here's the song I'm really excited about," I said. That's when I switched it to "You Will Always Be My Girls." The song started playing . . .

> *I'm in here counting the days*
> *While my mind is slippin' away*
> *I'll hold on as long as I can to you*
> *I may not remember your name*
> *Or the smell of the cool summer rain*
> *Everything and nothing has changed, nothing has changed*
> *And I will remember your smile and your laughter*
> *Long ever after this moment is gone.*

About the time the chorus started for the first time I heard sobbing in the backseat. I turned and saw tears pouring down Karyn's face. I could tell she was embarrassed, because she doesn't like to show a lot of emotion in front of people, but she couldn't help herself. The longer the song played, the harder she sobbed. Later she told me that the moment the song started playing she found herself wondering what it was going to be like for her twenty years from now when she listens to these words.

Not long after the visit to Chicago, a film crew descended on our suburban Minneapolis home to shoot a music video. From the moment I started writing the song I knew it was going to be a video, and I wanted Karyn and the girls in it. Karyn never hesitated. She was on board from the beginning. Even though acting out the events of the song was hard for her, she nailed it. Of course, the entire film crew was in tears through most of the shoot, but that was to be expected. However, once the video was shot and edited and ready to go, I did not release it. Something in me said it was not yet time. I think I was waiting to release it when we released the album.

This progression, from the letter to the song to the video, fully opened my eyes to a truth that I "knew" but didn't really know. As I wrestled with the very real possibility of losing my memories in the future, not just a few but all of them, I suddenly understood that these fragile memories that I always took for granted are the only things that connect me to the people I love. And that connection is what makes me who I am. My essence as a human being, everything I am, the person I've been, the man I hope to be in the future, all come down to my ability to remember. I am a living memory and without my memory I will cease to live even if my body keeps on functioning. If that day comes, I will be trapped in a coffin in my head with no way to get out.

As this realization hit me I came to understand I could not just sit back and wait for what may be inevitable. Nor could I retreat into the safety of my home with my family and cut myself off from the world while making the most of every moment with my wife and daughters. Believe me, that would be so easy, and I do now make the most of every moment I have with them. But making the most of this time means more than simply reading to them or wrestling on the floor with them or doing all the dad things I love so much. My girls need to see me set an example for them of faith in action. They need to see what we are to do when trouble and suffering strike our lives. And that's why I chose to take two very intentional steps in dealing head-on with my brain injuries.

First, I have to speak out. As I said earlier, for three years, beginning right after the Brickman tour, I served as a spokesman for the Minnesota Brain Injury Alliance. In 2013 Rick Barron connected me to guitarist Billy McLaughlin, who introduced me to the American Academy of Neurology (AAN) and the American Brain Foundation (ABF). Billy had worked with both groups, which are actually connected to one another, and had even been featured in the AAN's magazine, *Neurology Now*. Lauren Ross, the senior fund-raising manager for the ABF, contacted me about sharing my story. In the conversations that followed, the AAN and ABF learned I wanted to do a lot more than tell my story in one magazine article. I became a spokesman and an ambassador for the group.

Six years and counting after my last injury, I now realize that this issue goes far beyond football and the NFL. Brain disorder and disease affect one in six Americans every year, touching not only those who suffer traumatic brain injuries and disease but also their families. It is a silent epidemic. I believe the fact that I now find myself in this place is my opportunity to shine a light on the problem. I not only want to raise awareness, but increase funding to the American Brain Foundation for research for a cure. In neurology we believe that if you can find a cure for one disease, you will find a cure for many. I pray and believe that day is coming.

The truth that there is a possible connection between football, concussions, and brain disease has motivated me to take strong advocacy positions for the game that I still love and respect. I fight for current and former players' long-term health. I believe that billionaires making billions off concussions should pay premiums on a long-term health-care plan that will provide assistance for any player diagnosed with brain disorder and disease. Let's stay away from lawsuits and poorly structured settlements and ask the NFL to be the organization of integrity it has the potential be. More emphatically, I advocate for our children in youth contact sports. I would like to see state policies or a national mandate removing tackle football from schools until high school and, in return, follow the NFL's example of creating a national first-through-eighth-grade highly competitive noncontact flag football league. We would remove seven years of head trauma during the most important developmental stages of a child's brain, while at the same time allow our children to participate in a sport that can provide great life lessons.

On April 30, 2014, the AAN gave me the highest honor I have ever received when they presented me with their Public Leadership in Neurology Award for my work in advancing public understanding and awareness of neurologic disease. When I read the list of others who have received this award, I was floored. The list of past honorees includes former generals, vice presidents, and A-list actors and actresses, along with sports stars who were much more successful than I. The AAN flew me out to Philadelphia for the awards luncheon, where I had the privilege of delivering the keynote address. I just told my story. When I was finished this roomful of neurologists gave me a standing ovation.

Once I became a spokesman for AAN, my life as an advocate went to heights I never imagined possible. The NFLPA contacted me to see if I might be interested in appearing before the United

States Senate Special Committee on Aging. I'll let the irony of that statement sink in for a moment. Less than a week before my thirty-third birthday I appeared before a Senate committee investigating the impact of diseases and conditions normally associated with people forty and fifty years older than I and the connection of sports with those diseases. I was part of a four-person panel that included Chris Nowinski, a former college football player and professional wrestler who cofounded the Sports Legacy Institute at Boston University. After Dr. Omalu discovered CTE, Boston University took the lead in researching the disease, with Chris as its point man. The panel also included Dr. Robert Stern, professor of neurology, neurosurgery, and anatomy and neurobiology, and clinical core director of Boston University's Alzheimer's Disease Center. Dr. Stern is also one of the lead researchers into CTE at the Sports Legacy Institute. Finally, the fourth person on the panel was Jacob VanLandingham, PhD, director of neurobiological research at the Tallahassee Memorial HealthCare Neuroscience Center, and assistant professor of the Florida State University College of Medicine.

One person who did not testify before the committee but whose presence was greater than all the rest of us was Kevin Turner. Kevin played in the NFL for eight seasons, but now, at the age of forty, he suffers with amyotrophic lateral sclerosis, or ALS. His presence asked the question: Can the violence of the NFL lead to this disease? Kevin Turner passed away on March 24, 2016.

In the weeks prior to that appearance I had to write out my testimony. Using the piece I wrote for *Neurology Now* as my template, I wrote out a brief version of my story and talked about the uncertainty I now face as I look to the future. I also included a few lines from "You Will Always Be My Girls." On the day of my actual appearance I did not read my official testimony. Instead it is entered into the record. But I did speak. The committee gave me four minutes to talk, and by four minutes, they meant four minutes. There's a clock and a light that switches from green to yellow to red to make sure you don't go over. I had prayed a lot about what I should say. I started off with describing the high point of my career, the 2006 Super Bowl. Then I contrasted it with the low, waking up on the field after getting knocked out in a Bengals' training camp practice.

But the heart of what I wanted to say was summed up in a line that the newscasts that night picked up on. I told the committee, "It took losing my mind to care about my mind." I then went on to talk about my memory problems and how I discovered them. Then I mentioned the letter I wrote to my family and the song and video that grew out of it. As soon as the meeting adjourned, news crews from ABC, CBS, and NBC asked me about the video. Prior to my testimony the story had been about the NFL and possible conspiracies in the league to suppress information about concussions. But now, with my appearance before the Senate committee and the vulnerability I showed, the story moved to a real person struggling with the lasting effects of concussions and the uncertainty they bring.

I wasn't really prepared for questions about the video. I started praying, "Lord, what do I do?" I felt the answer in my spirit: it's time.

Less than twenty-four hours after the Senate hearing, I uploaded the video onto YouTube and put links to it on both my Twitter and Facebook pages. I thought some people might be interested in seeing it, but I never expected what happened next. The number of views climbed and climbed every day. In two or three days we were up to around sixty thousand. I was amazed by the reception.

But the video's impact had only begun.

Four days after I put the video on YouTube my wife and I went out to a movie for my birthday. We had just sat down and the previews started rolling when my phone buzzed. I had a message that the website for NFL on Fox had just posted my video. By the end of the night our number of views had jumped into six figures and kept climbing. The success of the video prompted interview requests with all sorts of news outlets. Rick Reilly from ESPN came out to our home and did a feature on Karyn, the girls, and me. All the while the video kept getting viewed time after time. To date, on YouTube, the video has been viewed 1.2 million times, with more views on other places where people have posted it.

I have to be honest: this was an incredibly emotional video shoot. As we filmed the scenes I couldn't help but imagine the worst for my future. Watching Karyn go deep into her role for the music video was painful. I won't forget the scene we shot when Karyn is looking through photos of our girls and me. We asked her, if she was willing, to imagine those memories being erased. She did, and it was beautiful and tragic all at the same time. The entire crew sat behind the camera and cried with her. As a speaker, I strongly believe that vulnerability equals connectivity. This music video was my opportunity to be completely vulnerable about my fears, praying that the song and video would somehow be used as a beacon of hope for the many in our world suffering from brain disorder and disease. The success of the video has given me peace because I know it has touched the lives of many who have watched it.

All of this brings me to the second response to my condition I want my daughters to see. Through my position with the American Academy of Neurology and all the interviews and video views and even this book, I'm speaking out, and I will continue to speak out for as long as I can. But I'm doing more than that.

All of my life I've been a competitor. I've been knocked down, and knocked out, but I always got back up and kept fighting. I think back to the first concussion I suffered in the NFL, where

I was hit in the head in a helmet-to-helmet blow. Even as I lost consciousness, I heard the guy who hit me standing over me, taunting me. My head cleared. I jumped up. And I made the first-down signal, which brought the house down at the old RCA Dome. I wanted that player and every other defensive player to know that they could hit me as hard as they could but I was going to get back up.

The concussions I suffered on the field ended my NFL career, but that doesn't mean I have conceded defeat to them. I am fighting back. How? First, I refuse to give up and lie down. Instead I get up every morning determined to make this day count. I treasure every moment I have with those I love. With every story I read to my girls, with every seemingly throwaway moment of laughter or tears or whatever the day may bring, I pause and reflect and grab hold of that memory with everything I have. I want my wife and daughters to know that I will never take them or our time together for granted. Ever.

But I am also fighting back by working to help raise funds and raise awareness for brain disease research. At the very end of the video for "You Will Always Be My Girls," you see me get up out of the hospital bed and surprise Karyn and the girls. The camera then moves back to the hospital room and the IV hanging above the bed. On the side of the IV bag are the words "Experimental Drug." That's my prayer and something for which I work every day. I pray that a cure can be found that will untangle the tau proteins that wreak havoc on the brain and cause CTE. Unfortunately, right now this disease can only be diagnosed posthumously. After speaking to multiple neurologists and neuroscientists I learned there is hope to be able to diagnose CTE in a living person within the next ten years. If a cure is found, I will be at the front of the line, ready for them to try it out on me.

However, a cure may never come. That is why I am also fighting back through cognitive fitness training. In the summer of

2015, I entered into a strenuous twenty-week program that was harder than any NFL training camp I ever went through, well, at least mentally. I'm not going to lie. When this company approached me for the first time I was a bit skeptical, but I agreed to take their neuropsychological assessment because it was based on the Woodcock-Johnson, a battery of cognitive tests that are medically credible. The test itself took between an hour and an hour and a half, and it was tough and tiring.

The results proved my concerns. My long-term memory (after five minutes) tested in the seventeenth percentile, and my delayed long-term memory (after sixty minutes) was even worse, testing in the twelfth percentile. Strangely enough, these results gave me peace, because they validated my complaints regarding memory.

Now another miracle! After twenty weeks of sitting across from a brain trainer for an hour and a half per day, four days a week, I was ready for my postprogram evaluation. My trainer, Brad Olson, mentally pushed me to my limits, much like one of my strength and conditioning coaches would do in the NFL. I'm overwhelmed with joy to share that I tested in the seventy-eighth percentile for long-term memory, and, remarkably, in the ninety-eighth percentile for delayed long-term memory. This result was the most overwhelming, because it meant I will potentially be able to retain and store new memories more efficiently moving forward. I also showed significant improvement in my verbal comprehension and logic and reasoning. My whole athletic career was built around training my body, so it made complete sense to learn I can also train my brain. We all have the potential to train and strengthen our cognitive abilities, and if the results have the potential to improve our long-term brain health, then we should all take action.

Does this mean my past memory issues have been cured? Not at all. The jury is still out as to what these results mean for my long-term future. However, the improvement shows that the brain is like a muscle; it is plastic and it can be stretched and strengthened. For the first time in years I feel like my memory has improved, and you'd better believe I will keep on training. After all, once an athlete, always an athlete.

I still don't know what the future may hold, none of us does, but I feel more confident now than I ever have. When I first discovered my memory problems I feared my life was over.

Now I know it has only just begun, and I refuse to take even a second of it for granted. If you're someone who has gone or is going through some suffering in your life, please believe that there is always hope and that you have the ability to choose to have faith in it.

As long as my mind stands strong I have dedicated myself to being the best husband to my wife, Karyn, that I can possibly be, and a loving dad and example of a godly man to my little girls, Elleora, Katriel, Amy, and Haven. Realizing that my mind and memories are what bring relevance to my life has inspired me to be the best man that I can be. Memories are the essence of what makes us matter as humans. They hold our identity. What has relevance in our lives if we can't remember it? Can we all grasp the importance of our mind and memories and no longer take for granted the most important things in our lives? If we can, then I believe we can all better ourselves. Pastor Wes Feltner, PhD, once said, "What we believe about our future directly impacts the way we live our lives today." So, what do you believe about your future, and how will it change the way you live today?

To my beautiful family, I believe in a future filled with new memories and a love that has no condition. No matter what that future may hold, I promise you will always be my girls, and I will always love you.

ACKNOWLEDGMENTS

THIS HAS BEEN QUITE A JOURNEY. I never set out to write my life story, nor one having to do with an injury that ended my football career, but providence seems to have a mind of its own, doesn't it? I hope I never forget the call I received from my literary agent, Steve Ross. "Hi, Ben—this is Steve Ross from Abrams Artists Agency in New York." I knew of Abrams through my endeavors in music and immediately thought the call was related to those. The conversation took an unexpected turn when Steve asked if I had ever thought about writing my story. "Uh . . . no, not really," was all I could say. At the same time I couldn't help but foresee where this line of questioning was headed. Steve had heard about my story from Mark Tabb, a *New York Times* bestselling author, and shared how much my story had impacted his life. He believed that, with the right writer, it could positively affect the lives of many others, too. I told him I was interested but challenged him on vetting a number of writers; Steve, however, calmly and strategically always brought me back to Mark Tabb. Well, I'm glad he did. I agreed to give Mark a call at Steve's request, and it was one of the most engaging calls of my life. I was so concerned that I wouldn't be able to find a writer who would truly connect with my life. I was involved in so many different things, and on top of that I had a unique past, having grown up as a pastor's son and now being a dad with four daughters—how could anyone relate? Enter Mark Tabb. Long story short, Mark was a former pastor turned full-time author. He grew up in Oklahoma and was a huge football fan; he'd followed my career since I was in college and was, ironically, living in Indiana, where he'd watched my professional career unfold from its origin. Okay, here's the best part: he's not a father of four daughters. He's a father of five daughters! It's hard to explain, but it felt like I was talking to a combination of my dad and me. I knew within ten minutes that this was the writer for my story. I'm happy to say that both Steve Ross and Mark Tabb are now, first and foremost, my friends and advocates. Thank you, Steve, for believing in me and helping my story become a voice for hope. Mark, you are so talented, and I thank God for your wanting to share my life story and for so eloquently putting it on paper. You are a stellar example of what it means to be a committed husband and father, and I appreciate your friendship.

I must also thank all my friends at Howard Books and Simon & Schuster for their hard work and expertise in making this experience truly special. My wish is that our project will provide hope and challenge where it is needed.

Many thanks to my friends Rick Barron and Tommy Barbarella for taking a day to write one of the most impactful songs I have ever heard and gotten the chance to sing.

Thank you, NFLPA, for representing my needs and fighting for my future security. Tim English, you are amazing, and your diligence and passion for accountability and justice in the league are inspiring. Many thanks also to my personal lawyer and mentor, Scott Hillstrom, for standing strong next to me. Your presence provided much-needed education, protection, and perspective. Thank you for mentoring me in many areas in my life. Your friendship has become very special to me, and I look forward to our future conversations.

My entire life up to age thirty revolved around a game. That game is football. I love football, and that will never change. I want to take this opportunity to thank the many coaches in my life who used the gridiron to mold me into the man I am today. Thank you to my high school coach, Bob Majeski, and his staff in Hastings, Minnesota; without you, none of this would have been possible. Thank you, Glen Mason and Vic Adamle, for seeing something special in a kid from a small river town in Minnesota. Coach Mason, without your handshake promise that I could come play for the Golden Gophers, my dream of playing in the NFL would've been shattered. Thank you, Tony Dungy and Bill Polian, for believing that an injury-broken tight end could be rehabilitated into a starting Super Bowl champion. Coach Dungy, your effect on my life is indescribable. Concussions may have dismantled our business relationship, but I respect and thank the Brown family and Marvin Lewis for giving me a chance to reach my potential as an athlete. The strongest part of the game is the men you share the field with. Thank you to all my teammates for the privilege of playing alongside you. I learned so much from many of you, and I will cherish every memory I can hold on to of the experiences we've shared together.

What a family. I am so blessed! Mom and Dad, you are my heartbeat. Thank you for being my first coaches, who trained and built me up the right way. I hope the path I have chosen is one that honors the endless hours you both put into helping me develop character and identity. I love you so much. Ashley, my soul twin, you are such a joy in my life, and I can't imagine a day or a memory without you. Thank you for loving me no matter the circumstances; I assure you that you will always have my heart.

Last, but certainly not least, my beauties. Oh, what a joy to be surrounded by exquisite women! I love you all so much that when I try to think of the right words to use to describe it I start to cry. Karyn, you are an angel in the flesh, and you love corny things, so I know you'll like that statement. Thank you for pouring your heart into this book with me. I know it must have been difficult for you to allow yourself to experience your greatest fears. But we did it together, just as we do everything, and that's why we will always be A-okay! Karyn, you are such an amazing wife and mother. I can't thank you enough for saying yes to me and for giving me the honor of being your husband and the father to your children. To my four miracles, Elleora, Katriel, Amy, and Haven: you have given my life purpose. My relevance lies within the structure of being your dad. I am so excited to watch you grow, learn, imagine, create, laugh, cry, win, lose, and turn into the women God has destined you to become. I will do my best to love you the way you deserve to be loved: unconditionally. No matter what the future may bring to my health and to my mind, know this truth and lock it away in the vault of your identity: I love you, and You Will Always Be My Girls.

—*Ben (Dad)*

SEP 0 0 2016